ASIAN TOFU

ASIAN TOFU

Discover the Best, Make Your Own, and Cook It at Home

ANDREA NGUYEN

Studio Photography by Maren Caruso

TEN SPEED PRESS

Berkeley

CONTENTS

Introduction   1

Tofu Buying Guide   7

Tofu Cooking Tips   14

17 Homemade Tofu Tutorial

Master Soy Milk Recipe   23

Silken Tofu   28

Tofu Pudding   30

Block Tofu   32

Seasoned Pressed Tofu   38

Tea-Smoked Pressed Tofu   40

White Fermented Tofu   41

Fresh Tofu Skin   44

Soy-Simmered Fried Tofu   46

FRESH AND SATISFYING

49 Snacks and Starters

Naked and Simple

Japanese Chilled Tofu   51

Chilled Tofu with Crunchy Baby Sardines   53

Chilled Tofu with Spicy Sauce   54

Tofu Skin Sashimi   55

Tofu with Century Eggs   56

Savory Tofu Pudding   59

Grilled and Fried

Miso-Glazed Broiled Tofu   61

Fermented Tofu, Lemongrass, and Goat Skewers   63

Grilled Crisp Tofu Pockets   67

Fried Tofu with Chile Peanut Sauce   69

Deep-Fried Tofu   70

Creative and Modern

Spiced Tofu and Vegetable Fritters   71

Tofu French Fries   74

Fresh Tofu with Sauces and Toppings   75

SOOTHING AND SOFT
77 Soups and Hot Pots

Casual and Special Soups

Tofu, Tomato, and Dill Soup   79

Miso Soup   80

Tofu, Seaweed, and Pork Soup   81

Hot-and-Sour Soup   82

Silken Tofu and Edamame Soup   84

Tofu Bamboo and Chicken Soup   86

Warming Hot Pots

Warm Simmered Tofu   87

Silken Tofu and Seasoned Soy Milk Hot Pot   89

Soy Milk Lees and Kimchi Hot Pot   91

Soft Tofu and Seafood Hot Pot   93

Stuffed Tofu in Broth   94

HOMEY AND WHOLESOME
97 Main Dishes

Stir-Fried, Panfried, and Braised

Stir-Fried Tofu, Shrimp, and Peas   100

Spicy Tofu with Beef and Sichuan Peppercorn   101

Panfried Tofu with Mushroom and Spicy Sesame Sauce   103

Tea-Smoked Tofu with Pepper and Pork   104

Bitter Melon with Tofu and Pork   106

Tofu with Tomato and Green Onion   107

Lemongrass Tofu with Chiles   108

Hakka-Style Stuffed Tofu   109

Deep-Fried and Roasted

Twice-Cooked Coriander Tofu   112

Soy Milk Lees and Vegetable Croquettes   114

Batter-Fried Tofu with Chile Soy Sauce   116

Roast Chicken with Red Fermented Tofu   117

Crisp Roasted Pork Belly   119

Poached, Simmered and Steamed

Simmered Greens with Fried Tofu   121

Tofu and Vegetables in Coconut Milk   124

Spiced Tofu and Coconut in Banana Leaf   127

Tofu Chicken Meatballs in Lemongrass Broth   129

VERSATILE AND DELICIOUS
131 Salads and Sides

Tossed

Tofu Noodle and Vegetable Salad   133

White Tofu, Sesame, and Vegetable Salad   135

Greens and Fried Tofu in Mustard Sauce   136

Spicy Lemongrass Tofu Salad   137

Pressed Tofu and Peanuts in Spicy Bean Sauce   138

Sauteed, Stir-fried, and Simmered

Spicy Yuba Ribbons   139

Savory Soy Milk Lees with Vegetables   142

Bean Sprouts with Panfried Tofu and Chinese Chives   143

Tofu with Kimchi and Pork Belly   145

Water Spinach with Fermented Tofu   147

Fermented Tofu Simmered in Coconut Milk   148

RELIGION AND ARTISTRY
151 Mock Meats

Tofu and Vegetable Fritters   154

Sweet and Savory Tofu Eel   157

Bear Paw Tofu   159

Cellophane Noodle and Tofu Rolls   161

Savory Okara Crumbles   163

BUILDING ON TRADITIONS

165 Buns, Dumplings, Crepes, Noodles, and Rice

Spicy-Sweet Fried Tofu Buns   167

Tofu Steak Burgers   170

Vegetarian Wontons in Chile Oil   172

Tofu, Pork, and Kimchi Dumplings   174

Chinese Chive and Pressed Tofu Turnovers   177

Spiced Chickpea Crepes with Soybean Paneer   179

Fried Shrimp Tofu Skin Rolls   182

Stir-Fried Thai Noodles   184

Foxy Tofu Noodle Soup   187

Sushi Rice in Tofu Pouches   188

Fried Rice with Fermented Red Tofu   191

AMAZING TRANSFORMATIONS

193 Sweets and Dessert

Solidified, Squeezed, and Grated

Sweet Tofu Pudding with Ginger Syrup   195

Tofu Blancmange with Cured Pineapple and Lime   196

Essence of Tofu Ice Cream   198

Tofu Tiramisu   199

Cashew and Cardamom Fudge   201

Byproduct Bonuses

Gingery Chocolate Chip Cookies   202

Okara Doughnuts   203

207 Basics

Chinese Sweet Fragrant Soy Sauce   207

Japanese Seasoned Soy Concentrate   208

Korean Seasoned Soy Sauce   209

Thai Sweet Chile Sauce   210

Chile and Sichuan Peppercorn Mix   211

Fermented Tofu, Lemongrass, and Chile Sauce   212

Chile Oil   213

Chicken Stock   214

Dashi Stock   215

Savory Kelp Relish   216

Tamarind Liquid   217

Green Chutney   218

Ingredients   219

Selected Bibliography   224

Acknowledgments   225

Index   226

Measurement Conversion Charts   231

INTRODUCTION

Despite all the terrible terms that have been attached to tofu, it is still considered a *good* four-letter word by countless people. As an Asian staple, it is beloved by rich and poor alike. Whether fresh and tender or aged and fermented, tofu denotes basic sustenance, culinary craftsmanship, time-honored traditions, good health, and more. Tofu pervades many aspects of Asian life and culture, as I discovered during my travels and research for this book.

For example, visit a country in East or Southeast Asia and you'll see tofu practically everywhere, on restaurant menus, as street food, and at cafeterias. You can buy it from open-air ("wet") food markets and neighborhood tofu shops as well as fancy food halls and superstores such as Walmart and Carrefour. Small packages of tofu snacks are often displayed as impulse buys at Chinese hypermarkets.

There are even ample opportunities for tofu tourism. A popular excursion from Taipei is to "The Capital of Tofu" in Shenkeng, renowned for its tender tofu and old-fashioned methods, such as cooking the soy milk over wood charcoal for a light smokiness. Under the archways that line the charming Old Town area, vendors sell a variety of tofu, including tofu ice cream, grilled stinky tofu on a stick, and salty-sweet fermented tofu.

Among the highlights of visiting Kyoto are elaborate multicourse tofu meals and tofu shops that date back to the 1800s. Tokyo offers elegant tofu fine dining restaurants, but in the outer stalls of the Tsukiji market, you'll come across the twenty-something Table-Mono tofu vendors hawking super rich soy milk, tofu, and ice cream to passersby.

Tofu is featured in many Asian cookbooks but it has also been spotlighted in comic books and children's books. It has inspired artists and designers to create posters, sculptures, and even tofu MP3 speakers and lamps! Few other foods can rival tofu's significance to so many people.

East Asian Stronghold

While people agree that tofu is an ancient food, no one is clear on when it was invented and by whom. Soybeans are native to China and were considered one of five sacred "grains." As a primary foodstuff, the soybean's main virtues were its ability to grow well in poor soil without depleting the land, and its consistently high yield. The little bean was a useful famine food and the Chinese took to transforming it. Initially it was made into a type of gruel, and later into palatable staples such as soybean sprouts, soy sauce, and tofu.

Legend holds that King Liu An of Huainan invented tofu, and excavated tomb carvings point to tofu being made as early as the Han Dynasty (206 BCE–220 CE). Scholars also suggest that the Han Chinese may have learned about rendering curds from milk through contact with nomads from the northern steppes. However, tofu did not catch on as a popular, commercially made food until the tenth century, when the Mandarin term *dou fu* (tofu) was mentioned numerous times in literature.

It was from the Song Dynasty (960–1279 CE) onward that tofu spread to other parts of the region. Wherever the Chinese exerted their influence, whether through religion, politics, or trade, tofu went with them. That's why so many Asian tofu dishes are Chinese in origin.

How tofu knowledge flowed from China to other cultures, however, is murky. For example, monks and scholars traveling between China and Japan may have transmitted tofu culture to Japan between the eighth and twelfth centuries. It was first mentioned in Japan in 1183 as a Shinto shrine offering, but the characters as we know them today were not written in Japan until 1489. What is generally agreed upon is that tofu was not part of everyday Japanese eating until the middle of the Edo Period (1603–1868). Some support the theory that the Japanese learned about tofu from the Koreans, as a result of the Japanese invasions of Korea between 1592 and 1598. In any event, Japan took to tofu in a big way, evidenced by the 1782 bestseller *Tofu Hyaku Chin* by Ka Hitsujun. Among the book's one hundred tofu recipes are enduring classics, such as *hiya yakko* (chilled tofu; page 51) and *yu dofu* (simmered tofu; page 87).

Korea and China share a border, and tofu was likely introduced to Korea in the thirteenth and fourteenth centuries. Historic records show that it even played a role in diplomacy. In 1434, as part of their tribute relationship, the Chinese emperor requested Korean cooks skilled at making *dubu* (tofu) preparations. By the fifteenth century, tofu had indeed become widespread in Korea, though it was mostly made by Buddhist monks as temple food. It was part of an annual ceremony to memorialize the deceased, a practice that continues today.

Wavering Southeast Asia

Vietnam was also a major player in China's tribute system and a Chinese colony for a millennium, from 111 BCE to 939 CE. Additionally, Vietnamese Buddhism is closely aligned with Chinese Buddhism. Given all of those factors, Vietnam stands out among the Southeast Asian countries as having a broad array of tofu (*dau phu* or *dau hu*) dishes, including Chinese favorites and many native preparations, such as Lemongrass Tofu with Chiles (page 108). The Vietnamese also developed an extensive vegetarian repertoire that included tofu-based mock meats and fake fish sauce.

While tofu is present in other parts of Southeast and South Asia, it is not a huge deal. According to Thai food authority David Thompson, tofu was a latecomer to the Thai table: "Bean curd is a Chinese import and stayed in that community up until the 1930s when the Chinese and their food became more accepted in Thailand. And so such a relatively short time has meant very little use in pure Thai food."

While tofu may be added to curries as a meat substitute, included in simple stir-fries and added to noodle dishes, the Thai repertoire includes few tofu-centric preparations. In general, tofu is treated in a Chinese manner, such as being deep-fried and eaten with sauce, or it plays supporting role, as exemplified in pad Thai (page 184). The fermented tofu preparation (*lon tao hu yi*, page 148) is an unusual dish that presents tofu in a Thai manner.

People living in Cambodia and Laos enjoy tofu dishes that are often borrowed from Chinese traditions. However, they also invent some of their own, such as the Hmong poached chicken and tofu meatballs on page 129.

In multicultural and multireligious Singapore and Malaysia, treats such as grilled stuffed tofu pockets (page 67) satisfy the dietary needs of Muslims, Buddhists, Christians, and others. While tempeh (fermented soybeans) is king in mostly Muslim Indonesia, tofu is a strong runner-up in terms of popular soy-based foods. Indonesia was part of the spice trade route, which explains original creations such as twice-cooked *tahu bacem* (page 112) from Java.

The Chinese brought tofu to the Philippines but locals didn't adapt it to their cuisine in a significant way. Filipino cookbooks rarely include tofu recipes. As contribution to my research, freelance writer and food blogger Tracey Paska informally polled relatives and tofu vendors at the popular Cubao wet market in Metro Manila. She asked them to name Filipino tofu preparations. Aside from *tokwa't baboy*, a dish of fried tofu, boiled pork, and vinegary soy sauce, people could not name any other traditional dishes that featured tofu. However, Chinese Sweet Tofu Pudding with Ginger Syrup (page 195) is a very popular snack.

Myanmar (formerly Burma) is something of a rogue tofu country. Burmese cooks employ a different kind of tofu. Irene Khin Wong, the owner of Saffron 59 Catering in New York City, explained that soybean-based tofu is a Chinese import that endures in her native country. However, the prevailing and more popular Burmese tofu (also called Shan tofu) is made from ground legumes that are cooked in a polenta-like manner and then cooled and cut. Tofu can be made from many kinds of legumes, including lentils and peanuts, but this book focuses on the soybean version.

South Asian Newcomer

Although soybeans had long been a minor crop in India, tofu didn't arrive until 1976 when a tofu shop was established near Auroville, an experimental utopia in southwest India. According to the SoyInfo Center, Westerners made that tofu.

Renowned author and teacher Julie Sahni explained that India was a late tofu adopter because initially soy milk and soybean curd were presented as substitutes for cow's milk and paneer. While Indians who had contact with the Chinese were open to those soybean products, many others took offense at the notion that a bean could replace the precious foods produced from cows, revered and sacred animals in their culture. "It was too close for comfort, too competitive, and very difficult to accept," she said.

Much had changed by 1985, Sahni noted in *Classic Indian Vegetarian and Grain Cooking*, as tofu was gaining popularity in India as a protein-rich, healthy substitute for traditional paneer cheese. Many Indian cooks have picked up on tofu since then. The *saag* tofu and cashew and tofu fudge recipes (pages 121 and 201) demonstrate how some people integrate tofu into traditional preparations. Today, India is the world's fifth largest producer of soybeans.

Tofu in America

I was born in Vietnam but grew up in America, and tofu was regularly on our family's table, a natural extension of my Asian heritage. This isn't the case for most Americans, despite the soybean's long history in the United States.

British colonist Samuel Bowen planted the first soybeans in Savannah, Georgia, in 1765 and made his own soy sauce. A few years later, Benjamin Franklin sent seeds from London to a botanist in Philadelphia, citing Italian friar Domingo Navarette's 1665 account of Chinese tofu. By the 1850s, Midwestern farmers were cultivating soybeans from Japanese seeds, thanks to precocious travelers and Commodore Matthew Perry's historic expedition and trade mission to Japan.

Though some Americans experimented with eating soybeans during the 1800s, people mostly knew only of soy sauce. The US soybean crop was mainly used to feed animals and enrich soil with nitrogen. However, Americans turned to soy as a source of nourishment during wartime and periods of deprivation. For example, Civil War soldiers in the southern states drank a coffee substitute made from ground roasted soybeans.

In the early part of the twentieth century, the USDA sent expeditions to Asia to investigate traditional soy foods and growing methods. Agricultural explorers Charles Piper and William Morse detailed their findings in *The Soybean* (1923), a historic publication that included recipes to encourage Americans to consume soy foods. Innovators George Washington Carver and Henry Ford both championed soybeans for cooking and also collaborated on developing soy-based plastics. Ford hosted multicourse soybean feasts and developed an experimental "Soybean Car."

Mildred Lager's *The Useful Soybean* (1945) presented well-researched and impassioned arguments for adopting soybeans as a natural food. Unfortunately, her efforts did not alter prevailing attitudes toward the bean. Americans still perceived it as a nonfood, though they indirectly consumed it via livestock raised on soybean meal, vegetable oil, and other processed foods. During and after World War II, farmers in the US began cultivating soy as a major cash crop, turning it into one of country's most important agricultural commodities. America is currently among the world's biggest soybean producers and exporters.

From Alternative to Mainstream

In 1958, Boys Market in Los Angeles became the first American supermarket to sell tofu. However, tofu did not get a real boost in the US until the 1970s, when it became part of the natural foods and sustainable eating movement. Frances Moore Lappe's *Diet for a Small Planet* (1971) and William Shurtleff and Akiko Aoyagi's *The Book of Tofu* (1975) detailed the ecological, health, and culinary benefits of tofu.

Shurtleff and Aoyagi's work encouraged people to make tofu and prepare vegetarian fare. Their extensive exploration of Japanese tofu shops and cuisine underscored how tofu was an efficient means to use the Earth's natural resources. "I wanted to make a contribution to the planet," Shurtleff explained in a 2010 conversation. Organic tofu pioneer Jeremiah Ridenour, who traveled with Shurtleff and Aoyagi in the 1970s and eventually cofounded Wildwood Natural Foods, succinctly put it this way: "It's about feeding the world. We have to be eating at the beginning of the

food chain." Tofu activists such as Shurtleff and entrepreneurs such as Ridenour helped reframe tofu for their generation. As a result, tofu took on a New Age aura of Asian trendiness and organic living. Before that, the American tofu scene remained in the realm of Asian American–owned tofu shops and vegetarian Seventh-day Adventists. The economic upheaval of the 1970s gave way to the boom years of Reaganomics, and many of the Americans who tasted tofu in the guise of Western fare disliked it. In fact, a 1986 Roper Poll published in *USA Today* listed tofu as the nation's most loathed food.

Burdened with a "bland white cake in water" image, tofu got a marketing makeover in the 1990s as manufacturers answered consumers' call for healthy foods. Non-dairy Western products such as Tofutti ice cream and tofu chocolate Americanized tofu and converted many skeptics. In 1990, *The Tofu Book* by John Paino and Lisa Messinger declared tofu the foundation for a new American cuisine.

The Los Angeles Tofu Festival debuted in 1996 and had a successful run until 2007, attracting thousands of people annually with clever themes and taglines such as "Tofuzilla" and "It's hip to be square." Over the past decades, tofu publications, better awareness of Asian cultures, and robust Asian American communities have contributed to greater appreciation for tofu as a healthy, affordable food source.

Tofu Today

In a 2008 survey of 1,000 adults, the United Soybean Board found that 85 percent of Americans understand that soy is healthy, a 26-point rise since 1997. The USDA's recently released 2010 dietary guidelines recommended soy products and soy milk as part of a good diet. On the flip side, there are many who believe that too much soy is harmful to health. Indeed, overconsuming anything can lead to adverse side effects. A wise strategy is to enjoy moderate amounts of minimally processed, natural soy foods, such as tofu, soy sauce, and miso.

That's easier nowadays because tofu can be found at most supermarkets and specialty grocers. Tofu makers such as Hodo Soy (page 131) are expanding people's palate for tofu and Dong Phuong Tofu (page 193) are preserving tofu traditions for their immigrant communities. The menus of Japanese *izakaya* pubs showcase fresh tofu to appreciative diners. At the same time, curious home cooks and chefs are beginning to experiment with making tofu from scratch.

Tofu is no longer either relegated to food co-ops or considered as a mere meat substitute. The widespread availability of tofu and the shift in mainstream attitudes toward tofu make it more relevant now than ever to the American kitchen. We are not in wartime or suffering extreme deprivation. However, there is increased interest in healthful eating, sustainable living, and authentic Asian flavors.

Many books focus on Western ways with tofu, but this one puts tofu in its original context, as an important Asian staple that people have made, cooked, and enjoyed for centuries. The recipes, stories, and images bridge the Pacific and convey tofu's timelessness as well as its modern incarnations. If tofu is going to evolve and succeed in the West, Asian approaches need to be involved.

As I "chased the bean curd" for this book, a few food-savvy friends declared a hatred for tofu, but many more (thank goodness) revealed a curiosity about it and even a love of it. *Asian Tofu* does not aim to convert, but rather to present tofu traditions as they exist and as they continue to deliciously develop.

I encourage you to explore the techniques and recipes herein. There is much to savor, as tofu can be eaten from morning until night, in no-meat, low-meat, and meaty preparations. It is a flexible food that is open to endless possibilities.

TOFU BUYING GUIDE

Most recipes in this book can be made with tofu sold at supermarkets, health food stores, and specialty grocers. However, a few dishes require a trip to an Asian market. And a handful of preparations call for making your own—see the Homemade Tofu Tutorial (page 17) for guidance. The world of tofu is vast and this section does not cover it all. The types of tofu here are what you will need to prepare the foods in this book.

Tofu Types

Tofu Blocks

Tofu is made by coagulating hot soy milk with mineral salt or acid coagulants. By varying the richness of the soy milk, coagulation method, and pressure used to weight the curds, a tofu maker regulates how much whey (liquid) is left in the tofu. The amount of residual whey determines tofu texture and density. Tofu is typically identified as silken, medium, medium firm, firm, extra firm, and super firm. These categories of tofu are like clothing sizes. While there are industry definitions for tofu densities and textures, manufacturers have latitude within each one, so there are different levels of "firm," for example. In general, Japanese-style tofu is softer than other kinds.

Recipes, personal tastes, and availability dictate which tofu texture to buy. In general, the firmer the tofu, the harder the texture, and the more protein it contains by weight.

While there are other factors involved in the texture of a block of tofu, you can guesstimate its density by the amount of protein contained in a standard 3-ounce serving. Look at the nutritional label. My benchmarks for buying tofu that is neither too soft nor too hard for its class are:

Texture	Grams of protein per 3-ounce serving
Silken/Soft	4–5
Medium/Medium-firm/Regular	6–8
Firm	8–9
Extra-firm	9–10
Super-firm	14+

The overlapping numbers highlight the gray areas of tofu textures. Cook with various brands and textures to understand what each is like, then find brands that match your preferences.

Look for tofu blocks in the refrigerated area of a market, perhaps in a "health food section" or refrigerated Asian foods area. Boxed tofu is only useful in an emergency. Refrigerate tofu in its sealed tub or plastic packaging. Vietnamese tofu, typically encased in flimsy plastic wrap, should be transferred to a tub of water. So should any leftover tofu from an opened container. Replace the water every other day to ensure freshness for about a week.

SILKEN (SOFT)

Aptly named for its mouthfeel, this type of tofu cuts very smoothly. It is made by coagulating rich soy milk over low heat and not weighted down at all. No curds are visible in silken tofu because they are never separated from the whey. Most commercially made silken tofu has been solidified in its plastic tub packaging; a minority is cut into blocks and packaged in water. The precut type of silken tofu tends to be firmer than the kind that requires unmolding. Coagulants are decent indicators of silken tofu texture: glucono delta lactone signals a firm texture; magnesium chloride (nigari) and calcium sulfate (gypsum) signal a softer texture.

MEDIUM, MEDIUM-FIRM

For many Asian cooks, this is their standard tofu. It is rougher textured than silken tofu—the curds are visible. When you pick up a block of medium tofu with one hand, it feels delicate, as if it will break apart. Do the same with medium-firm tofu and it may bend slightly or crack. Firm tofu that's on the soft side can be used as medium-firm tofu.

Tofu labeled medium or medium firm is great for dishes that require little manipulation of the tofu. Eat it chilled, simmer it in broth, or braise it in sauce. Because there is relatively more whey in this type of tofu, panfrying and deep-frying it can be messy and/or result in deflated fried tofu.

FIRM

This is what most recipes in this book call for. Ideally, firm tofu is denser than medium or medium-firm tofu. The curds are clearly visible when you cut the block. If you poke at firm tofu, it should feel relatively solid with a little give, like the flesh at the base of your thumb. It can take a little more physical handling than medium, which makes it perfect for panfrying, deep-frying, and stuffing.

Firm tofu for Asian cooking *does not* mean super dense or hard tofu. As noted earlier, some versions of firm tofu verge on medium firm; others tilt toward extra firm or ultra-dense super firm.

EXTRA-FIRM

As the name suggests, extra-firm tofu is more solid than firm tofu. You can still make out the curds, but the entire block feels very substantial. In a pinch, use firm and extra-firm tofu interchangeably. Extra-firm tofu that seems dense and finely textured skews toward super firm.

SUPER-FIRM

You can barely see the curds in this type of tofu, which is bricklike with a very dense texture akin to a rubber eraser. You can throw a block of super-firm tofu back and forth between your hands without it breaking. It's terrific for homemade pressed or smoked tofu. It grates well, making it a vegan substitute for paneer. At health food markets and specialty grocers, super-firm tofu is typically sold in vacuum-sealed packages. They are often labeled "high protein."

Pressed Tofu

Put a lot of pressure on curds and they become meatlike. In Mandarin Chinese, such tofu is called *dou fu gan* (dry bean curd) and it is typically featured in vegetarian fare because it's substantive in texture and loaded with nutrients.

Pressed tofu is so compacted that you cannot see the curds. It does not require draining because there is little liquid left—cut it up and it's ready to go. It can be thinly sliced and stir-fried with vegetables, cubed and tossed with seasonings, or dropped into soup. I've even had it finely slivered and poached so that it resembled orzo pasta.

In China and Taiwan, pressed tofu comes in myriad shapes, sizes, and textures. Chinese markets abroad mostly sell two varieties of pressed tofu, unseasoned white and seasoned brown. Usually labled as "baked tofu," brown pressed tofu is typically flavored by Chinese five-spice powder, sugar, and soy sauce. The brown variety is what's used in this book.

At the market in the refrigerated foods section, pressed tofu is sold in vacuum-sealed packages or bulk boxes (unless you know the origin and age of the latter, avoid it). Each piece is about 1/2 to 3/4 inch thick and can be shaped as 3-inch squares or 6-inch rectangles or square slabs. Pressed tofu ranges in texture from firm-soft—good for cutting up into small pieces—and firm-hard, which won't break when thinly sliced and stir-fried. For the most part, they are interchangeable. Refrigerate and use pressed tofu within a week of purchase. Sliminess signals spoilage. Or, buy super-firm tofu and make your own seasoned tofu (see pages 38 to 39).

Tofu Noodles

At the Chinese market near the pressed tofu, there are usually 8-ounce packages of squiggly, chewy-tender white tofu noodles. They are cut from pressed tofu and are terrific in salad (page 133). The vacuum-sealed packages can be refrigerated for several weeks, and the noodles can be frozen, though they tend to break after thawing.

Tofu Skin

When soy milk is heated in a pot, it forms a film on top just like regular milk. Pull off that film and you have tofu skin, called *dou pi* in Mandarin and *yuba* in Japanese. Freshly made tofu skin (page 44) is worth savoring at least once in every tofu lover's lifetime. The Japanese, particularly in Kyoto, have a wonderful repertoire of fresh tofu skin dishes.

GENERAL TIPS

There is a lot of variability in tofu, so keep these things in mind when you are shopping:

- Whenever possible, go natural. Buy organic or non-GMO soy products—they are better for the Earth and tastier.

- Be persnickety. Tofu is like bread. Know the brands sold in your area; try them out and find one that you like. If you have an artisanal tofu shop nearby, support it. Asian cooks traditionally have their favorite tofu brands, neighborhood shops, or market vendors. Make it your quest to find one, too.

- You never know where good tofu may be sold. Trader Joe's and Whole Foods carry excellent tofu, which may be labeled under different brands at other stores. Asian markets may sell artisanal tofu that's not widely distributed, and farmers' markets may also have locally made tofu.

- At an Asian market, depending on the type of tofu, it may be shelved in the refrigerated section, frozen foods area, dairy case, dried vegetables aisle, or fermented foods aisle.

- The amount of tofu in a package can differ from the stated weight on the label. For example, a typical 14-ounce package of firm tofu often contains 16 ounces. The marginal difference will usually not affect the outcome of your dish. However, if a recipe requires 1 pound, get as close to that as possible.

- Check the "best by" date to help you select the freshest package.

- In most cases, your recipe will not fail if you do not have the right kind of tofu.

Tofu noodles

Fried tofu slices (sushi-age)

Dried tofu sticks

Fried tofu slices (abura-age)

Tofu skin rounds

Fresh tofu skin packets

But it's the Chinese who have mastered the art of manipulating tofu skin into various dishes.

With the exception of the *nama yuba* (page 55) that you make yourself, the remaining recipes require tofu skin purchased from a Chinese market. Look for buff-colored **fresh tofu skin packets** (*dou fu bao*, often labeled "fresh bean curd skin") packaged on Styrofoam trays or in bulk containers covered by water; purchase the latter only if it looks and smells fresh. The packets are roughly 4- by 5-inch rectangles that resemble pads of wrinkly gauze. Their shape is the result of a large sheet of tofu skin having been folded up. I like to cut the packets for Spicy Yuba Ribbons (page 139). Tofu skin has a chewy, tender texture that is vaguely meaty. It can be chopped and seasoned for making mock fish and the like.

Tofu skin also comes in the form of giant partially dried **tofu skin rounds** (*dou fu pi* or *fu pi*, often labeled "fresh bean curd sheets" or "bean curd spring roll skin"). The translucent 24-inch-wide golden pieces look like oilcloth. Each one represents a single film of soymilk. They are sold in 8- or 16-ounce plastic packages in the refrigerated foods or frozen foods section of Chinese markets. In this book, these pliable skins are used as a dim sum wrapper to encase a shrimp filling (page 182) or for the *yuba* ribbons mentioned above. Thaw frozen tofu skin rounds in the refrigerator. If they are unwieldy, you can fold them into a smaller size; slide the package into a large plastic grocery bag to keep moist. They keep refrigerated for several weeks. They dry out quickly, so keep them covered as you work.

In the dried vegetables aisle at a Chinese market (usually near the dried mushrooms), look for packages of brittle yellow **dried tofu sticks** (*fu zhu*, "tofu bamboo"), which are the entire tofu skin gathered up and dried over a pole. That's why some sticks are in narrow U-shapes. They are wonderful broken into shorter lengths and dropped into simmering broth (see the chicken soup recipe on page 86), where they turn soft and impart a unique earthy edge. They can be transformed into a version of the *yuba* ribbons (page 139), too. Select packages with the most intact-looking sticks. The thicker-looking tofu sticks tend to open up easier and cook up softer than the tightly rolled ones. Store dried tofu sticks in a dry spot and they will last indefinitely.

Fried Tofu

Artisanal tofu shops and Asian markets sell prefried tofu for cooks who are short on time. With the exception of puffy or spongy fried tofu, which are difficult to make at home, I generally do not purchase fried tofu because I am not sure what kind of tofu or oil was used.

For puffy **fried tofu slices**, head to a Japanese, Korean, or Chinese market. Large rectangles are called *abura-age*; smaller squares may instead be labeled *sushi-age*. The Japanese market will likely have both sizes; Korean and Chinese markets mostly have the square ones. Japanese and Korean markets stock it in the tofu area; Chinese markets will keep it in a refrigerated Japanese foods section.

Packaged *abura-age* can be preseasoned. The recipes in this book require the unseasoned ones, which are blond in color and sold in clear plastic packages. Do not confuse spongy slices of *abura-age* with firm slabs of *atsu-age*, which are made from regular block tofu. Keep the fried tofu refrigerated in its packaging or freeze it in a zip-top bag for up to three months. Puffy cubes of fried tofu are typically used in Chinese or Southeast Asian recipes. No recipes in this book use them, but they can add richness and protein to a bowl of noodle soup or stir-fry, as they absorb flavors like a sponge.

Tofu Pudding

Look for quart-size tubs of creamy, custardy tofu pudding at Chinese or Southeast Asian markets. They typically are sold with a small container of ginger sugar syrup. You can use the tofu pudding as a sweet (page 195) or savory (page 59). It can also be scooped up and employed like a soft

Tofu pudding

White fermented tofu

Red fermented tofu

tofu. Some Vietnamese tofu shops, such as Dong Phuong (page 193), make a *pandan*-flavored green tofu pudding that should only be eaten as a dessert-type snack. If the pudding is warm, eat it as soon as you can! To reheat it, spoon it into serving bowls and warm in a microwave oven. Keep the pudding refrigerated.

Fermented Tofu

When cubes of tofu are allowed to age and ferment in a brine of salt, rice wine, and water, they develop a rich creaminess and deep savory flavor. It is one of the most remarkable transformations of tofu that the Chinese came up with. Intensely flavored fermented tofu is not eaten alone; rather, it is used as an umami-rich seasoning or condiment.

There are two basic kinds, white and red. The white kind (called *bai fu ru*, *fu ru*, and *su fu* in Chinese; *chao* in Vietnamese) occupies the most shelf space at Chinese and Vietnamese markets, typically near other jarred sauces, seasonings, and vegetables. Look for jars containing white cubes of tofu in liquid.

I typically select **white fermented tofu** made in Taiwan, such as Hwang Ryh Shiang brand. The ingredients should be tofu, water, wine, and salt. Many brands contain sesame oil, which lends a viscous quality and pleasant aroma. You can buy the tofu with or without chile flakes—it does not matter with the recipes in this book. A higher-priced brand is likely to be of better quality. Regardless, press on the cap to make sure that it is flat, firm, and tight. Avoid slightly bulging lids or cubes of tofu with dots of mold. Choose a jar with a best-by date that's as far away as you can find and avoid jars with dust on them. Once opened, refrigerate the tofu. It will continue to age and may turn an unattractive gray color but it will still be edible. For a delicious experiment, make your own White Fermented Tofu (see page 41).

Red fermented tofu (called *hong fu ru* or *nan ru* in Chinese; *chao do* in Vietnamese) ferments in a deep red brine that mostly contains red yeast rice (*hong qu mi*, or red kojic rice), rice wine, and water. It's very hard to make red fermented tofu. Instead, I rely on excellent brands from China, particularly Treasure and Red Diamond in ceramic containers. Labeled "Shanghai Red Beancurd" and "Fermented Bean Sauce," respectively, their flavor is salty with a slight sweetness.

Whatever brand you select, make sure the seal and/or ribbon are tightly in place. Tofu packaged in plastic bags will continue to age and turn saltier as it sits out. You can slow down that process under refrigeration: transfer both tofu and brine to a glass jar and refrigerate. I use basic fermented red tofu for the recipes in this book. If you develop a fondness for it, check out the Taiwanese brands that also have rice and soybeans in the jar. They are milder and practically tasty enough to snack on.

With any kind of fermented tofu, both the tofu cubes and the brine may be used in cooking. Use a fork or spoon to retrieve a chunk of tofu and mash it lightly into your measuring spoon or cup. Use the brine from red fermented tofu as a glaze for grilled meats (see the Note on page 120).

Soy Milk

Soy milk is the precursor to tofu. For a discussion on using purchased fresh soy milk as a tofu making shortcut, see page 22. In the sweets chapter, feel free to use commercially made soy milk in the recipes. At the store, peruse the nutrition label carefully to make sure that there is no sweetener or flavoring. Then examine the fat and protein content: you want about 4.5 grams of fat and around 9 grams of protein per cup, no less.

TOFU COOKING TIPS

An extremely versatile ingredient, tofu can be used for countless dishes. These pointers prepare you for the recipes ahead and beyond.

Cutting

Because each block or piece of tofu differs in size, use the recipe's measurements for cutting tofu as a guide. You may have to stand the block on its side to obtain nice sized pieces. Not every piece needs to be the same size; however, take extra care if the tofu has to be stuffed, because the thickness of each piece matters. Liquid starts draining soon after you cut tofu, so be prepared.

Draining

Tofu is a great sponge for absorbing seasonings, as long as it has had some of its liquid removed before cooking. Recipe instructions often include information on draining tofu, and there are many ways to go about it, from pressing it between boards to boiling it to microwaving it. I use several methods in this book, depending on how the tofu will be cooked. Depending on the size of the pieces, draining tofu takes perhaps 15 minutes.

DRAIN NATURALLY

Some cooks cut their tofu at the beginning of their ingredient prep work, letting it sit on their cutting board to drain. Others place the tofu atop a bamboo tray or flat strainer positioned over a bowl to catch the liquid. I prefer to cut the tofu, then transfer the pieces to a clean, dry, non-terry dishtowel placed on a tray or large plate.

A waffle-weave dishtowel works extra well because it raises the tofu up slightly so it doesn't sit on an overly damp surface. I put the tofu on half of the dishtowel and later use the drier half to blot excess moisture right before cooking. You can use paper towels, but you'll need a lot.

SOAK, THEN DRAIN

When tofu is destined to be simmered in liquid, Chinese cooks often blanch it first. The tofu softens in the hot water, but once it's removed from the water, it drains and firms up in about 15 minutes. Tofu drained this way can better withstand vigorous simmering for dishes such as spicy *ma po dou fu* (page 101); the tofu doesn't fall apart and each piece becomes velvety soft and absorbs the seasonings during cooking. Soaking cut tofu briefly in a bowl of very hot water does the trick, too.

When tofu will be deep-fried, I like to soak it in very hot salted water. That firms up the outer surface of the tofu, facilitates draining, and lightly seasons the tofu, coaxing out its savory flavor. After draining, the tofu fries up beautifully and quickly with a fine, even yellow surface.

PRESS

To firm up tofu so it's no longer jiggly, cut up the tofu, then weight it down. I use two waffle-weave dishtowels, laying one on a baking sheet (or other flat-bottomed implement), placing the tofu on top, then covering it with another dishtowel. A second baking sheet goes on top of the second towel to create a sandwich of sorts. Finally, weight (food cans) is positioned on top. This method multitasks by draining the tofu while firming it up. It is used in the seasoned pressed tofu and fermented tofu recipes (pages 38 and 41). Use this technique when you want to transform tender tofu into firm tofu.

SQUEEZE

Breaking up a block of tofu and squeezing it in a piece of fabric (muslin works really well) is the fastest way of draining. This approach works best when the tofu will be mashed for a dumpling filling or mixed with other ingredients, such as in the Indonesian banana leaf packets on page 127. The recipes have an approximate yield for you to aim for while squeezing.

Frying

Many Asian tofu recipes call for fried tofu, so I urge you to overcome any fears of frying. Cooking tofu in hot oil creates a wonderful chewy-crisp coating on each piece of tofu, adds a rich fattiness, and creates a lovely golden color.

Deep-frying or **shallow-frying** tofu is easy, fast, and not overly dramatic. Unless a recipe requires immediate crispness, you can deep-fry a big batch and refrigerate it for five days.

Use a wok to deep-fry if you want to save on oil. A deep-fry thermometer is the best tool for gauging oil temperature; you want a moderately-high temperature (between 360° and 370°F) to quickly fry the tofu, so the dried chopstick test does not work here. After deep-frying, let the oil cool, then strain it through paper towels, saving it for another use. Discard used oil when it has darkened or smells off.

Panfrying tofu does not create an even crisp texture all over the tofu pieces. However, you use less oil and can fry large slabs of tofu. A large nonstick skillet works well for panfrying. Because the tofu is not quickly coated in hot oil, there tends to be some sputtering of oil during panfrying; be sure to blot excess moisture from the surface of the pieces before panfrying. Panfried tofu can often be substituted for deep-fried or shallow-fried tofu, but the result will not be the same in texture and flavor.

Soy milk lees

Soy milk

Block tofu

Silken tofu

Seasoned pressed tofu

Fresh tofu skin

HOMEMADE TOFU TUTORIAL

Why make tofu yourself? Because you want to experience it at its peak—freshly made, creamy, and subtly sweet. Homemade tofu is as precious as homemade bread.

In parts of Asia where tofu is a mainstay, most people rely on local producers and market vendors; they don't typically make their own tofu. This is probably why a number of Asian people reacted with pleased surprise when I mentioned I was making my own tofu at home. One day while I was shopping for a cedar tofu mold at the Soko Hardware store in San Francisco's Japantown, several older women overheard my conversation with the store clerks and peppered me with delighted questions. One of them rhapsodically recalled growing up in Fremont, California, where the neighborhood tofu maker cooked huge quantities of soy milk in a cauldron set over a backyard wood fire.

Still, some home cooks do take on tofu making. In Japan, supermarkets sell bottled soy milk with tiny packages of coagulant for this purpose. And a few years ago, a family friend asked how to make fresh tofu; she wanted to relay the information to a Vietnamese woman who had immigrated to Africa. (For a story of how tofu comforts and connects people, read about the Lim family on page 77.) And nowadays many people are talking about making tofu at home. It no longer seems so arcane. In fact, when I brought homemade tofu to a dinner party, our Swedish-born hostess without hesitation remarked, "Oh, making tofu is like making yogurt."

You can prepare most of the recipes in this book with purchased tofu. However, if you want to further explore the subtle flavors and textures of tofu, doing it from scratch is for you; there are many options for getting started. Most of the ingredients and equipment are surprisingly accessible. Review the section on essential ingredients and equipment, then embark on your own tofu adventure.

Tofu Essentials: Ingredients

Making tofu requires only three ingredients: dried soybeans, water, and coagulant. With so little involved, it's important to start out with good ingredients to ensure results that are worth your effort.

Dried Soybeans

Selecting good soybeans is part of the tofu maker's craft, but you do not have to struggle with it. Tofu is *not* made from the green edamame beans that are boiled up for snacking. You need mature, dried soybeans.

There are countless varieties of dried soybeans, and their seed coats come in many colors—buff, yellow, green, brown, black, and mottled. Most are yellow inside (some green or black soybeans have light green interiors). They are roundish and range from tiny lentil-size to giants the size of blueberries. When purchasing soybeans:

- Choose handsome, clean beans with uniform size and shape. The light beige or pale yellow ones are most commonly used for making tofu.

- Check for the soybean's hilum, the "eye" that indicates where the seed was attached to the pod. The hilum varies in color, but on the choicest soybeans for making tofu it's nearly invisible.

- Look for large beans (think of a regular-size frozen pea); they generally contain more protein and fat, resulting in a higher yield. However, huge beans do not necessarily mean better tofu. When comparing soybeans, peruse the nutritional labels, if present, to determine fat and protein content.

- Buy organic or non-GMO dried soybeans: they are cultivated in a healthy and sustainable way, and they make exceptionally tasty soy milk and tofu.

- Shop for dried soybeans at health food markets and Asian grocers, or in the bulk section of some supermarkets.

- Consider buying soybeans directly from a grower. Iowa's Fairview Farms cultivates Laura Soybeans, an excellent non-GMO bean.

- Try different kinds of soybeans from a variety of sources. The price is extremely reasonable, so your experimentation won't break the bank.

- Taste beans that have been soaked but *do not* swallow them because they are hard to digest. Good soybeans should have a pleasant, fresh flavor.

- Store dried soybeans in an airtight container at room temperature. They will keep indefinitely.

Water

Use water that you regularly drink to soak the beans and render the soy milk. I use filtered tap water, but you may prefer spring or well water. Rinse the beans and wash equipment with regular tap water, but the water used for making soy milk, and subsequently to yield tofu, should taste good.

Coagulant

A handful of coagulants can be used to make tofu, from everyday vinegar and lemon juice to gypsum, Epsom salts, and boiled-down seawater. Japanese producers traditionally preferred *nigari* extracted from seawater to coagulate their soy milk, while Chinese tofu makers favored gypsum and Vietnamese tofu makers used the whey from previous batches as a coagulant. Nowadays, those divisions are blurred and tofu makers use what they deem to be optimal for their customers. For example, some people use gypsum for silken tofu while others prefer the ease of glucono delta-lactone (GDL), a white crystalline powder that is acidic in nature. Read commercial tofu labels and you may see a combination of coagulants. Regardless of what is used, the coagulant works to solidify the protein and oil in hot soy milk.

In trying out most of the coagulants listed above, I've found that gypsum and *nigari* are the best (and equally good), with Epsom salts coming in third. All three are common minerals classified as types of salt. They are also easy for home cooks to obtain. Vinegar and lemon juice produce tofu that is grainy in texture and slightly sour tasting. Some people like that tang and say that the acid helps preserve the tofu. GDL is a pricey industrial product. Using recycled whey works best if you are a professional producer with space to store the whey and are making tofu every day.

The yield of tofu solids is about the same regardless, but there are subtle flavor and texture differences in the end product. Gypsum is the most versatile coagulant for the recipes in this book.

THE TOP THREE TOFU COAGULANTS

Coagulant	Characteristics	Availability
Nigari (magnesium chloride)	Produces slightly sweet flavor; firmer tofu than gypsum yields. Can be taken with water as a health supplement, but the flavor can be very bitter. *Nigari* comes from the Japanese *nigai,* which means "bitter."	Clear liquid *nigari* is sold at many Japanese markets in small plastic bottles, such as the one below on the left. Purchase crystalline or granulated *nigari* from online vendors, who may also carry liquid *nigari*. Check health food stores with macrobiotic sections.
Gypsum (calcium sulfate)	Yields mild-tasting tofu that is slightly more tender than *nigari* tofu. Adds a significant amount of calcium to tofu.	Use food-grade gypsum, which is also used in beer making. Home brewing suppliers sell gypsum and it is available online. The gypsum sold at Chinese markets tends to have an odd perfume.
Epsom salts (magnesium sulfate)	Functions like gypsum but the resulting texture is slightly grainy. Can be used to alleviate body aches, exfoliate, and relieve constipation. Soak, drink, or scrub with it.	Widely available and reasonably priced at drugstores and supermarkets.

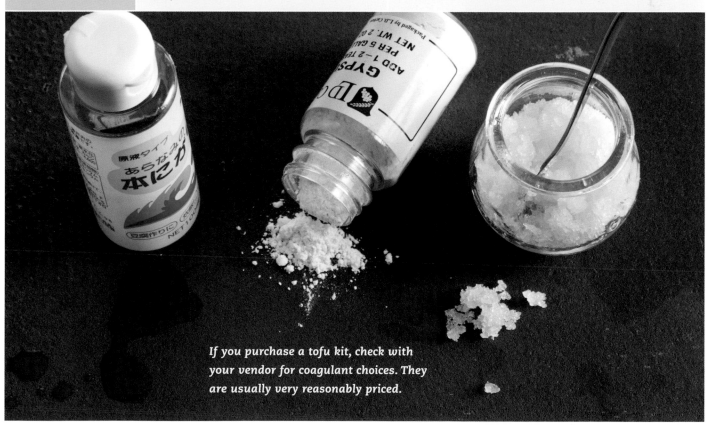

If you purchase a tofu kit, check with your vendor for coagulant choices. They are usually very reasonably priced.

Tofu Essentials: Equipment

Unless you are planning to make rectangular blocks of tofu, you can get by with basic kitchen equipment to make tofu. Silken tofu and soft tofu pudding are prepared in a variety of containers and no special mold or mold lining cloth is required. However, you'll need the following items to handle the tasks involved.

Grinding Beans

BLENDER

A regular countertop blender, *not* the hand-held immersion kind, renders the soaked beans and water to a silky, thick mixture in no time. A food processor can be used, too.

Cooking Soy Milk

LARGE POT

To initially cook the soybean slurry, use a pot with a capacity of about two and a half times the amount of water that will be used. For example, rich soy milk calls for 6 cups of water, so use a 4-quart pot. A 6-quart pot is perfect for a batch of light soy milk. If you double a recipe, remember to use larger pots. A nonstick pot makes cleaning easier.

SMALLER POT

To simmer the strained soy milk, find a pot that holds about 1 quart less than the larger pot. For example, a 3-quart pot is plenty sufficient for a 3 1/4-cup batch of rich soy milk. A 5-quart pot will accommodate a batch of light soy milk just fine. Again, a nonstick pot helps reduce cleanup.

WOODEN SPATULA

The shape of the spatula mimics a tofu maker's stirring paddle; its flat edge is perfect for effectively stirring a pot of soy milk, cooling the soy milk, and adding coagulant.

Straining Soy Milk

LARGE COLANDER OR MESH STRAINER

Choose a colander that is a little bigger than the smaller pot so that it fits inside but extends over the pot's rim by about 1 inch. Or use a sturdy mesh strainer.

PRESSING CLOTH

Have a large piece of cotton cloth to press the soy milk through—a big square of lightweight unbleached muslin or an oversized non-terry cotton dishtowel.

PRESSING TOOL

Use a potato masher; clean, empty wine bottle; or quart jar.

TOFU TOOL DISCOVERIES

While writing this book, one of my go-to kitchen helpers was a stash of **unbleached muslin** squares—my better alternative to cheesecloth. I used them for rendering soy milk, lining molds, squeezing tofu, and straining stocks. They laundered beautifully in the washing machine, their unfinished edges developing character as I developed my tofu making skills. At the fabric store, look for lightweight unbleached muslin. It comes in varying widths; the ideal yardage is about 48 inches wide, enough to yield two 24-inch-square pieces. Buy a generous 2/3 yard and tear it in half along the grain.

On the other hand, **soy milk machines** disappointed. They are good for making soy milk that you drink but do not have a large enough capacity to handle the larger volume needed for making tofu. Plus, they are designed for a particular ratio of beans to milk. I tried manipulating one machine to produce different kinds of soy milks but my efforts resulted in lots of cleanup and burnt milk. Additionally, I had to strain the milk to remove lingering fine solids. The machine was not a huge time-saver for making tofu.

Wooden tofu mold

Mold-liner cloth

Pressing cloth

Plastic tofu mold

Shaping Regular and Firm Tofu

MOLD

Use a tofu pressing box made of wood or plastic, Japanese bamboo colander (*zaru*), or a small colander. You can fashion a mold from two disposable aluminum loaf pans. Use the tip of a paring knife to perforate the bottom and sides of one pan with holes, spaced about 1 inch apart, for drainage; employ the other to weight down the curds.

For beautiful, neat block tofu, purchase a dedicated mold. Search online for "tofu kit" and "tofu box." Plastic molds, such as the Soya Joy (the wooden option is pictured on page 21), are great for beginners and are what I provided to my recipe testers; it works well for a batch of tofu made from 6 ounces of dried soybeans. Wooden ones are larger and have a removable bottom for easy unmolding. The one I often use has an opening that spans 4 inches wide, 5³/4 inches long, and a scant 3¹/2 inches deep. The larger wooden mold measuring 4³/4 inches wide, 6³/4 inches long, and 3³/4 inches deep is good for tofu made from 12 ounces of dried beans. Japanese wooden molds, such as the Mitoku, are pricey but beautifully constructed and worth owning if you regularly make tofu.

MOLD-LINER CLOTH

Use the fabric that came with the purchased mold or a piece of lightweight fabric, such as cotton voile or unbleached muslin; trim the fabric to a size roughly three times the length and width of your mold.

TOFU SHORTCUTS: CANNED SOYBEANS, SOY FLOUR, OR PURCHASED SOY MILK?

With all the soaking, grinding, and cooking involved in making tofu, are there any time-saving shortcuts? Canned soybeans have been cooked, so they won't work. Reconstituting soy flour to make soy milk only saves on the initial soaking time as you still have to strain and cook it twice. Regular blocks of tofu made from soy flour are unpleasantly grainy. Mass-marketed soy milks sold in boxes and cartons do not coagulate well.

The most viable tofu making shortcut is to purchase freshly made soy milk from an Asian grocery store or artisanal tofu shop. Look for 1- or 2-quart plastic containers in the refrigerated section with the dairy products.

If the soy milk is as thick as regular whole milk, it is like medium soy milk and is great for tofu pudding (page 30). It will work for block tofu but you may need to add extra coagulant because there is more fat and protein in this richer milk; your yield will be higher than normal.

Most fresh soy milk has a richness that's akin to lowfat milk, which works perfectly for block tofu (page 32) but *not* for tofu pudding. Let 8 cups of the soy milk come to room temperature, then bring it to a strong simmer in a large pot. Turn off the heat and stir for about 1 minute to cool to about 170°F; because you don't simmer the soy milk for long, it doesn't get as hot as the scratch method. Then add the coagulant as directed in step 3 of the block tofu recipe. The rest is the same.

Do your best to find organic soy milk with no flavoring. This semihomemade approach is good for beginners and experimenters who want to practice or tinker. For the ultimate quality control, make soy milk yourself.

Master Soy Milk Recipe

Certain tofu products, such as tofu noodles, cannot be made at home; however, you can prepare many kinds of tofu yourself. Regardless of the type of tofu, rendering soy milk is the crucial first step. It is not difficult to do, and it allows you to control the quality of the beans and water used, and the thickness of the soy milk.

With regard to timing, if you aim to make silken tofu, tofu pudding, or tofu skin (pages 28, 30, and 44), the soy milk should be cooled first, allowing the flavor to concentrate. In the case of silken tofu, the soy milk should be slightly chilled or at room temperature to solidify well. It's advantageous to prepare the rich and medium soy milk in advance.

For block tofu, the finished soy milk is typically coagulated right away while the soy milk is still hot. Review the instructions beginning on page 32 and have your coagulant and tools ready. You could prepare the light soy milk in advance up through step 10, let it cool, and then continue later with simmering and adding the coagulant to form the curds and whey. But it's a lot of soy milk to store and there is no huge benefit to not making block tofu right away. For those reasons, plan on making it as an extension to this recipe.

I've designed this set of instructions as a master recipe that will enable you to experience the leeway you have when making tofu from scratch. The first step is to decide what kind of tofu you want to prepare, because that determines what kind of soy milk you'll be making. Use the following table as a guide.

Application	Soy Milk Type
Silken tofu, tofu skin (pages 28 and 44)	Rich
Tofu pudding (page 30)	Medium
Block tofu (page 32)	Light

The differences between rich, medium, and light soy milk are similar to those between heavy cream, whole milk, and lowfat milk. I've designed this recipe so that you use the same amount of soybeans but vary the quantity of water to make the different types of soy milk.

Soy milk type	Rich	Medium	Light
Dried soybeans	6 ounces	6 ounces	6 ounces
Water*, plus more for soaking	4 cups	6 cups	8 cups
Yield after extraction	4 cups	6 cups	8 cups
Yield after simmering and cooling	3¼ cups	5 cups	N/A

* Use good drinking water, such as filtered or spring.

Note that 6 ounces of dried soybeans is about 1 scant cup; if you accidentally measure a little more beans, your milk will be slightly thicker. Light soy milk is typically used after it has been extracted. It is not cooled before it is coagulated for tofu.

CONTINUED

Master Soy Milk Recipe

Read this entire recipe before making your first batch. You can pace yourself by soaking the beans days in advance. After making soy milk and tofu a few times, you'll have a routine down. It will take less time and cleanup will be easier. I've learned to rinse the equipment soon after using it to remove some of the clinging bits. A plastic dough scraper is handy for removing the film of soy milk that clings to the pot. Once you become familiar with your soybeans, tinker with the ratio of beans to water, just like the pros do!

SOAK THE BEANS

1 Put the dried beans in a colander and rinse under tap water to remove any surface dirt. Transfer the beans to a bowl. Add water (such as filtered or spring) to cover by 2 to 3 inches, then set aside to soak at room temperature. The soaking time varies by season, and below is a rough estimate of the time required.

Air Temperature	Approximate Time
80°F	8 hours
70°F	10 hours
60°F	13 1/2 hours
50°F	17 1/2 hours

2 Test the beans to determine their readiness. Squeeze one between your fingertips and it should split apart into two long halves. The beans are sufficiently soaked if the surfaces of the halves are flat with an even buttercup yellow color *and* if you can easily break one of the halves crosswise. If the surfaces are concave and/or darker in the middle than at the edge (on the left in the photo), and if halves bend in a rubbery manner, soak longer. Adequately

soaked beans (on the right in the photo) are softer, and easier to grind. Drain the soaked beans in a colander. (Feel free to save the soaking liquid to use in the next steps.) It is possible, but not easy, to oversoak the beans. I've never done it, but some people say that bubbles or foam appear on the surface. If you see these, discard the water, then use the beans.

When soaking the beans in advance, transfer the drained beans to an airtight container and refrigerate for up to 5 days; discard or keep the soaking water refrigerated in a separate container, if you like. Refrigerating the beans in the soaking liquid is fine for 2 days; beyond that, the flavor may be compromised. If the beans look suspect, rinse them before using; throw out the soaking liquid if it smells funky. Regardless, return both beans and liquid to room temperature before proceeding. Soaked soybeans can be frozen but

Soy Milk Type	WATER USE				
	Heating in Larger Pot	Grinding Beans	Rinsing Blender	Second Pressing	Total Used
Rich	1 cup	2 cups	1/2 cup	1/2 cup	4 cups
Medium	3 cups	2 cups	1/2 cup	1/2 cup	6 cups
Light	5 cups	2 cups	1/2 cup	1/2 cup	8 cups

the soy milk and tofu produced from them are not as super-lative as those produced from soaked, unfrozen beans. Each 6 ounces of dried beans weighs about 14 ounces (and measures about 2 1/4 cups) after soaking.

RENDER THE SOY MILK

3 Set up your soy milk making equipment. For the straining station, put the smaller pot (see page 20) in the sink and place the colander (or mesh strainer) inside it. Put the soy milk pressing cloth in the colander, letting its edges drape over the rim. Have your pressing tool nearby.

4 Now use the table above as a guide on how much water to use at the various stages in making soy milk. It's okay if you use slightly different amounts of water in the next steps, but, overall, try to utilize the total amount specified. All the water and soybeans should eventually end up in the pot.

5 Put the larger pot (see page 20) on the stove. To kick-start the cooking process, heat some water in the pot. The amount you need is in the column labeled "heating in larger pot." Use high or medium-high heat. If the water comes to a boil before you've ground all the beans, lower the heat and cover the pot; raise the heat once you've added the ground beans.

6 Meanwhile, use a blender to grind the soybeans with 2 cups of water. Run the blender on the highest speed for 1 to 2 minutes to yield a thick, smooth, ivory white puree—a beany milkshake. (If you scale up this recipe, grind in several batches. A 6-cup blender can handle about 2 1/4 cups of soybeans and 2 cups of water at a time.)

Add the mixture to the pot of water. If there are whole beans left at the bottom of the blender container, pause the pouring and run the blender for 30 seconds before adding it to the larger pot. A few unblended soybeans won't ruin the tofu, but try to grind up as much as you can. To rinse out the blender container, add 1/2 cup of water and run the blender for 10 to 15 seconds. Pour into the larger pot and scrape out any residual bits.

7 Cook the soybean mixture, stirring the bottom frequently with a wooden spatula to avoid scorching, until frothy foam forms and begins to rise, 3 to 6 minutes. This can suddenly sneak up on you, so monitor the pot. Look for a very thick layer of foam that resembles softly whipped egg whites. When you see the foam rise like a beer head, turn off the heat and remove the pot from the heat to prevent

CONTINUED

Master Soy Milk Recipe

boiling over. Stir the pot a few times and wait for the foam to deflate a bit.

8 To strain out the milk, pour the hot mixture into the pressing cloth, pausing when the colander is full and waiting for the milk to pass through before adding more from the larger pot. Scrape out any soybeans remaining in the pot. (The rich soy milk is super thick and takes longer to pass through the cloth than the other milks.)

9 Gather up the pressing cloth and twist it closed into a sack. It will be hot; it's fine to wait a few minutes for the contents to cool slightly. Use your pressing tool to mash the sack against the colander and extract more soy milk.

10 To extract additional milk, do a second pressing. Open up the pressing cloth and spread the solids (lees) out. Add 1/2 cup of water to the lees; stir to combine into a polenta-like mixture. If the lees are still steaming hot, let them cool for 3 to 5 minutes. When you are able, twist the cloth closed and wring out more soy milk.

Open up the pressing cloth, and transfer the soft white lees to a bowl. Let cool before using or refrigerating. See "Tofu Byproduct Bonus," opposite, for details on using the lees.

Remove the colander and pressing cloth to reveal the soy milk in the smaller pot.

RECOOK THE SOY MILK

11 Soybean protein needs to be cooked for a certain amount of time to ensure that it is fully digestible and ready to be coagulated. Bring the smaller pot of soy milk to a gentle simmer over medium-high or high heat, stirring the bottom frequently with a wooden spatula. When bubbles percolate at the surface, lower the heat slightly to maintain that pace of gentle cooking for 5 minutes, minding the pot and stirring. If a light film forms at the top, remove it; you can eat it as a super delicate fresh tofu skin. Should the milk scorch, your tofu will have a certain rustic smoky taste, as if it were made over a wood fire. After this second cooking, the soy milk is ready to be used for tofu making, cooking, or drinking. See the individual recipes for details.

When making soy milk in advance, remove it from the heat and set it aside to cool. A skin forms quickly on hot soy milk, so during the first 15 minutes use the spatula to frequently stir the milk; run the exhaust fan to facilitate air flow and trace a "Z" or an "N" pattern to introduce cool air into the milk. When you can keep your finger on the side of the pot for 3 to 5 seconds, the soy milk has cooled down enough so that a skin won't form (around 130°F). You can stop stirring, partially cover the soy milk, and let it finish cooling naturally.

If the soy milk overevaporates and is thicker than you like (use the yield in the table on page 23 as your guide), add back some water to dilute it. If it is too thin, simmer it down, stirring often. Rich and medium soy milk can be refrigerated for up to 5 days. Let them sit out for about 30 minutes to remove the chill before preparing tofu. Light soy milk should be used to make tofu right after it is made.

TOFU BYPRODUCT BONUS: SOY MILK LEES

Don't discard the crumbly soft lees from the pressing cloth after you've wrung out all the soy milk! What you may consider the dregs is a valuable food source. Called *dou fu zha* or *xue hua cai*, okara, and *biji* in Mandarin, Japanese, and Korean, respectively, the lees are loaded with dietary fiber and nutrients. They are low in fat too, and contain about 17 percent of the protein from the original soybeans.

To inspire you to use the lees (pictured on page 16) in Asian ways, I've included it in a few recipes in this cookbook. If you prepare the deep-fried croquettes on page 114, you'll notice how the lees absorb whatever wet ingredients—stock and/or condiments—that you set upon them. Add some to a Korean hot pot (page 87), and you'll thicken it into a creamy chowderlike consistency. Season and sauté them with vegetables for *unohana* (page 142), an old-fashioned Japanese favorite. Or bake cookies or make doughnuts (pages 202 and 203) with *okara* for a modern hybrid twist. Beyond the Asian kitchen, employ the lees as a meat extender for dishes. Tester Dave Weinstein incorporated *okara* into panfried potato and chicken croquettes.

Most modern-day tofu operations, in Asia and abroad, sell their lees as animal feed—there is not enough human demand for the lees. But home cooks' batches of soy milk and tofu yield manageable amounts of lees (6 ounces of dried soybeans yields about 7 ounces, 1 firmly packed cup, of lees) that can be refrigerated for up to one week and put to delicious use. It freezes well for several months, too; thaw it at room temperature or in the refrigerator before using.

Silken Tofu

Silken tofu, unlike regular tofu, does not entail pressing the whey out during the tofu making process. Rather, the soy milk is solidified in its final container. The curds and whey never separate, resulting in the velvety soft texture of silken tofu, called *kinugoshi-dofu* (silk-strained tofu) in Japanese.

This tofu's rich and fatty flavor derives from the fact that it is made from soy milk that's thicker than that used for block tofu. Think of the difference between ice creams made from milk versus those made from cream. Each has its own merits, but the flavors and textures are different. Silken tofu (pictured on page 16) reveals its elegant creaminess when eaten slightly chilled with a few simple garnishes, such as for *hiya yakko* (page 51), a Japanese classic.

The trick to making silken tofu is to prevent curds and whey from forming, which happens if the soy milk gets too hot. Commercial producers use a carbohydrate called glucono delta-lactone, which is not widely available to home cooks. However, some small-scale tofu producers and chefs steam cold soy milk with *nigari* until it's just set, then serve it chilled in its container.

I tried the slow and gentle steaming technique with my favorite coagulants and found that *nigari*, both liquid and refined crystals, and Epsom salts produce slightly weepy tofu that's cloudy at the bottom when the soy milk is cooked in large quantities. However, gypsum produces a gorgeous, silky texture that molds well with no weepiness, even when I steam the entire quantity of soy milk in a glass loaf pan; it is the best overall coagulant for this type of tofu. The artisanal tofu makers I met in Japan also use gypsum for their silken tofu.

Feel free to steam as little soy milk as 1 cup at a time. Just use a third of the coagulant and water. Remember to make the soy milk in advance and refrigerate it until you need it. It is fine if the soy milk is cold, slightly chilled, or at room temperature; it should *not* be warm or hot. That is, don't make the soy milk and then move right into this recipe. If you do, the moment you add the coagulant to the warm or hot soy milk, it will separate into curds and whey.

3 cups Rich Soy Milk (page 23), chilled or at room temperature

1¹/₂ teaspoons packed gypsum

2 teaspoons water, filtered or spring preferred

1 Choose a large mold or several small molds to steam the soy milk in. Glass or ceramic containers with straight, smooth inner walls work best for unmolding; make sure the mold fits in your steamer tray. If you want easy cooking and storage, and don't mind if the tofu is served in imperfect shapes and irregular sizes, select a vessel such as a glass loaf pan. For individual servings, use 3- or 4-ounce ramekins. There is no need to oil the mold for silken tofu.

2 Get a pot of water boiling for steaming. Stir together the gypsum and water to dissolve.

3 When the water comes to a rolling boil, lower the heat to steady the flow of steam. Give the soy milk a stir and if it is not totally smooth, pass it through a coarse-mesh strainer. Now, combine the soy milk and coagulant liquid, stirring to blend well. Pour into the molds to a depth between 1 and 2¹/₂ inches.

4 Place the molds in the steamer tray and position the lid slightly ajar to minimize the amount of condensation dripping down. Gently steam the soy milk until the tofu has set. The amount of time required depends on the quantity of soy milk and the size of the mold. In general, it takes about 6 minutes to set 1 inch of soy milk. The tofu is done if it jiggles when you shake the mold; if you pick up the mold and slightly tilt it, the tofu may slide around. A toothpick inserted into the center will leave a tiny visible hole on the surface. You may steam the tofu for a few more minutes because the gentle heat will not harm the outcome.

5 Detach the steamer tray and cool for a few minutes before removing the molds. Cool the molds completely at room temperature. To unmold the tofu with ease, cover and chill in the refrigerator for at least 4 hours. You can keep the tofu refrigerated for up to 3 days. Let it sit at room temperature for about 15 minutes, then run a knife around the edge (just like a cake) and invert it onto a flat surface. The water that releases as the unmolded tofu sits is the whey.

VARIATION: CITRUS-SCENTED SILKEN TOFU

When I visited Tokyo to do research for this book, Japanese food expert and author Elizabeth Andoh took me to visit Toshio and Kyoko Kanemoto, the proprietors of her neighborhood tofu shop, Nitto Tofu. Among the couple's superb offerings was an amazing *yuzu*-flavored silken tofu. Once I tasted it, I had to recreate it. It turned out to be easy.

Choose an aromatic citrus, such as Meyer lemon, lime, orange, or Buddha's hand. Grate just the skin, using a Japanese ginger grater, if possible, to obtain the finest texture. For every cup of rich soy milk, use 1/2 teaspoon grated zest (the amount from an average lemon). Stir in the zest before adding the gypsum coagulant. Then steam as directed above.

The citrus oils are spotlighted when the tofu is simply presented. Tester Makiko Tsuzuki enjoyed it as small chunks with a light drizzle of soy sauce. I also like to feature it in the creamy edamame soup (page 84).

Tofu Pudding

If you're new to making tofu, this recipe is a great one to start off with. It doesn't require as much finesse as silken tofu, nor do you need to obtain or rig up a tofu mold. The technique is simple. Heat the soy milk, then pour it from a height of about 12 inches into a deep pot containing gypsum and tapioca starch dissolved in water. The strong gush of soy milk ensures that the ingredients commingle well. As the soy milk sits, the coagulant solution sets it to a tender-yet-firm texture.

Gypsum is the traditional coagulant for tofu pudding; used alone, it yields a good tofu flavor and delicate, slightly coarse texture. However, it weeps a lot of whey. For less whey and a silkier and firmer finish, add tapioca starch. Less whey also means a milder flavor. As you learn about your soy milk and personal preferences, play with the texture. For example, try 2 teaspoons of gypsum with 1 teaspoon of starch, or vary those ingredients by 1/4- to 1/2-teaspoon increments.

This tofu pudding is usually featured as a warm savory or sweet snack (pages 59 and 195, respectively). You can also serve it chilled with savory garnishes such as grated ginger, green onion, and soy sauce (page 51). Or, let it enrich hot pots like Korean *soon dubu chigae* (page 91).

You have to scoop the tofu pudding out of the pot that it is made in; consider it whenever you need a soft tofu that does not need to be cut into neat shapes. Tofu pudding can be purchased at some Asian markets, but homemade is fabulous.

5 cups Medium Soy Milk (page 23), at room temperature
2 1/2 teaspoons packed gypsum, or 1 1/2 teaspoons packed
    gypsum plus 1 1/2 teaspoons tapioca starch
1/4 cup water, filtered or spring preferred

1 Put the soy milk in a medium saucepan (a lip makes pouring easier). Over medium-high heat, bring to a boil, stirring often with a wooden spoon to prevent scorching and keep a skin from forming.

2 Meanwhile, choose a larger, tallish pot, such as a deep 4-quart pot, to hold the finished tofu. In the pot, whisk together the gypsum and water to create a milky liquid. Position the pot somewhere low enough so you can pour the soy milk into it from about 12 inches above—on a chair seat or opened oven door. If you like, put the pot on a baking sheet or dishtowel to minimize mess from any splashing. Keep the whisk nearby.

3 When the soy milk reaches a rolling boil, turn the heat off. Whisk the coagulant because the solids tend to settle. Holding the saucepan about 12 inches above the pot, pour the hot soy milk into the coagulant; the gush of turbulence will mix the ingredients together. (You can start low and raise the saucepan higher as you pour.) Cover immediately with a lid and move the pot if necessary. Let the tofu sit, undisturbed, for 15 minutes.

The tofu can be used once it has set. However, let it sit for another 30 minutes and the flavor will have developed further. Check recipes for information on using the tofu. If there are a lot of residual bubbles on the surface of the set tofu, use a spoon to gently remove them. Once you scoop the tofu, you break it up and it begins releasing whey. That is its nature. The longer it sits, the more it will drain, just like regular tofu. Use a slotted spoon to scoop if you want to leave some of the whey behind. To minimize the amount of whey that seeps out, scoop large pieces of the tofu and do it right before serving as savory or sweet tofu pudding.

To store the tofu pudding for up to 3 days, replace the lid on the pot and refrigerate after the tofu has completely cooled. When reheating for warm tofu dishes, gently pour water into the pot around the tofu's edges (to avoid breaking it up) to cover by 1/4 inch. Heat over medium-low heat until the tofu is warm to the touch. Avoid boiling because that may break up the tofu or make it unpleasantly firm. To keep the tofu warm, use the lowest heat.

Block Tofu

MAKES 1 TO 1¹/₄ POUNDS, DEPENDING ON THE BEANS

Think of soy milk like cow's milk and you'll understand that making block tofu—the kind that is sold in cut pieces, submerged in water or sealed up in a packaged tub—is akin to making cheese. It's simply a matter of separating the protein and fat out of the milk by forming curds and whey.

To draw out the protein and fat, diluted coagulant (see page 18) is added to fresh, hot soy milk. Within minutes, clouds of curds and pale yellow whey form. They are ladled into a cloth-lined mold, and the liquid whey drains out, leaving the curds. A little weight placed on top helps the curds stick together to form the tofu. Adding the coagulant to the soy milk can require finessing—see the troubleshooting tips on page 33 for help. The temperature of just-cooked soy milk is about 180°F. Its temperature when coagulant is added affects how much coagulant is needed as well as the size of the curds. In general, lower temperatures require more coagulant but can yield beautiful lofty curds. I aim for around 170°F, so I let the soy milk cool for 2 or 3 minutes before I add coagulant.

For draining and shaping the tofu, you will need a mold and a piece of thin, lightweight cloth to line it. See page 20 for details and options.

About 8 cups Light Soy Milk (page 23), prepared through step 10, after the second pressing of the lees

About 1¹/₂ teaspoons packed refined nigari crystals, gypsum, or Epsom salts, or 2 teaspoons liquid nigari

¹/₂ cup water, filtered or spring preferred, plus more as needed

1 Keep the soy milk in the smaller pot you just used for rendering it. Bring to a gentle simmer over medium-high or high heat, stirring the bottom frequently with a wooden spatula. Allow the soy milk to softly percolate for 5 minutes, adjusting the heat as needed. Remember to mind the pot and stir during this period. If a light skin forms, remove it as it may break up the tofu during shaping; you can eat the skin (see page 9).

2 Meanwhile, combine the coagulant with the water, stirring with a spoon to dissolve. Put the mold in the sink (or rimmed baking sheet or roasting pan) and arrange the liner cloth inside, letting its edges drape over the side. Be sure to have a lid that fits the pot well, a ladle, a fine-mesh strainer, and a bowl nearby.

3 When the soy milk is cooked, turn off the heat. Let it sit for 2 to 3 minutes, frequently tracing a "Z" or an "N" through the milk to help it cool down a little and prevent a skin from forming. (If you are measuring the temperature, wait for the soy milk to stop moving before sticking a thermometer in.) Now add the coagulant in 3 additions.

Addition 1: Moving the spatula in a vigorous back and forth movement (a "Z" or an "N" pattern) across the pot bottom, stir the soy milk 6 to 8 times to rev up the liquid so that the coagulant can be well distributed. Still stirring, pour in a third of the coagulant. Then stop the spatula in the center of the pot and hold it there, upright, to slow down the activity. Once the soy milk stops moving, gently lift the spatula out. (The speed and direction of the stirring produces nice curds and a better overall texture.)

Addition 2: Use the spoon to sprinkle another third of the coagulant onto the surface of the soy milk. Cover the pot and wait for 3 minutes.

Addition 3: Give the remaining third of the coagulant a final stir with your spoon, uncover the pot, then sprinkle the coagulant onto the surface of the soy milk. Use the wooden spatula to gently stir back and forth across the topmost 1/2-inch layer of the soy milk for about 20 seconds. If there is milky liquid at the edge, give that area extra attention. The soy milk should be curdling. You'll feel the coagulating curds as you move the spatula and/or see them form into cumulus-like clouds, with the pale yellow whey beginning to separate.

Re-cover the pot and wait for 3 minutes (6 minutes if using gypsum or Epsom salts). Uncover, and if there is still milky liquid, gently stir the surface for about 20 seconds to further distribute the coagulant and complete the curdling. You should now see curds in pale yellow whey with no milkiness remaining.

Troubleshooting: If there is still milky liquid after the final round of stirring, cover the pot and wait for 1 minute, then gently stir the surface again. If the pot is no longer hot (you can touch it without flinching), put it over the lowest heat possible for 2 to 3 minutes to reheat. Gently stir back and forth across the surface and you should begin to see the curds separate from the whey. Turn off the heat, cover, and set aside for 2 minutes. Should the milky liquid still remain, mix a quarter of the original amount of coagulant in 1/3 cup of water, sprinkle it onto the milky areas, and gently stir the surface. That should do the trick.

CONTINUED

Block Tofu

CONTINUED

4 You will end up with a pot of white curds and pale yellow whey. The curds resemble those of fresh ricotta or cottage cheese. To remove some of the whey from the pot and make ladling out the curds easier, first gently press a fine-mesh strainer on the curds. The whey naturally moves into the strainer. Ladle some of the whey into the mold to moisten the liner cloth. Ladle more into the waiting, empty bowl. Remove as much whey as possible; when the curds feel firm against the strainer, stop ladling and remove the strainer. (See page 36 for uses for whey.)

5 Ladle the curds and any remaining whey into the mold. Be gentle to preserve as much of the curds' structure and texture as possible. Neatly fold in the liner cloth to cover the curds. Put the top of the press in place.

6 Weight the tofu to compress it. The amount of weight and the pressing time depend on the size of the curds, the tofu texture you want, and the size and shape of your mold. Below are some guidelines I use for a 3-inch-deep wooden mold with an opening measuring 4 by 5³/₄ inches.

Texture	Weight*	Time
Medium	1 pound	15 minutes
Medium-firm	1¹/₂ to 2 pounds	15 minutes
Firm	3 pounds	20 minutes

* For weights, use food cans or a small bowl filled with water.

Midway through, check that the weight is not lopsided so as to unevenly distribute its pressure.

When I use the slightly smaller plastic tofu mold that measures 3³/₄ by 4³/₄ inches wide and 2³/₄ inches deep, I put a small cutting board or plate on the top piece of the mold to stabilize and prevent the weight from slipping or falling off during pressing, and use a smaller weight (so, for medium-firm tofu, I use an 8-ounce cutting board and a 1-pound food can).

To gauge the texture of the tofu, I look at how compacted the curds have gotten. For example, when the curds are down to half their original thickness, the tofu has a medium density; at a third of their original thickness, the tofu is medium-firm or firm. The difference between medium-firm and firm is more or less determined by the weight and the pressing time. Keep in mind that you can always keep the weight on longer to yield firmer tofu, but the reverse is not true. If you like, open the cloth and press the surface with your finger to gauge texture. In the mold the tofu will feel soft and squiggly. However, it will firm up once fully cooled. Don't be afraid to experiment, as that's what tofu makers do. When you're satisfied, remove the weight.

7 Just-pressed tofu is very delicate and needs to cool and firm up. Before removing it from its mold, partially fill a bowl, pot, or sink with cold water (tap water is fine). Your mold dictates how you can remove the cloth-wrapped tofu. Wooden tofu molds have removable bottoms; with a plastic tofu mold or loaf pan, slowly invert the wrapped tofu into the water. If the tofu was molded in a colander, submerge it in the water to loosen and remove the tofu and cloth.

Once tofu and cloth are free of the mold, unwrap the tofu. If your tofu was made in one large piece and seems unwieldy, cut it into two or three pieces. Let it sit under water for about 5 minutes, until it has firmed up.

8 To remove the tofu from the water, simply slide a small plate or large spatula underneath and lift it up. Place the tofu on a plate, and if using within 8 hours, cover and keep it in a cool spot. You can use it as soon has it has completely cooled, though many people say tofu needs 2 hours to rest to develop its full umami. If you are not using it soon, refrigerate it in an airtight container, with water to cover, for up to 1 week. Change the water every other day.

CONTINUED

Block Tofu

VARIATION: CONFETTI TOFU

Once you get the hang of making tofu, suspend chopped vegetables to produce a colorful confetti-like tofu. Mix 6 to 7 tablespoons of finely diced assorted vegetables into the soy milk right before coagulation: for example, try equal parts carrot, reconstituted wood ear or shiitake mushrooms, and cooked edamame for a Japanese take. Or go for a Viet approach by combining finely chopped wood ear mushroom, green onion (the green part only), and shallot in a 3:2:2 ratio. Aim for a balance of color and use vegetables that are relatively low in moisture (no zucchini!).

Have the prepped vegetables near the stove, and when the soy milk has finished simmering, turn off the heat and add the vegetables. Proceed as for regular block tofu, adding coagulant, ladling out whey, and ladling the tofu solids into the mold; do your best to distribute the goodies evenly—when you see a clump of vegetables, break it up. Use a 1½- or 3-pound weight to press the tofu into a medium-firm or firm texture. Unmold, cool, and store the tofu in water as usual.

This kind of tofu is terrific as a panfried tofu steak. See the Korean panfried tofu recipe (page 103) for cutting and cooking guidance. Enjoy with soy sauce and chile sauce.

TOFU BYPRODUCT BONUS: WHEY

From each block of tofu, you can capture about 2 cups of whey, depending on the coagulant and the beans. Just like the lees, the whey offers valuable nutrition—it contains 9 percent of the protein in the original soybeans. Between the whey and the lees, you have more than 25 percent of the soybeans' total protein.

What to do with the whey? It has a delicate tangy sweetness and pale yellow color. It's neutral enough to use like water as a base in soups, hot pots, and sauces. (Whey is unsuitable for dashi stock, page 215, because it turns slimy when the seaweed soaks in it.) Boil vegetables in whey and they will absorb even more nutrition and flavor. Vietnamese tofu makers traditionally used their tofu whey to coagulate new tofu. If you don't have space to store the whey or desire to cook with it, don't discard it. Treat it like a mild soap to wash utensils and pots and pans. Water plants with it to add supplemental nitrogen, vitamins, and minerals to the ground. Suggestions for using the lees are on page 27.

BLOCK TOFU ALTERNATIVES: BEAN FLOWER, OBORO TOFU, AND ZARU TOFU

Though we tend to think of tofu in block shapes, the curds do not have to be pressed and shaped to be tofu. In fact, some people enjoy the delicate unpressed curds, which are often referred to as **bean flower** (*dou hua*) or **tofu brains** (*dou fu nao*) in Chinese; note that tofu pudding goes by the same names. The curds can be added to soup or enjoyed dressed with savory or sweet garnishes. Try it out by transferring some of the curds to a small bowl with a slotted spoon; drizzle on good soy sauce or sprinkle on some sugar. It's lovely.

If you like the unpressed curds, take a more formal approach by making Japanese *oboro* tofu. Deposit the curds into small shallow bowls and let them cool and settle in the bowls. Pour out any whey before eating the tofu.

For slightly denser *zaru* tofu, drain the curds through a bamboo strainer basket (*zaru*), available at Asian markets, houseware shops, and restaurant supply shops; you can also use a small strainer or colander that you already have. Place the strainer over a bowl or in the sink to avoid making a mess. To minimize cleanup, line the strainer with thin cloth; or, without the cloth, the tofu takes on the woven pattern of the bamboo strainer.

Whether you make *oboro* or *zaru* tofu, let gravity unite the curds into one mass. Serve the tofu the day you make it (for optimal flavor and texture), either fresh and warm or chilled. Keep it simple, like Japanese *hiya yakko* (page 51), or use one of the tofu topping ideas in the snacks and starters recipe chapter (page 75).

Practice efficient tofu making by preparing a double batch of light soy milk and, after coagulating it for block tofu, scoop out about half of the curds to enjoy as bean flower, *oboro* tofu, and/or *zaru* tofu. Put the rest into the press.

Seasoned Pressed Tofu

MAKES ABOUT 14 OUNCES

Meaty and flavorful pressed tofu is a wonderful Chinese convenience food. It keeps well in the refrigerator and can be sliced and eaten as is—cold, at room temperature, or hot. It can be stir-fried, coated with seasonings for a salad, tucked into *banh mi* sandwiches and rice paper rolls, dropped into noodle soups, and encased in dumpling dough.

Pressed tofu comes in plain (white) or it can be simmered with seasonings, which inject savor and outer color. When the simmered tofu is baked afterward, an appealing chewy skin forms and the flavor deepens. Most pressed tofu sold at Chinese markets and health food stores have been simmered and baked.

Seasoned pressed tofu is very firm because it is typically sliced thin for cooking or serving. Homemade tofu for this recipe is too tender. Instead, I purchase organic super-firm tofu (see page 8), which is extremely dense and takes to the simmering-and-baking process well. Make this at least a day before you need it; it can be refrigerated for weeks.

Once you've tried this basic Chinese seasoned pressed tofu (pictured on page 16), try smoking it. Or consider the spicy lemongrass and lime leaf version (page 39) for a Southeast Asian take. Feel free to alter the seasonings; the cooking process will remain the same.

1 pound super-firm tofu
3 cups water, filtered or spring preferred
3/4 teaspoon salt
2 teaspoons sugar
1 1/2 tablespoons light (regular) soy sauce
1 1/2 teaspoons dark (black) soy sauce
2 star anise (16 robust points total)

Chubby 3/4-inch piece fresh ginger, peeled and cut into
3 slices and bruised with the side of the knife
1 tablespoon sesame oil

1 Cut the tofu into slices that are roughly the size and thickness (a generous 1/2 inch thick) of a deck of playing cards. However, let the block of tofu determine the size. You may have 6 to 10 pieces total.

2 To press excess liquid from the tofu, use 2 baking sheets (or other flat-bottomed implements). Lay a non-terry dishtowel (or a double layer of paper towel) on one of the sheets and arrange the tofu slices on top, then lay another non-terry dishtowel (or more paper towels) atop the tofu to absorb moisture. Place the other baking sheet on top to create a sandwiching effect. Finish with a 4-pound weight (I use two 28-ounce food cans). Set aside at room temperature for 3 to 4 hours. The tofu is ready when it is only slightly moist to the touch and feels very firm—you can hold a piece on one side and wiggle it without fear of it falling apart.

3 In a medium saucepan, combine the water, salt, sugar, both soy sauces, star anise, and ginger. Put the tofu in the pan in two layers. They should be covered by liquid. Over medium-high heat, bring the water to a simmer. Lower the heat to medium or medium-low and gently simmer for 15 to 20 minutes to allow the tofu to absorb the seasoning liquid; the tofu will expand slightly. Remove from the heat and set aside, uncovered, to completely cool. Some of the liquid will evaporate, concentrating the flavor. Once cooled, cover and refrigerate the pan overnight to marinate the tofu.

4 The next day, remove the tofu from the marinade; discard the marinade. Air-dry the tofu for about 15 minutes, leaning the pieces up against the rim of a plate. This also helps take the chill off the tofu. Meanwhile, position a rack in the middle of the oven and preheat to 450°F. Line a baking sheet with parchment paper.

Right before baking, put the sesame oil on a small plate. Put each piece of tofu in the oil, then flip it over to coat the other side. Put the pieces on the baking sheet as you work.

5 Bake for 10 to 12 minutes, until the pieces are gently sizzling and have darkened at the edges; the longer time yields slightly drier results. Use a spatula to turn each piece over. Bake for another 5 minutes to further brown. Remove from the oven and put the baking sheet on a rack to cool. (If you are making the smoked tofu on page 40, transfer the just-baked pieces to the wok for smoking.) When cool enough to handle, about 10 minutes, lean the tofu pieces up against the rim of the baking sheet to facilitate airflow and form a nice skin on the bottom. The tofu will firm up, dry, and darken with a lovely rich patina as it rests. Once completely cooled, it is ready to be used or refrigerated in an airtight container for up to 2 weeks.

VARIATION: SPICY LEMONGRASS PRESSED TOFU

You can infuse pressed tofu with different kinds of ingredients to create new flavor combinations. In the refrigerated section at health food markets and specialty food stores you'll see a broad range of seasonings, from classic soy sauce and five spices to Thai and barbecue. To do it at home, you create a strong-flavored marinating liquid to infuse the tofu with lots of flavor. For a Southeast Asian twist, combine chile, lemongrass, and kaffir lime. The result is great on its own as a snack, added to fried rice, and showcased in a tart-spicy *laap* (page 137).

Begin by following the instructions for Seasoned Pressed Tofu. To prepare the marinade, in a saucepan, combine 3 1/4 cups water (filtered or spring), 1 1/8 teaspoons salt, 2 teaspoons packed brown sugar, 1/4 teaspoon turmeric, 1 tablespoon light (regular) soy sauce, 3 large cloves garlic (smashed), 1 hefty stalk lemongrass (cut into 3- to 4-inch lengths and smashed), 6 to 8 kaffir lime leaves, and 4 Thai or serrano chiles (halved lengthwise). If kaffir lime leaf is unavailable, double up on the lemongrass. Bring to a boil, then simmer for 5 minutes. Turn off the heat, cover, and let steep for 30 minutes. Remove the lemongrass and lime leaves before using the marinade to simmer the tofu. Substitute canola oil for the sesame oil before baking.

Tea-Smoked Pressed Tofu

MAKES ABOUT 14 OUNCES

In China, pressed tofu is sometimes set on a rack and smoked. To mimic that at home, you need a 14-inch wok, its lid, and a round cake rack that fits into the wok; an inexpensive mesh splatter screen (about 11 inches wide) works too, if you break off the handle with pliers.

14 ounces Seasoned Pressed Tofu (page 38), baking in the oven as directed in step 5 of the recipe
1 tablespoon packed light or dark brown sugar
1/3 cup black tea (Lapsang Souchon yields extra-bold smokiness)
1/3 cup raw white rice, any kind

1 While the seasoned pressed tofu bakes, line the wok with aluminum foil, making sure the foil tightly lines the pan or the tea mixture won't smoke.

2 Stir together the smoking mixture of sugar, tea, and rice. Pour it into the foil-lined wok, spreading it out evenly. Place the cake rack over the tea mixture.

3 When the tofu is done baking, remove it from the oven and let the sizzling subside. Use a metal spatula to transfer the hot tofu pieces to the rack. Loosely cover the wok with its lid and set the wok over high heat. After a few minutes, the tea mixture will start to smoke. At that point, press down on the wok lid to secure it in place. Reduce the heat slightly and smoke the tofu for 3 minutes. Longer, and the tofu may turn bitter. Remove the wok from the heat.

Carefully remove the lid, turning it away from you. Use the spatula to transfer the tofu back to the baking sheet or to a plate to cool. When the wok has cooled, remove the foil and discard. Store just like regular seasoned pressed tofu.

White Fermented Tofu

Chinese fermented tofu mystified me for years. I used to spend too much time at Asian markets trying to make sense of the many brands and types. It's strange-looking stuff that can smell funky or be slightly slimy but still tastes great. But when I set out to make my own, I not only discovered that it's easy to make a delicious "Chinese cheese," but I also better understood tofu's transformation into this very traditional soy-based staple.

Among the many kinds of fermented tofu, the most versatile one is the white variety that's seasoned with salt and rice wine. As suggested in *Florence Lin's Chinese Vegetarian Cookbook*, you can add extra spices, such as chile flakes (my favorite) or crushed Sichuan peppercorns and/or fennel seeds. Commercially made fermented white tofu often contains sesame oil, but I prefer to keep the seasonings simple. (Note: I've attempted to make red fermented tofu but to no avail. See page 13 for buying tips.)

In its transformation to *bai fu ru*, tofu undergoes incubation, salting, and fermentation. During the ripening process, which I prefer to do slowly (and safely) in the refrigerator, the soybean proteins break down into peptides and amino acids. Mature fermented tofu tastes good because it contains lots of free amino acids, including glutamic acid. Be observant during incubation to make sure that the tofu is adequately prepared, and then be patient with the fermentation. Tester Diane Carlson aptly described this recipe as a fun chemistry project. In general, a moderate room temperature (65–75°F) works well for incubation.

The firmer the tofu, the better the cubes will hold their shape over time. Tofu with some tenderness, such as homemade tofu, ripens a bit faster but is more prone to breaking down and losing its looks (though you can still use it). I often purchase organic tofu for this. Do not replace the rice wine with sherry, or the taste will be off.

Intensely savory and slightly sweet, white fermented tofu is often used as a condiment for adding punchy flavor to creamy rice soup or plain rice, or as a seasoning to lend umami depth and creaminess to foods such as stir-fried water spinach (page 147).

8 ounces firm or extra-firm tofu

1 1/2 tablespoons fine sea salt

1/2 teaspoon dried red chile flakes (optional)

1/4 cup Shaoxing rice wine, plus more as needed

1/2 cup water, filtered or spring preferred, plus more as needed

1 Cut the tofu into 1-inch cubes. To press excess liquid from the tofu, use two small baking sheets or flat-bottomed plastic trays. Lay a non-terry dishtowel (or a triple layer of paper towel) on one of the baking sheets, then arrange the tofu cubes on top and lay another non-terry dishtowel (or more paper towels) atop the tofu. Place the other baking sheet on top and finish with an approximately 2-pound weight, such as a 28-ounce food can. Set aside at room temperature for 1 to 2 hours. The tofu is ready when it is only slightly moist to the touch and feels very firm. You should be able to pick up a cube and wiggle it without fear of it falling apart. Blot away moisture, if needed.

2 To grow the mold on the tofu, create a Petri dish–like environment. Use a shallow rectangular or square

CONTINUED

White Fermented Tofu

glass baking dish to hold the tofu; it is easier to observe the changes in the tofu through glass. Arrange the tofu cubes in the baking dish, spacing them 1/2 to 1 inch apart. Cover tightly with plastic wrap. Then use a skewer to poke 5 to 8 holes on the top for air ventilation.

Keep the tofu at room temperature for 2 to 4 days, maybe even 5 days if temperatures are below 65°F. Expect condensation to gather on the plastic wrap and clear circles to form around the ventilation holes. You are ready to move to the next step when the tofu has taken on a slippery wet appearance, developed orange-yellow splotches of mold on the top and sides, *and* smells pungent. If you pierce a piece of tofu with a toothpick, there should be some resistance but it should feel a little soft, maybe even creamy. It should not feel firm like when it first started. If furry gray mold forms, it is okay and an indication that it is time to proceed to the next step; the mold sloughs off during ripening, though I sometimes gently scrape it off with a knife.

The amount of time it takes to achieve the "3S" criteria—slime, splotches, and stink—depends on air temperature and humidity. Check on the progress daily, lifting the plastic wrap to peek and sniff.

3 Select a wide-mouth, 2-cup glass jar to hold the tofu. In a small bowl, combine the salt and chile flakes. Lightly coat each cube of tofu with the seasoning mixture. This is best done if you use a skewer or long toothpick to pick up each cube (go in from the side) and then spoon the seasonings on all sides. Use another skewer to dislodge the cube into the glass jar. Do your best to position the cubes flat.

4 Combine the wine and water and pour it into the jar. There should be enough to just cover. Mix up more, if needed. Cap the jar tightly and refrigerate for at least 4 weeks before using. If you underincubated the tofu, it may take twice that time to ripen.

You can use the tofu when it is young and a tad sharp tasting. However, it turns creamier and develops a wonderfully mellow, complex flavor with age. Try tiny samples of it weekly to gauge its progress, if you like. Or, stick the jar in the back of the fridge and forget about it for several months; I've eaten some straight at 6 months old! Fermented tofu keeps indefinitely in the refrigerator.

FROZEN TOFU

When you have excess tofu on hand, don't let it go to waste. You can preserve it by fermenting it or freezing it. Frozen tofu is sold at Chinese markets but you can make your own.

Cut it into chunks of about 2 inches. Let them drain for about 10 minutes atop a non-terry towel or a double layer of paper towels, then put them about 1/2 inch apart on a parchment paper–lined tray. Freeze until hard, then transfer to a zip-top bag and keep frozen for up to 3 months.

Thaw at room temperature. Before using, expel excess moisture by gently pressing the tofu between your palms. Thawed tofu has a slightly chewy, alluring texture. It also soaks up flavors like a sponge. I like to drop cubes of thawed silken or medium tofu into soups and hot pots. Firm, extra firm, and super firm can be seared and then stir-fried or braised.

Fresh Tofu Skin

MAKES ABOUT 4 OUNCES

Once you've made soy milk, you understand how quickly and easily a skin forms on the surface. For the most part, that skin is a delicious serendipity that becomes an instant snack for the tofu maker. But Chinese and Japanese tofu makers also prepare tofu skin on purpose. The resulting light tan sheets can be dried and transformed into myriad foods, from mock meats to dumpling wrappers.

Freshly prepared tofu skin is heavenly, with a silky texture and super delicate flavor. Unless you happen to be at a tofu shop where freshly made tofu skin is available, the best bet for getting this prime tofu experience is to make it yourself. And if you're going to spend the time to make tofu skin, eat it straight and simply dressed; see Tofu Skin Sashimi (page 51), a Japanese favorite.

You don't need any special equipment or coagulant to produce a truly rare and artisanal food. You can heat the soy milk in a nonstick skillet directly on a burner until a skin forms and then pull it off. That works fine if the burner has even, steady heat. I prefer to place the skillet atop a pot of simmering water to let the steam provide consistent heat. The most difficult aspect of making tofu skin is the wait time in between sheets; however, you can certainly multitask as the skin forms.

3¼ cups Rich Soy Milk (page 23), at room temperature

1 Select a heavy medium nonstick skillet and a pot for it to sit on. For example, I use a 10-inch skillet and a 3½- or 4-quart pot. The skillet does not have to fit snugly like a regular lid, but it should perch nicely on the pot's rim. It's natural for some steam to escape during cooking.

2 Fill the pot with water to about 1 inch of the rim. Bring to a boil over high heat. Meanwhile, check the consistency of the soy milk. If it is not totally smooth, pass it through a fine-mesh strainer. Reserve any remaining solids to add to the delectable dregs later, if you like. After the water boils, lower the heat to a strong simmer. Put the skillet on top, then pour in the soy milk.

3 Now wait. The water should be bubbling away as the skillet and soy milk heat up. Meanwhile, find a wide bowl or pot and position a long chopstick, wooden spoon, or spatula across the top. Place this "drying station" near the stove. The soy milk will sit placidly and then slowly form a tan-colored skin, often starting at the center and radiating outward. It will quiver and patterned wrinkles will appear.

The first tofu skin takes about 10 minutes to set, as the milk needs to heat to about 150°F; subsequent ones will take about 7 minutes.

Use the first skin to test the thickness of the milk. Sometimes if the soy milk is too rich and thick, the skins take longer to form and they are thicker. Ideal skins are translucent. You can certainly eat thicker skins but they are not as ethereal. If 15 to 20 minutes pass before a skin forms, the milk is too thick. For thinner skins, dilute the soy milk by adding water by the tablespoon; if there are bits of skin in the soy milk you're diluting, strain it into a container before diluting and returning it in the skillet. Soy milk about the thickness of cream or half-and-half usually works well.

4 When a tan-colored skin has stretched across the surface, or nearly across, use a rubber spatula to detach it from the skillet. A gentle downward push all the way around the edge should do it.

Now imagine the skin like the face of a clock. Position your thumbs and index fingers about 1 inch from the edges, at 2 and 10 o'clock. Now pinch gently to pick up the skin. It should not be that hot. Hold it above the soy milk for a few seconds for any excess to drip back into the skillet. Now drape the skin, drier side down, on your chopstick or wooden spoon. (Alternatively, use an extra long chopstick or the handle of a wooden spoon to scoop under and lift up the skin, then rest it across the bowl to hang the skin.)

Troubleshooting: Sometimes the tofu skin that forms does not completely cover the surface. That's okay. Detach it wherever needed, then lift it from the skillet. If the skin is so misshapen that it doesn't hang well, place it on a plate to cool. It is edible, so don't discard it. If there are residual bits of skin clinging at the skillet's edge, remove them and set them aside to cook up with the last of the milk for a treat.

Let the tofu skin dry and cool for 4 to 5 minutes, then remove it from its hanging position before you're ready to pull off a new skin. Put the drier side down on a work surface and fold up the skin in quarters in a square or rectangle shape. Place the finished skin on a plate. Invert a bowl on top to prevent drying.

5 Repeat this process to make more tofu skins. Midway through, replenish the water in the pot, if needed; I keep a hot kettle of water on the stove for this purpose. You may have to raise the heat toward the end if the water is low—about 3 inches below the skillet. The last few tofu skins will not be "perfect," but they'll be tasty nonetheless.

You won't be able to use up all the soy milk; stop when you see the skillet bottom. Remove the skillet from the pot. There will be about $1/4$ cup of soy milk left. It may be fairly thick, loose, and creamy, or there may be a pockmarked film at the bottom. Whatever you do, don't discard it—it has a super concentrated nutty-sweet flavor. Scrape it up and cook it over medium or medium-low heat. If it's creamy and wet, stir it around the skillet until it resembles wet scrambled eggs. If it's more of a film, cook it to a toasty state; it may look dry and unattractive. Regardless, save these delectable dregs for yourself. It is the tofu skin maker's bonus.

Freshly made tofu skin is precious and should be eaten within 48 hours of being made. If you are planning to enjoy it soon, keep it at room temperature covered by the bowl or plastic. Otherwise, refrigerate the skins in an airtight container, returning them to room temperature before using.

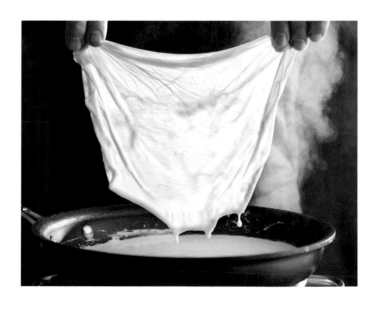

Soy-Simmered Fried Tofu

MAKES 3 LARGE RECTANGLES, 6 LARGE SQUARES, OR 12 MEDIUM RECTANGLES OR TRIANGLES

These sweet-and-salty slices of fried tofu are a standby in the Japanese kitchen, where they can be added to a bowl of steaming udon noodle soup (page 187), pried open into pouches and stuffed with sushi rice (page 188), or shredded and scattered atop *chirashi* sushi rice. You can buy the tofu preseasoned at Japanese, Korean, and Chinese markets, but it will taste more vibrant if you purchase prefried slices of tofu and add the flavoring yourself. It's easy to make *abura-age no nimono*, and the result keeps for a good 5 days in the refrigerator, where it's ready to be used at your whim.

Making the puffy fried tofu (called *abura-age* or *sushi-age*, depending on size) is complicated and best left to the pros, who often add leavening during coagulation. The finished tofu is sliced and pressed, after which it is carefully deep-fried, first at low then at high temperature, to force it to swell. Japanese cooks employ slices of puffy tofu whereas Chinese cooks tend to use cubes. You want the thin spongy slices for this application. See the buying guide on page 11 for guidance. Note that depending on your end use, you may or may not have to cut the tofu before searing or simmering it.

3 rectangular fried tofu slices (about 6 by 3¹/₂ inches),
    or 6 square fried tofu slices (about 3 inches)
1 tablespoon sugar
2 teaspoons sake
1¹/₂ tablespoons Japanese or Korean soy sauce
6 tablespoons Dashi Stock (page 215)

1 To remove some of the residual oil from the tofu, bring a pot of water to a rolling boil. Add all the tofu slices. Let them blanch in the water, which should still be bubbling, for 10 to 15 seconds. If the tofu bobs around in the pot, gently press down on it with a skimmer or slotted spoon to ensure even exposure to the hot water. Transfer the tofu to a colander to drain.

2 When the tofu is cool enough to handle, about 10 minutes, stand over the sink and give each piece a few moderate squeezes to remove excess water.

If the tofu will be used for the Foxy Tofu Noodle Soup (*kitsune udon*, page 187), leave the tofu slices *uncut* and proceed to step 3. If the tofu is destined for rice-stuffed tofu pouches (*inari-zushi*, page 188), you need to cut the tofu and pry the pieces open. With the rectangles, cut each one crosswise to yield large squares. With the squares, you have several options. Cut off ¹/₈ inch from one side if you want large squarish *inari-zushi*. For smaller portions, halve the tofu crosswise into rectangles or on the diagonal into triangles; once stuffed and closed, they'll be log-shaped or ear-shaped, respectively.

Regardless of the size or shape, open the tofu to form a pouch. Some brands open up naturally. If yours doesn't, hold each piece in the palm of one hand and use your other hand to slap down on the tofu; this pushes air out. Use your fingers to gently pry it open. (Alternatively, roll a chopstick or dowel rolling pin over each piece from fold to opening, then pry it open.) Set on a plate near the stove.

3 In a measuring cup, stir together the sugar, sake, soy sauce, and dashi stock. Set near the tofu. Heat a large nonstick skillet over medium-high heat. Add the tofu slices or pouches, arranging them in one layer. Use a spatula to press on them, flipping them once or twice, until you hear a steady sizzle; don't worry if the tofu discolors in places. Lower the heat to medium, then pour in the seasoned dashi stock.

Cook for about 3 minutes, turning the tofu pieces after 30 to 45 seconds, when half the liquid has disappeared. The tofu is done when nearly all of the liquid is gone. Set the skillet aside to cool completely. After a few minutes, flip the tofu over to allow the top side to soak up the residual liquid in the skillet. The tofu will absorb more flavor during cooling.

Use immediately or refrigerate in an airtight container for up to 5 days, bringing it to room temperature before using.

Snacks and Starters

Tokyo subways are renowned for being punctual and I was counting on their efficiency to make a 5:30 a.m. appointment with food writer Junko Nakahama. She had arranged a special visit to Takeya Tofu, her neighborhood tofu maker in the Bunkyo ward. The owners, Mr. Katsuji Ishijima and Mrs. Masako Ishijima, typically began their workday in the wee early hours but agreed to delay their routine for us. Jet-lagged and bleary eyed, I took the first train, at 5:10 a.m.

"Mr. Ishijima is nervous about representing Japanese tofu to you," Junko told me as we walked from the Sendagi station. The Japanese take tofu seriously; I assured Junko that I just wanted to observe and learn from a typical mom-and-pop shop.

Takeya Tofu turned out to be a modest operation the size of a large single-car garage. People tend to think of Tokyo as glitzy but the tofu shop highlighted the city's homey and humble side. The Ishijimas lived on the second floor, dried their equipment outside, and sold their soy milk and tofu through a small glass window. Another larger set of windows permitted airflow into the workplace, which tended to get steamy. Tokyo suffered a brutal heat wave when I visited in September 2010 and everything was wide open when we arrived at 6 a.m.

After the formal introductions, Mr. Ishijima went into action. A sturdy man with an easy smile, he had been waiting for us and had an entire lesson plan for the morning. His soybeans had sufficiently soaked and he flipped a switch to grind the beans and transform it into hot soy milk. As the machines whirred, Mr. Ishijima reflected on the dwindling number of small-scale tofu makers left in Tokyo. Tofu is an integral part of Japanese culture, much like the baguette is to the French. In 2008, a Tokyo Foundation article estimated that 980 tofu shops remained in the city.

"Today, there are about 750 tofu makers in Tokyo. Every month, two or three close down," he said. "In our Bunkyo ward, there were sixty tofu makers during my father's time. Now only twenty-three remain. We are becoming endangered."

Mr. Ishijima, seventy, is a second-generation tofu maker who inherited the trade from his parents. Because he was an only child, there were no other career options for him at the time. "I was not lucky to have this kind of hard work," he joked. While Junko and I were in the shop, Mr. Ishijima's ninety-two-year-old mother came to the back door to say hello. His son, dressed in business attire, greeted us before leaving for work. Mr. Ishijima did not expect his son to continue the family business.

Our conversation stopped once the hot soy milk began flowing into an industrial-size stockpot. Mrs. Ishijima quickly filled a dozen small containers for their regular customers and placed them by the window for pickup.

"The soy milk will take extra time to cool in this heat. It is seasonal and you learn to work with it," Mr. Ishijima said, taking the milk's temperature. He then stirred it with a long wooden paddle to hasten the cooling, waited a bit, then rechecked and stirred again.

When Mrs. Ishijima spotted a layer of nama yuba (fresh tofu skin) on the milk, she plucked it off with chopsticks and divided it between two bowls for Junko and me. It was ethereal.

When the soy milk was ready, Mr. Ishijima stood over it with purpose and began stirring it with the paddle, speed-ing up the rotations to form a deep vortex into which he poured his coagulant of diluted gypsum. He then stirred the soy milk backward slowly before pausing the paddle in the center and lifting it out. He knew exactly how much coagulant to add so he only had to do it once, he explained.

When the soy milk had coagulated, the husband-and-wife team swiftly began scooping the curds with a large round ladle, depositing the mounds into plastic containers for unpressed oboro tofu. Mrs. Ishijima put a lid on each and slid it into a sink of cold water to cool. Barely stopping, Mr. Ishijima set up two tall metal molds for block tofu. Working with the speed, confidence, and agility of a true craftsman, he scooped the remaining curds and filled the molds. Then he weighted them down with a wood plank and a bucket of water.

It was 8 a.m. by then, and the Ishijimas started the arduous task of cleaning their equipment. "Tofu takes three hours to make and three hours to clean up," Mr. Ishijima said. His wife offered Junko and me oboro tofu, which was creamy like a fresh cheese.

About thirty minutes later, Mr. Ishijima unmolded the tofu into another sink of water, dumping out the tofu and removing the cloth liner. He then used well-worn wood planks to support the tofu as he deftly cut it into blocks with a special cleaver-shaped piece of stainless steel. "It is done. The tofu now needs to rest and develop its flavor," he said, pronouncing the lesson over. It was barely 9 a.m.

Walking back to the subway, Junko admitted she'd never realized all the skill and effort involved in making tofu. I totally concurred but was also bowled over by the deliciousness of the fresh tofu that we sampled.

That morning with the Ishijimas underscored for me that the best way to savor well-made tofu is to just add some toppings or sauce. That's why this recipe collection kicks off with straightforward classics that celebrate tofu excellence. From there, the recipes showcase how tofu can be transformed into marvelous morsels.

Japanese Chilled Tofu HIYA YAKKO

SERVES 4 AS AN APPETIZER

People who are passionate about tofu seek out the freshest and treat it simply. A drizzle of high-quality soy sauce, such as the kind you use for topnotch sushi or sashimi, may be all that's needed to make the tofu sing. However, you can embellish the tofu with fresh ginger, green onion, and other garnishes. This is a classic Japanese approach. Korean and Chinese renditions follow.

While you can make this preparation with purchased tofu, you will truly savor tofu's brilliance if it's homemade. *Hiya yakko* is often presented with silken tofu but it can also be prepared with tofu pudding or block tofu pressed to a medium texture. Unpressed *oboro* and *zaru* tofu (page 37) are marvelous, too.

Chilled tofu is typically a summertime dish, but I enjoy it year-round. I usually present it with two basic garnishes (not including soy sauce), and if I feel extravagant I add a third one. Green *shiso* (*Perilla frutescens*) is sold at Japanese markets. More robustly flavored *tia to*, a *shiso* relative with green and garnet leaves, is a less pricey stand-in sold at Viet markets.

1 green onion, white and green parts, cut into thin rings
1 pound silken tofu or medium tofu, or 2 cups tofu
    pudding, chilled
1 tablespoon grated, peeled fresh ginger
High-quality Japanese soy sauce or Japanese Seasoned Soy
    Concentrate (page 208)

OPTIONAL GARNISHES (CHOOSE ONE OR NONE)
2 tablespoons dried bonito flakes (katsuo-bushi)
2 tablespoons finely shredded green shiso leaves
1 full-size sheet toasted nori, briefly held over an open
    flame to recrisp, and cut into thin, 2- to 3-inch-long
    strips (use scissors)

1 Put the green onion in a small bowl and add water to cover. Set aside for 10 minutes to soak and reduce some of its harshness.

2 Meanwhile, ready the tofu. If using silken tofu, run a knife around the edge of the mold or package and invert onto a plate to unmold. Pour off the excess liquid or use a paper towel to blot it away. If using regular block tofu, drain it on a non-terry dishtowel or double thickness of paper towels placed atop a plate. Cut the silken or block tofu into 1-inch cubes or husky 1-inch-thick dominoes and arrange them in a shallow bowl or individual dishes. If using tofu pudding, scoop up large shards with a metal spoon, putting them into a shallow bowl or individual dishes. Before serving, pour off any whey that gathers.

3 Drain the green onion well, patting it with a paper towel to remove excess water.

The most expeditious way to serve the tofu is to simply top it with the green onion, ginger, and any optional garnish and drizzle the soy sauce around the edge.

Alternatively, present the tofu naked with all the garnishes in separate little dishes and the soy sauce on the side. Let guests choose their own garnishes. Chopsticks are traditionally used to eat this tofu but you may find that a spoon or fork is better for grabbing the tofu and all the other goodies.

Chilled Tofu with Crunchy Baby Sardines JAKO HIYA YAKKO

SERVES 4 AS AN APPETIZER

This is a wonderful Japanese way to combine the softness of tofu with a contrasting crunch of tiny fried sardines. Called *chirimen jako*, the dried young sardines are pearl gray and about a millimeter wide and less than an inch long. They are sold at Japanese markets in plastic bags. Out of the packaging, they are slightly soft, but they perk up in hot oil and turn wonderfully crispy—like oceanic bacon bits.

Shreds of *shiso* add earthiness and crushed toasted sesame seeds contribute richness; if *shiso* is unavailable, substitute thinly sliced green onion, just like with regular *hiya yakko* (page 51). A light drizzle of Japanese seasoned soy sauce brings it all together. This preparation is spectacular with homemade tofu.

2 tablespoons canola oil

1/4 cup dried baby sardines

1 pound silken tofu or medium tofu, or 2 cups tofu pudding, chilled

4 or 5 green shiso leaves, cut into very thin strips (about 1/4 cup total)

1 1/2 tablespoons white sesame seeds, toasted and slightly crushed with a mortar and pestle

Japanese Seasoned Soy Concentrate (page 208) or high-quality Japanese soy sauce

1 In a small skillet, heat the oil over medium-high heat. Meanwhile, position a mesh strainer over a bowl and have this set up near the stove; you'll use it to quickly drain the fish.

The oil is ready when you drop in a fish and it immediately sizzles. Add all the fish and gently fry, stirring constantly, for about 1 minute, until they are fragrant and crisp. During cooking, they'll darken, then turn golden. If you like, pick up the skillet toward the end to prevent overcooking.

Pour the contents of the skillet into the strainer. Give the strainer a good shake, then transfer the fish to a paper towel–lined plate to further drain and cool. Keep at room temperature if using within hours. Or, transfer to an airtight container and refrigerate for up to a week; return the fish to room temperature before serving.

2 If using silken tofu, run a knife around the edge of the mold or package and invert onto a plate to unmold. Pour off the excess liquid or use a paper towel to blot it away. If using block tofu, drain it on a dishtowel or double thickness of paper towels placed atop a plate. Cut the silken or block tofu into husky 1-inch-thick dominoes or 2-inch squares. Arrange them on individual dishes or in shallow bowls. If using tofu pudding, scoop up large shards with a metal spoon, putting them into a shallow bowl or individual dishes. Before serving, pour off any whey that gathers.

3 Top the tofu with some *shiso* and sesame seeds, and a crown of the fried fish. Serve the seasoned soy sauce on the side. If you have leftover fish, save it for a rice topping.

Chilled Tofu with Spicy Sauce YANGNYUM DUBU

SERVES 4 AS AN APPETIZER

Whereas Japanese chilled tofu is full of playful subtleties, Korean chilled tofu is gutsy and lusty. The thickish spicy-sweet soy sauce, enriched by crushed toasted sesame seeds, envelops the block of tofu to generously coat it with flavor. If you are using silken tofu, try cutting it with a crinkle cutter to carve out grooves that will catch the sauce.

Chilled tofu is a great palate cleanser and pairs well with boldly flavored foods such as Korean barbecue. If you have firm tofu on hand, warm it up and enjoy it with the sauce; see the instructions in the tofu and kimchi stir-fry recipe on page 145.

1 small green onion, white and green parts, cut into thin rings
1 pound silken tofu or medium tofu, chilled
1/3 cup Korean Seasoned Soy Sauce (page 209)
1/2 moderately hot red chile, such as Fresno, stemmed, seeded, and finely chopped

1 Put the green onion in a small bowl and add water to cover. Set aside for 10 minutes to soak and reduce some of its harshness.

2 Meanwhile, ready the tofu. If using silken tofu, scoop it into individual shallow bowls, or run a knife around the edge of the mold or package and invert onto a plate to unmold. Pour off the excess liquid or use a paper towel to blot it away, then cut it into 1-inch cubes or 3/4-inch-thick slabs. If using block tofu, drain it on a non-terry dishtowel or double thickness of paper towels placed atop a plate. Cut into 1-inch cubes or husky 1-inch-thick dominoes and arrange them in a shallow bowl or individual dishes.

3 Drain the green onion well, patting it with a paper towel to remove excess water.

To serve, top the tofu with the sauce and sprinkle with the green onion and chile. Chopsticks are traditionally used to eat this tofu but a spoon or fork may be better for getting at a bit of everything in each bite.

Tofu Skin Sashimi NAMA YUBA

SERVES 4 AS AN APPETIZER

Freshly made tofu skin, called *nama yuba* in Japanese, is one of the soybean's greatest gifts to mankind. My first taste was during a tour of the Hodo Soy Beanery factory in Oakland, California. Just plucked from the hot soymilk, the tender sheets of soymilk were divine. Hodo co-founder Dean Ku drizzled a little savory-sweet soy sauce onto the *yuba* before handing each of us a portion. That simple preparation was mind-blowing: nutty, sweet, creamy, and salty all at once.

I was hooked, and when I visited Kyoto, an artisanal *yuba* hot spot, I ate all the freshly made tofu skins I could handle. At the end of the line, I return to this very pure presentation, which many people describe as being sashimi-like. Sashimi is about experiencing the freshness and vividness of excellent ingredients. That's what you experience with *nama yuba*. Just add a bit of wasabi and soy concentrate. Grated ginger can stand in for the wasabi.

4 ounces Fresh Tofu Skin (page 44), at room temperature
1/2 to 1 teaspoon prepared wasabi
Japanese Seasoned Soy Concentrate (page 208) or
    high-quality Japanese soy sauce

1 You can serve the tofu skins in their flat, folded state, but for an artful presentation, unfold each sheet from a quartered to a half fold. Then either roll it up into a delicate log, or pull up the skin at the center and give it a slight twist to form a small teepee. As you work, divide the tofu skins among 4 small plates.

2 Near each serving of tofu skin, place a tiny knob or pyramid of wasabi. Pour a small amount of the seasoned soy concentrate into individual dipping sauce bowls. (If your tofu skin turned out creamy and not sheetlike, serve it in small shallow bowls. Have the wasabi in another dish, or put a swab of it on the rim of each dipping sauce bowl.)

3 Serve immediately. Invite guests to treat it like sashimi: add a bit of wasabi to the soy sauce, use chopsticks to grasp a sheet of tofu skin, momentarily rest it in the sauce, then eat.

Tofu with Century Eggs PI DAN DOU FU

"May I buy a few pieces of tofu to take with me?" I asked Le Thi Phuong, a very pretty Vietnamese woman I met at an artisanal tofu shop in Shiding, a mountainous village near Taipei. Phuong was married to Wang Fen Ji, a fifth-generation tofu maker whose family-owned shop was renowned for its delicious tofu prepared with fresh spring water.

"No," she surprisingly responded. "Our tofu is very fresh and spoils quickly. If you're going to other places today, the tofu will spoil by the time you get back to the city." When I revealed my plan of eating the tofu in the car, Phuong insisted on making me a midmorning snack. She dashed across the narrow street and came back with two century eggs (*pi dan*). Then she quickly assembled a rendition of this classic Chinese tofu dish, a favorite in Shanghai and Taiwan. Phuong's nontraditional Viet touch was adding a drizzle of mild hot sauce.

It was dynamite. Preserved century egg has an intensely fatty yolk that amplifies tofu's richness. The garnish of slightly sweet thickened soy sauce, often called Taiwanese soy sauce paste, and flourish of chopped cilantro balanced the egg's pungency. My five companions and I stood in front of the tofu shop and spooned up every bit.

At home when I prepare this dish, I use homemade tofu and concoct a version of the soy sauce paste, which is actually saucy rather than pasty. Medium or medium-firm tofu's tenderness marries best with the egg, though you could use silken. Top with dried bonito flakes (*katsuo-bushi*) to savor the Japanese influence on Taiwan. The sauce can be made hours in advance, then covered and kept at room temperature. If you don't want to make the special soy sauce, use regular soy sauce and a touch of sesame oil. You can add zip with lots of shredded young ginger and green onion.

SAUCE

4 teaspoons sugar

2 tablespoons light (regular) soy sauce

1 teaspoon sesame oil

1 tablespoon water

1/2 teaspoon cornstarch dissolved in 1 tablespoon water

1 pound medium or medium-firm tofu, at room temperature

2 century eggs

1 to 2 tablespoons chopped cilantro, leafy tops only

1 To make the sauce, in an extra-small saucepan, stir together the sugar, soy sauce, sesame oil, and water. Bring to a boil over medium heat. Give the cornstarch a last stir, then swirl it in. Stir the sauce for about 20 seconds, until it has thickened. Transfer to a small bowl and let cool to room temperature, about 15 minutes; you should have 1/4 cup.

2 Cut the tofu into chunky matchbooks, about 11/2 inches wide, 2 inches long, and 1/2 inch thick. Line a plate or tray with a non-terry dishtowel or double layer of paper towels. Let the tofu drain on top for 5 to 10 minutes.

3 Meanwhile, peel the century eggs and rinse briefly under cold water to remove their lingering ammonia-like smell. Halve and cut each egg lengthwise into 8 wedges, then cut the wedges crosswise to yield 1/2-inch chunks. Set aside. Arrange the tofu on individual plates or one communal plate. Sprinkle the egg on top. Drizzle on the sauce. Finish with the cilantro. Serve with spoons.

CENTURY EGGS: BUYING, STORING, AND USING

I didn't appreciate Chinese century eggs (*pi dan*, also called thousand-year-old eggs) until I tasted them as a tofu topping. Despite their name and ancient appearance, the eggs undergo a preservation process that does not take years. They are covered in a mixture that includes lime, clay, ash, and salt, then cured for several weeks or months. The lime causes the white to turn gelatinous in texture and amber in color. The yolk becomes super rich and creamy, taking on a blue-gray color. Half of one is all I can manage at a time.

Well-stocked Chinese markets are the source for these eggs. They are typically packaged in plastic or paper and plastic, and stored at room temperature though they may be kept with regular eggs. Select the higher priced ones because price reflects quality. The ones I buy are preserved duck eggs from Taiwan and clearly say "lead free," meaning that they were not processed with lead oxide, a poisonous shortcut used by some lesser producers.

I used to refrigerate them until I read the instructions on the Taiwanese packaging that suggested room temperature storage to prevent drying and hardening. Expect a mild ammonia-like odor once the egg is peeled. That can usually be rinsed off. If the odor is strong and you're concerned about getting ill, then don't eat it. Aside from a tofu topping, the eggs are a typical accompaniment to creamy rice soups (jook/congee).

Savory Tofu Pudding DOU HUA

SERVES 6 AS A SNACK

One of the popular Chinese tofu snacks is warm soft tofu topped with a variety of piquant toppings that range from mild green onion, soy sauce, and sesame oil to intensely flavored chile oil, pickled vegetables, and stir-fried meat mixtures. Sometimes *dou hua* is served with noodles, but I prefer to let the custardy tofu take center stage.

The toppings below have a certain Sichuan bent—the cooks of that province prepare exceptionally good renditions. The toppings may be savory-spicy, savory-spicy-tart, or savory-spicy-rich. In Chengdu, Xiao Tan Dou Hua (Mr. Tan's Bean Flower) has specialized in tofu pudding since 1924. Three generations have endured through the tumultuous twentieth century to continue their delectable craft today. Unfortunately, few street hawkers remain and their Sichuanese cry, "*Dou huar! Dou huar!*" is seldom heard anymore.

For wonderful earthy depth, head to a Chinese markets for preserved mustard tuber (*zha cai*). It is sold in cans labeled "Sichuan preserved vegetable." Maling is a reliable brand. At home, buy or simply prepare the tofu pudding (page 28) and lay out a bunch of different toppings for your guests to choose among.

SAUCE

2 tablespoons regular (light) soy sauce

1½ tablespoons Chile Oil (page 213), with chile flakes

1½ teaspoons sesame oil

1 teaspoon Sichuan peppercorn, toasted and ground

1½ tablespoons Chinkiang or balsamic vinegar, optional

GARNISHES

½ cup chopped green onion, green part only

¼ cup unsalted roasted soybeans (soy nuts) or peanuts

⅓ cup chopped preserved mustard tuber (zha cai), rinsed if overly salty, optional

2 ounces wonton or pot sticker skins or fresh flat Chinese noodles or linguine pasta, optional

Canola oil for deep-frying, optional

4 cups Tofu Pudding (page 30)

1 To make the sauce, combine the soy sauce, chile oil, and sesame oil. Add Sichuan peppercorn to taste. If you'd like a hot-and-sour finish, add the vinegar (or set it out and let your guests add it to their sauce themselves).

2 Prepare the garnishes. Put the green onion, roasted soybeans, and mustard tuber in separate small dishes.

For extra crunch, deep-fry strips of wonton skin or short lengths of noodles. If using wonton or pot sticker skins, cut them into narrow strips, about ⅓ inch wide. With the noodles, cut them into 2- to 3-inch lengths. Heat about ¾ inch of oil in a saucepan over medium-high heat to about 350°F on a deep-fry thermometer. If you don't have a deep-fry thermometer, stick a *dry* bamboo chopstick into the oil; if bubbles rise immediately to the surface, the oil is ready. Fry the noodles or wonton strips in batches for 1 to 2 minutes, until golden brown. Drain on paper towels, then transfer to a serving bowl. Set at the table with the garnishes and sauce.

3 If your tofu pudding is cold, reheat it as directed in step 3 of the tofu pudding recipe on page 30; see page 11

CONTINUED

Savory Tofu Pudding

of the buying guide if you purchased the tofu. Use a metal spoon to scoop up shards of the tofu into individual serving bowls. Expect liquid (whey) to accumulate in the bowls. While you can pour it off, it is nutritious and has a tangy flavor that commingles well with the garnishes. Invite guests to add garnishes and drizzle on the sauce themselves. Enjoy with spoons.

VARIATION: SPICY MEAT TOPPING

Heat 1½ teaspoons of canola oil in a wok or skillet over medium heat. Add 4 ounces ground pork or chicken and cook, stirring and mashing the meat into small pieces, for about 1 minute, until it is just cooked through. Add 2 tablespoons chile bean sauce and 2 minced garlic cloves. Keep stir-frying for another minute until the mixture is super fragrant. Stir in 1 chopped green onion (use the white and green parts) and remove from the heat. Transfer to a small bowl and offer it along with the other garnishes. Include the sauce too, if you like.

VARIATION: SWEET, SOUR, AND SPICY TOFU PUDDING

Instead of the sauce in the main recipe, set out small dishes each containing about ¼ cup Chinese Sweet Fragrant Soy Sauce (page 207), 1 to 2 tablespoons Chile and Sichuan Peppercorn Mix (page 211), and 1 to 2 tablespoons of Chinkiang or balsamic vinegar. Offer the same set of garnishes.

Miso-Glazed Broiled Tofu TOFU DENGAKU

MAKES 12 PIECES, TO SERVE 4 TO 6

I've yet to meet a person who doesn't like nibbling food on a stick, whether it's an ice pop, a hot dog, or a meaty morsel. Tofu on a stick is a popular snack in parts of Asia. For example, many Taiwanese swoon at the sight and smell of grilling skewers of stinky tofu brushed with a saté-like sauce.

In Japan, there are countless renditions of this miso-topped tofu, which originated in the 1400s. It is related to acrobatic characters known as *dengaku hoshi,* who, as part of popular rural folk dramas, performed special dances while standing on single short stilts. This skewered tofu preparation was conceived around the same time, and people connected the iconic flat skewer to the stilt. The name *tofu dengaku* stuck.

By 1782, the Japanese bestseller *Tofu Hyaku Chin* (One Hundred Delicacies Made with Bean Curd) included a dozen versions of *tofu dengaku*, but you can start with just two. They are easy to make and easy to love. With the gingery and lemony miso sauces prepared in advance and kept in the refrigerator, these little hot tofu lollipops come together in a flash.

Charcoal grilling of small tofu pieces is hard to do well at home. Oven broiling the tofu after it's been lightly coated with soy sauce and oil results in crusty edges and terrific flavor.

14 to 16 ounces firm tofu
2 teaspoons Japanese or Korean soy sauce
2 teaspoons canola oil
About 1½ tablespoons gingery miso sauce (see Note)
About 1½ tablespoons citrusy miso sauce (see Note)
1 teaspoon white sesame seeds, toasted
1 teaspoon black sesame seeds, toasted
½ teaspoon ground sansho or Sichuan peppercorn, optional

1 Cut the tofu crosswise and then crosswise again to yield 4 small blocks. Now cut each block into 3 squarish pieces, each about ¾ inch thick. If you position the block so one of its longer cut sides faces up, it is easier to eyeball handsome pieces. You'll have 12 pieces total.

2 To press excess liquid from the tofu, use two flat-bottomed implements, such as a set of baking sheets. To absorb moisture from the tofu, lay a non-terry dishtowel (or double layer of paper towels) on one of the baking sheets, then arrange the tofu slices on top. Lay another non-terry dishtowel (or more paper towels) atop the tofu. Place the other baking sheet on top and finish with a 2-pound weight, such as a 28-ounce food can. Set aside at room temperature for 10 to 15 minutes, until the tofu has firmed up. It does not need to be as firm as for pressed tofu, so the pressing time is shorter.

3 Position a rack about 4 inches away from the broiler element. Preheat the broiler. Line a baking sheet with aluminum foil.

4 On a small plate or shallow bowl, combine the soy sauce and oil. Put each piece of tofu in the mixture, then flip it over to coat the other side. Put the tofu on the baking sheet as you work.

5 Broil the tofu for about 3 minutes, until the tops have turned golden brown in places; the edges may have browned, too. Remove from the oven (keep the broiler on),

CONTINUED

then let the sizzling subside. Use a metal spatula to turn each piece of tofu. Broil the tofu on the other side for 1 minute, until the edges are tinged golden brown; a little crustiness is good.

Remove from the oven and, again, wait for the sizzling to calm down. Use a butter knife or small spatula to spread 3/4 teaspoon of miso sauce (in an 1/8-inch-thick layer) on top of each piece. Use the gingery miso for half and the citrusy miso for the other half.

Slide the baking sheet back under the broiler for 30 to 45 seconds, until the miso is bubbling. Remove from the oven. Sprinkle white sesame seeds on the gingery miso and black sesame seeds on the citrusy miso. If you like some zing, add a small pinch of ground *sansho* to each of the citrusy miso *tofu dengaku*.

Let cool for a few minutes before sliding two parallel bamboo skewers or a single two-pronged pick (such as a flat bamboo cocktail fork) into each tofu piece. Transfer to a serving platter and enjoy hot.

NOTE

Sweetened miso sauces are a staple in Japanese kitchens. Their generic name, *neri* miso, means "stirred bean paste," which describes how they are made. Many kinds exist, and you can accent them with various flavors to enjoy with broiled tofu and simmered tofu (*yu dofu*, page 87); they're good spread on crackers too. Here are two of my favorites to keep on hand. Each makes about 3 tablespoons.

For a **gingery miso sauce**, in an extra-small saucepan, combine 2 1/2 to 3 tablespoons red (*aka*) miso, 1 tablespoon sugar, 1 tablespoon sake, and 1 1/2 teaspoons water. Cook over medium heat, stirring constantly, for 1 to 3 minutes, until it is the texture of ketchup. Remove from the heat and set aside to cool for about 30 seconds, stirring frequently. Taste and add extra miso for saltiness, sugar for sweetness, or water to dilute. Stir in 1/4 teaspoon fresh ginger juice (see Note, page 72), then transfer to a small bowl and let cool completely.

To make a **citrusy miso sauce**, in an extra-small saucepan, combine 2 1/2 to 3 tablespoons white (*shiro* or *Saikyo*) miso with 1 tablespoon sake, 1 teaspoon mirin, 1 1/2 teaspoons water, 1/4 teaspoon sugar, and 1/4 teaspoon grated fresh lemon (or *yuzu*) zest. Cook over medium heat, stirring for 1 to 3 minutes, until it is the texture of thick hollandaise. Remove from the heat, briefly cool, then taste and adjust the flavor with extra miso, sugar, or water. Transfer to a bowl and cool completely before stirring in an additional 1/8 teaspoon of lemon (or *yuzu*) zest.

If you're going to use the sauces within an hour, cover the bowls with plastic wrap and keep at room temperature. Or, refrigerate in airtight containers for up to 4 weeks. Return to room temperature before using.

Fermented Tofu, Lemongrass, and Goat Skewers

DE NUONG CHAO

Fermented tofu is a Chinese invention, but here it gets a Vietnamese treatment, with lemongrass, fish sauce, and lime juice. The combination seasons thin slices of goat that are then skewered and grilled. The smart layering of flavors in this dish is a great example of southern Viet flair, and I'm thankful to Vietnamese-Australian chef Luke Nguyen for turning me on to it.

Because fermented tofu differs from one another, you must taste the marinade and tweak it. Don't be put off by the thought of it, because the flavor will be pleasant. Halal markets are good sources for quality goat, though Vietnamese and Latin grocers also carry goat. Leg meat works well, but the flesh from the shoulder or sirloin is fine, too. Despite goat's increasing popularity in the United States, it is still not widely sold. My go-to substitute is gamier lamb; a big Saratoga lamb chop or thick sirloin chop should do it. Regardless of meat, remove any silver skin present before using it.

Turn these skewers into a meal for two by tossing some extra vegetables on the grill along with the meat. Enjoy it all with the sauce and some rice, or even a baguette or pita bread.

1 tablespoon mashed white fermented tofu, with or without chile

2 teaspoons packed light or dark brown sugar

1 1/2 teaspoons fresh lime juice

1 1/2 tablespoons minced lemongrass (use white and/or pale green parts)

1 teaspoon grated, peeled fresh ginger

1 large clove garlic, finely chopped and crushed with the broad side of the knife

1/2 teaspoon dried red chile flakes

1/4 teaspoon salt

1 teaspoon fish sauce

1 1/2 tablespoons Shaoxing rice wine or dry sherry

1 tablespoon plus 1/2 teaspoon canola oil

8 ounces boneless goat or lamb, preferably cut from the leg, sirloin, or shoulder

4 to 6 large green onions, trimmed with about 3 inches of the greens still attached

6 tablespoons Fermented Tofu, Lemongrass, and Chile Sauce (page 212)

1 For the marinade, put the tofu in a bowl. Add the brown sugar and lime juice, stirring with a fork to blend well. Taste and balance out the tangy-sweet-savory flavors with extra lime juice, sugar, or tofu. Add the lemongrass, ginger, garlic, red chile flakes, salt, fish sauce, and rice wine. Stir to combine. Taste and make sure you like the flavors. Then add 1 tablespoon of the oil and blend together.

2 If you have time, place the meat in the freezer for about 15 minutes. It will firm up, making it easier to cut. Slice the meat across the grain into thin strips a scant 1/4 inch thick, about 1 inch wide, and 2 to 3 inches long.

3 Add the meat to the marinade. Use your fingers to coat and massage the seasonings into the meat. Cover with plastic wrap and set aside at room temperature for 30 minutes. Meanwhile, soak 10 bamboo skewers, each about 10 inches long, in water.

CONTINUED

Fermented Tofu, Lemongrass, and Goat Skewers

CONTINUED

4 To grill the skewers, prepare a medium-high fire in a charcoal grill (it's the right temperature when you can hold your hand over the rack for no more than 3 or 4 seconds) or preheat a gas grill to medium-high. To broil the skewers, position a rack about 4 inches from the heat source and preheat the oven for 20 minutes so it is nice and hot.

5 While the grill or broiler heats, drain the skewers. Toss the green onions with the remaining 1/2 teaspoon of oil, then thread them onto 2 of the skewers. Line up the green onions and individually insert each skewer crosswise, 1 to 2 inches from the root ends. You can use 1 skewer but doubling up gives you better control of the onions while grilling. Set aside.

Thread the meat onto the remaining 8 skewers, putting 3 or 4 strips on each. Squish the meat together as you thread so that it is compact. Cup your hand around the meat and gently squeeze to make sure that it hugs the skewer well. This allows for some charring of the surface but also preserves some of the flavors of the marinade. If you are broiling, put the skewers on an aluminum foil–lined baking sheet.

6 Place the meat skewers on the grill rack or slip the baking sheet under the broiler. Grill or broil, turning the skewers once, for 3 to 4 minutes on each side, or until the meat is browned and a little charred at the edges. After turning the skewers, add the onion skewer and cook for about 2 minutes, turning frequently, until they have softened and acquired a little character.

7 Arrange the meat skewers on a platter. Remove the skewers from the onions and offer them alongside the meat with the sauce. Serve immediately. Invite guests to enjoy the meat unadorned to savor the intricate flavors, or with a light dip in the sauce; you can also spoon the sauce onto the skewers. The onion is great dunked into the sauce as a chaser.

Grilled Crisp Tofu Pockets TAHU BAKAR

MAKES 12 PIECES, TO SERVE 4 TO 6

You may wonder why this Malaysian snack requires cooking tofu two ways. Indeed, the tofu is delicious when it's freshly deep-fried, stuffed with crisp vegetables, and garnished with a spunky sauce. Grilling the fried tofu, however, refreshes and crisps the tofu beautifully, and adds an earthy char that pairs perfectly with the sauce, making the pockets out-of-this-world good.

Penang-based food journalist Robyn Eckhardt tells me that the sauce can vary. Chinese vendors lean toward the *rojak* sauce, below, whereas Malay sellers often use a peanut sauce. For a vegetarian alternative, mix Thai Sweet Chile Sauce (page 210) with salt and/or Indonesian sweet soy sauce (*kecap manis*). As for the vegetables, think of a crunchy shredded salad: finely julienned carrot and jicama would be great instead of the cucumber and bean sprouts. See the ingredients guide on page 219 for details on dried shrimp paste, dark palm sugar, and sweet soy sauce.

ROJAK SAUCE
1 tablespoon dried shrimp paste or 2 teaspoons preroasted dried shrimp paste
3 tablespoons packed dark palm sugar or dark brown sugar
1 or 2 moderately hot red chiles, such as Fresno, coarsely chopped
2 tablespoons Tamarind Liquid (page 217)
3 tablespoons Indonesian sweet soy sauce

1¹/2 pounds firm tofu
4 ounces (1¹/2 cups) bean sprouts
5 cups water
2¹/4 teaspoons salt

Canola oil for deep-frying
1 large Kirby or Persian cucumber, quartered lengthwise, seeded, and cut on the diagonal into thin strips, each about 2 inches long
2 to 3 tablespoons unsalted roasted peanuts, chopped

1 To make the sauce, if using unroasted dried shrimp paste for the sauce, wrap it up in a 3-inch-square piece of aluminum foil like an envelope. Flatten the packet with the heel of your hand. Roast the packet on the stovetop directly over a medium-high flame for 2 to 3 minutes, turning occasionally with tongs, until it is briny smelling; expect steam to shoot from the foil. Remove from the heat and let cool. Blast your exhaust to get rid of odor. (If using preroasted shrimp paste, skip this step.)

2 Use a small food processor to grind the shrimp paste, palm sugar, and chiles to a fine texture. Add the tamarind and sweet soy sauce and process until smooth (you'll have about ¹/2 cup). Transfer to a bowl if using soon. Or, refrigerate in a tightly capped jar for up to a week; return to room temperature before using.

3 Halve the tofu crosswise, then cut each half into squarish pieces about 2¹/4 inches wide and ³/4 inch thick. You should have 12 pieces total. Put in a bowl. Put the bean sprouts in another bowl. Set aside.

4 Bring the water to a boil. Turn off the heat. After the boiling subsides, measure 3 cups and add the salt, stirring

CONTINUED

Grilled Crisp Tofu Pockets
CONTINUED

to dissolve. Pour this salted water over the tofu, covering it. Set aside for 15 minutes.

Pour the remaining (unsalted) hot water over the bean sprouts to cover. When the sprouts have softened, about 2 minutes, drain, flush with cold water, and set aside to drain well. The bean sprouts can be prepped several days in advance and refrigerated.

5 When the tofu is ready, pour off the water, then transfer the pieces to a non-terry dishtowel or double layer of paper towels placed atop a plate. Let drain for about 15 minutes.

6 Heat 1½ inches of oil in a wok, deep skillet, or saucepan over high heat to between 360° and 370°F. Blot excess water from the tofu one last time, then fry in batches of 4 to 6 pieces, sliding them into the oil, then gently stirring them with chopsticks or a skimmer to fry evenly and prevent them from sticking. If they stick, let them fry until they are light golden before nudging them apart, or remove the pieces from the oil, separate, then quickly replace them in the oil to finish frying. The tofu should be crisp and deep golden after 2 to 3 minutes. Drain the fried tofu on paper towels. Return the oil to temperature before frying another batch. Set aside to cool. The tofu may be fried and refrigerated up to 5 days ahead; return it to room temperature before grilling.

7 To grill the tofu, prepare a very hot charcoal fire (it's ready when you can hold your hand over the rack for only 2 to 3 seconds) or heat a gas grill to high. Grill the tofu for about 3 minutes on each side, until hot and crisp with some dark charring. Dab some sauce on the tofu before it comes off the grill, for caramelization, if you like. Transfer to a plate and let cool for a few minutes. (Alternatively, broil the tofu in a toaster oven directly on the rack for about 6 minutes, turning midway, until hot and slightly crisp at the edges.)

8 Lay each piece of tofu on your work surface and use a paring knife to cut a pocket into one side. To assemble, drizzle about ½ teaspoon of sauce into each pocket before stuffing in the bean sprouts and cucumber, letting a few hang out of the opening for flair.

9 Serve the pockets on individual plates or a platter. Drizzle on some of the sauce and sprinkle on the peanuts. Offer extra sauce on the side. These pockets are best eaten as a finger food.

Fried Tofu with Chile Peanut Sauce TAO HU THOT

SERVES 4

Whether you're a vegan or an omnivore, you'll love this Thai tofu snack of deep-fried tofu paired with a sweet chile sauce accented by peanutty crunch and cilantro bite. Many Thai restaurants abroad carry the popular street food, but you can prepare it at home, too.

It's particularly easy and fast if you have Thai sweet chile sauce on hand. Just mix in the salt, peanuts, and cilantro for the sauce. Though this dish is best enjoyed with just-fried tofu, you can fry it in advance. It will be convenient, but not stellar. Refrigerate the prefried tofu for up to 5 days and return it to room temperature before reheating it in a 400°F toaster oven for about 6 minutes, turning midway, until hot and gently sizzling.

14 to 16 ounces firm tofu
1^1/$_2$ teaspoons salt
2 cups very hot or just-boiled water

CHILE PEANUT SAUCE
1/3 cup Thai Sweet Chile Sauce, homemade (page 210)
    or purchased
About 1/4 teaspoon salt
1 generous tablespoon unsalted roasted peanuts, chopped
1 generous tablespoon finely chopped cilantro

Canola oil for deep-frying

1 Halve the tofu crosswise, then cut each half into thick dominoes, each about 1 inch wide, 2 inches long, and 1 inch thick. Put the tofu in a bowl. Dissolve 1^1/$_2$ teaspoons salt in the hot water, then pour over the tofu to cover. Set aside for 15 minutes to season the tofu.

2 Meanwhile, make the sauce in a small bowl. Season the sweet chile sauce with enough salt to give it a savory edge; with the homemade sauce, I use about 1/4 teaspoon. If the sauce is cold, wait for a few minutes for the flavors to develop before you taste and make adjustments. Add the peanuts and cilantro and set aside.

3 Pour off the water from the tofu, then transfer the pieces to a non-terry dishtowel or double layer of paper towels placed atop a plate, baking sheet, or tray. Let drain for about 15 minutes.

4 Pour oil to a depth of 1^1/$_2$ inches into a wok, deep skillet, or saucepan. Heat the oil over high heat to between 360° and 370°F.

Blot excess water from the tofu one last time, then fry in batches of 3 or 4 pieces, sliding the pieces into the oil, then gently stirring them with chopsticks or a skimmer to fry evenly and prevent them from sticking. If they stick, let them fry until they are light golden before nudging them apart; if that's hard to do, remove the tofu from the oil, separate the pieces, then quickly replace them in the oil to finish frying. The tofu should be crisp and deep golden after 2 to 3 minutes. Drain the fried tofu on paper towels. Return the oil to temperature before frying another batch.

5 Serve the tofu on a small plate with the sauce. Invite guests to dip the tofu into the sauce or spoon it over. They can use their fingers or forks to pick up the tofu.

Deep-Fried Tofu AGEDASHI DOFU

SERVES 4 AS A SNACK

A classic Japanese preparation included in *Tofu Hyaku Chin*, a 1782 bestseller, *agedashi dofu* remains on countless restaurant menus today. It is heavenly when the tofu is fried to a slight crisp and the delicate sauce just lightly cloaks. Most often, the tofu is soggy from waiting too long to be delivered to your table. If you make *agedashi dofu* at home, you can simply eat the tofu as soon as it is done! Additionally, thickening the sauce keeps the tofu from soaking up too much.

14 to 16 ounces firm tofu

1 teaspoon salt

1½ cups very hot or just-boiled water

¼ cup chopped green onion, green part only

1 cup Dashi Stock (page 215)

2 tablespoons Japanese or Korean soy sauce

1½ tablespoons mirin

2 teaspoons sugar

1 tablespoon cornstarch dissolved in 1½ tablespoons water

Canola oil for deep-frying

About ⅓ cup potato starch

1 tablespoon finely grated fresh ginger

2 or 3 tablespoons dried bonito flakes (katsuo-bushi), optional

1 Cut the tofu crosswise, then into 8 to 10 matchbox-size pieces, each about ¾ inch thick. Put all the pieces of tofu in a bowl. Dissolve the salt in the hot water, then pour over the tofu. The tofu should be covered. Set aside for 15 minutes to season the tofu.

2 Put the green onion in a small bowl and add water to cover. Let soak for 10 minutes to reduce its harshness.

3 Meanwhile, in a saucepan, combine the dashi, soy sauce, mirin, and sugar. Bring to a simmer, then add the cornstarch slurry. This is a thickish sauce that sticks well; don't pour in all of the slurry if you prefer a runnier sauce. Cook for about 30 seconds to thicken. Partially cover to keep warm.

4 When the tofu is ready, pour off the water, then transfer the pieces to a non-terry dishtowel or double layer of paper towels placed atop a plate. Let drain for about 15 minutes. Drain the green onion well, patting it with paper towels to remove excess water. Transfer to a bowl and set aside.

5 Meanwhile, heat 2 inches of oil in a wok or saucepan over high heat to between 360° and 370°F. As the oil heats up, blot excess moisture from the tofu. Because the potato starch can turn gummy if it sits too long on the tofu, wait until the oil temperature approaches 340°F before dredging each piece of tofu in the starch to coat well. Shake off excess starch, then set aside on a plate near the stove.

When the oil is ready, fry the tofu in batches of 3 or 4 pieces, sliding them into the oil, then gently stirring them with chopsticks or a skimmer to fry evenly and prevent them from sticking. They should be very crisp after 2 to 3 minutes. It's okay if they get just slightly golden. Drain on paper towels. Return the oil to temperature before frying another batch.

6 To serve, divide the sauce among individual shallow bowls or plates; offer some on the side too, if you like. Arrange the tofu on top. Garnish with the green onion, ginger, and bonito flakes. Eat with chopsticks.

Spiced Tofu and Vegetable Fritters SOY PANEER PAKORAS

MAKES ABOUT 24 FRITTERS, TO SERVE 4 TO 6

A modern ingredient in India, tofu is often employed as a substitute for paneer cheese. You may be familiar with it in simmered dishes such as *saag* tofu (page 121) with creamy greens and spices. Here it's featured in a deep-fried fritter.

While you can coat large chunks of tofu in the batter and fry it up tempura-style, it is tastier to cut it into small pieces and combine it with chopped vegetables and spices. There are more varied textures and flavors. Ketchup is a popular accompaniment for *pakoras*. I add fresh ginger juice to tilt the ketchup toward being an Indian condiment. Green chutney injects a vibrant herby contrast.

Garbanzo bean flour (*besan*) is sold at South Asian and many health food markets. Use an Indian or a Thai brand of rice flour, or a widely distributed one such as Bob's Red Mill.

10 ounces firm tofu

1/4 cup ketchup

2 teaspoons fresh ginger juice (see Notes)

Salt

BATTER

2 ounces (1/2 cup) garbanzo bean flour

21/4 ounces (1/2 cup) rice flour

1/2 teaspoon ground cumin

1/2 teaspoon cayenne

1/8 teaspoon turmeric

1/4 teaspoon baking soda

Generous 1/2 teaspoon salt

About 1/2 cup water

1 tablespoon coriander seed, toasted until fragrant in a skillet, optional

1/4 cup chopped seeded mild green chile, such as pasilla

1/4 cup finely chopped red onion

Canola oil for deep-frying

1/3 cup Green Chutney (page 218), optional

1 Initially, cut the tofu crosswise and then into matchbox-size pieces about 1/3 inch thick. This makes the tofu easier to manage for draining. Lay the tofu on a non-terry dishtowel or double layer of paper towels atop a plate. Let drain for about 10 minutes.

2 Meanwhile, in a dipping sauce dish, stir together the ketchup, ginger juice, and a big pinch of salt. As the sauce sits, the ginger bite will be a little more pronounced, which is what you want. The salt amplifies the ginger flavor, so taste before serving and add more salt if you must. Set aside.

3 To make the batter, in a bowl, stir together the garbanzo bean flour, rice flour, cumin, cayenne, turmeric, baking soda, and salt. Make a well in the center, then pour in the water. Stir to create a thick batter resembling pancake batter. Set aside.

4 Blot the tofu pieces dry again, then cut each into small cubes about 1/4 inch. Add to the batter, along with the coriander, chile, and onion. Use a spatula to combine the ingredients into a thick mixture. You'll have about 2 cups.

CONTINUED

Spiced Tofu and Vegetable Fritters
CONTINUED

5 Pour the oil to a depth of 1 inch into a medium saucepan, flat-bottomed wok, deep skillet, or 5-quart Dutch oven. Heat over medium-high heat to about 350°F. If you don't have a deep-fry thermometer, stick a *dry* bamboo chopstick into the oil; if bubbles rise immediately to the surface, the oil is ready.

For each fritter, use two spoons to scoop up a good tablespoon of batter and scoot it into the hot oil. Fry only as many as will fit without crowding. Fry, turning the fritters over once or twice, for about 3 minutes total, or until puffed slightly, golden brown, and crisp. Use a skimmer or slotted spoon to transfer to a paper towel–lined plate.

The fritters soften just a tad after frying. If you'd like to recrisp them, raise the oil's heat to just above 375°F (use a thermometer or guess) and refry in batches for 15 to 30 seconds. Drain briefly before serving.

6 Arrange the *pakoras* on a plate and serve hot as finger food along with the gingery tomato ketchup and the green chutney.

NOTES

To extract ginger juice, grate unpeeled fresh ginger with a Microplane or Japanese grater, then press the solids through a fine-mesh sieve to obtain the cloudy yellow liquid. Use 1 inch of ginger for every teaspoon of juice you want.

Leftover *pakoras* can be reheated in a 350°F toaster oven or regular oven. Bake them for about 6 minutes, turning midway, until hot and slightly crisp.

Tofu French Fries

SERVES 3 OR 4 AS A SNACK

The Japanese have a charming knack for merging Western and Eastern cultures. At the Santa Monica, California, outpost of Musha, an *izakaya* pub, there is a quirky menu section called "Tofu World" with dishes such as "pure tofu" and "cheese tofu." My favorite is the tofu french fry, which is essentially *agedashi* tofu (page 70) served with wasabi mayonnaise and sweet chile sauce.

The delicately crisp batons of tofu are always delivered piping hot to the table with their accompaniments. No matter how many times I remind myself to wait for the fries to cool, I never do and end up burning the roof of my mouth. Thank goodness for beer.

I've replicated Musha's tofu french fries on numerous afternoons as a snack with drinks. Use a full-fat mayonnaise, or be authentic with Japanese Kewpie brand.

8 to 10 ounces extra-firm tofu

1 1/2 teaspoons salt

2 cups very hot or just-boiled water

Canola oil for deep-frying

About 1/3 cup potato starch

1 to 2 tablespoons mayonnaise or wasabi mayonnaise (see Note)

1 to 2 tablespoons Thai Sweet Chile Sauce, homemade (page 210) or purchased

1 Cut the tofu into batons about 1/2 inch thick and 3 inches long. Given their delicate shape, put them in a wide shallow dish to prevent them from breaking. Dissolve the salt in the water, then pour over the tofu. Set aside for 15 minutes to season.

2 Pour the water from the tofu, then transfer the pieces to a non-terry dishtowel or double layer of paper towels placed atop a plate. Let drain for about 15 minutes.

3 Meanwhile, heat 1 inch of oil in a wok or saucepan over high heat to between 350° and 360°F. As the oil heats up, blot excess moisture from the tofu. When the temperature approaches 325°F, dredge each piece of tofu in the potato starch to coat well. Shake off excess starch, then set aside on a plate near the stove.

When the oil is ready, fry the tofu in 2 batches, sliding the pieces into the oil, then gently stirring them with chopsticks or a skimmer to fry evenly and prevent them from sticking. They should be crisp after about 1 minute. It's okay if they get slightly golden; if they burst, they will still be delicious. Drain on paper towels. When you're done, if any pieces have softened, raise the oil temperature to slightly above 360°F and refry for about 15 seconds.

Serve immediately with mayonnaise and chile sauce for dipping.

NOTE

To make wasabi mayonnaise, mix 1 teaspoon wasabi powder with 1/2 teaspoon water and let the mixture stand for a few minutes. (Or use 3/4 teaspoon prepared wasabi.) Then stir in 2 tablespoons mayonnaise and 1 or 2 pinches of salt.

Fresh Tofu with Sauces and Toppings

SERVES 4

As you work through the recipes in this book, you are likely to amass sauces and toppings in the fridge. Set them out with some freshly made tofu and have a cross-cultural experience. That's what Beijing-based chef Max Levy does as part of his tofu tasting menu at Bei, one of the city's best contemporary restaurants. Max is fanatical about tofu and makes his own from northern Chinese soybeans and *nigari* that he personally carts back from Japan. His first course is comprised of tofu surrounded by six different sauces, oils, and seasonings.

At home, use what you have on hand, trying for a broad range of flavors and colors. Use 1 to 1¼ pounds of silken, medium, or medium-firm tofu, slightly chilled or at room temperature. Cut it into 1-inch cubes or ½-inch-thick matchbook-size pieces. Aim to make them easy to pick up with chopsticks or forks. Arrange on individual plates or a platter. Present three to six of the following garnishes, 1 to 2 tablespoons of each unless otherwise specified, in dipping bowls alongside. Provide little spoons, if needed. Invite guests to dip, swipe, and/or sprinkle.

SPICY AND/OR NUMBING

- Chile and Sichuan Peppercorn Mix (page 211)
- Fermented Tofu, Lemongrass, and Chile Sauce (page 212)
- Chile Oil (page 213)
- Green Chutney (page 218)

SALTY

- Chinese Sweet Fragrant Soy Sauce (page 207)
- Japanese Seasoned Soy Concentrate (page 208)
- Korean Seasoned Soy Sauce (page 209)
- Taiwanese soy sauce paste (see Tofu with Century Eggs, page 56, step 1)
- Your favorite soy sauce

SWEET AND/OR RICH

- Gingery Miso Sauce (see Note, page 62)
- Citrusy Miso Sauce (see Note, page 62)
- Rojak Sauce (see Grilled Crisp Tofu Pockets, page 67, steps 1 and 2)
- Chile Peanut Sauce (see Fried Tofu with Chile Peanut Sauce, page 69, step 2)
- Toasted white or black sesame seeds pounded with a few pinches of salt

FRESH AND HERBY

- Thinly sliced green onion, green part only
- Finely shredded green *shiso* leaves
- 1½ teaspoons grated fresh ginger

Soups and Hot Pots

The first time I went out to eat with my friend Linda Lim, she picked a Korean tofu restaurant. "Tofu is comfort food for me and I *have* to eat it at least once a week," she explained with a certain tone of fanaticism. Over the years, she talked of her upbringing in Kansas, an Asian food desert back in the 1970s, as she described it. One of the bright spots in her childhood turned out to be tofu related.

Economic opportunity and the prospects of a better life brought the Lim family from Seoul to the American Heartland. In 1965, historic changes to US immigration law established equal entry quotas for all nations, opening the door for greater immigration from non-European countries. People in occupations with labor shortages were given priority.

Many South Koreans were leaving for the States and Linda's parents wanted their family to go, too. In the late 1960s, they learned about an American need for chicken sexers, people skilled at differentiating between male and female chicks, a difficult and critical task to hatcheries. Mr. Lim decided to give up his accounting career and apply to immigrate to the States and be retrained.

He arrived in 1969 and quickly mastered the trade. His wife and daughters, Linda and Ann, joined him in 1971. Initially, the family lived in Jasper, Indiana. They moved all over the Midwest, wherever there was work to be had at a hatchery, and finally settled in Wichita, Kansas. "There were few Asians, let alone Koreans, in the area back then," Linda said. "The only Asian grocery store was in Junction City, over 100 miles away. They didn't have many Korean staples, such as *gochu garu* (ground red pepper), so my grandfather shipped those ingredients from Korea."

Her mother marshaled Linda and Ann to prepare innumerable batches of kimchi, fresh *mandu* dumpling skins, and *gochujang* chile paste. Mrs. Lim packed Korean *kimbap* sushi rolls in her children's lunchboxes, though they would have preferred peanut butter and jelly sandwiches. Every night she presented a meal of traditional Korean fare, including a soup, which the family sipped on, as many Asians do, in lieu of drinking a beverage.

As first-generation immigrants, the Lims did their best to still eat like Koreans in America, not like Korean Americans. Their annual foray into American dining was at a local Pizza Hut. "Meatloaf, hamburgers, and ambrosia salads were exotic to us," Linda said.

In 1984, after years of paperwork and waiting, Mrs. Lim successfully sponsored her sister and brother-in-law to the United States. While Korean ingredients were more readily available by then, good tofu was not. After trying supermarket tofu, Linda's uncle was dissatisfied and began making it from scratch. He'd never done it before but was a handy fellow who managed to figure it out. Her uncle made tofu every week and would drive thirty miles from his home in Newton to deliver a large tub full of fresh tofu to the Lims in Wichita.

Mrs. Lim cut up the tender square blocks to add to her family's daily soups or *chigae* hot pots. She would also pan-fry tofu and simmer it with diluted *yangnyumjang* sauce (page 209) for *dubu jorim*, a *banchan* type of side dish. "Emobu's [uncle's] homemade tofu had a wonderful texture and richness that I can still recall," Linda wistfully said.

Living in San Francisco nowadays, Linda is responsible for her tofu fix. She prepares *chigae* and other Korean dishes when she has time, but most often snacks on fresh tofu and kimchi. Her sister Ann in New Jersey enjoys tofu daily and has taught her ten-year-old daughter how to distinguish between excellent and mediocre tofu. "My uncle's tofu laid the foundation for our appreciation of it," Linda remarked. "When people say that tofu has no taste, I say no, it *does* have taste. It's a shame that so few people have ever experienced tofu's freshness."

Like Linda, I grew up with a soup as part of our daily supper—it's typical of most Asian cuisines. This collection of recipes showcases some classics as well as a few remarkable new discoveries. Most of the soups are perfect for everyday meals while others can be showstoppers.

Tofu, Tomato, and Dill Soup CANH DAU PHU

SERVES 4 TO 6 WITH 2 OR 3 OTHER DISHES

No matter how hot it got in Southern California, my mother would serve soup to start off our dinner, and she often prepared this classic combination of tofu and tomato. The ripe tomato adds tanginess and savory depth and the tofu contributes protein and texture while absorbing the other flavors. Slowly cooked onion gives sweetness; fresh dill injects color and fragrance.

If you like, cook 2 to 3 ounces of ground pork along with the tomato. Or, after turning off the heat, pour 2 beaten eggs onto the soup in a wide circle, and then stir gently to break it up into chiffonlike pieces. Vietnamese *canh* are enjoyed throughout the meal, so let guests help themselves. I often begin and end my Viet dinners with some soup.

12 to 14 ounces medium or medium-firm tofu

1 tablespoon canola oil

1 small yellow onion, thinly sliced

12 ounces ripe tomatoes, cored and coarsely chopped

3/4 teaspoon salt

1 1/2 tablespoons fish sauce

4 cups water

2 tablespoons chopped fresh dill or cilantro, feathery or leafy tops only

Black pepper

1 Cut the tofu into bite-size cubes, each about 3/4 inch. Set aside on a plate.

2 In a 3-quart saucepan, heat the oil over medium heat. Add the onion and cook gently, stirring occasionally, for 4 to 5 minutes, until fragrant and soft. Add the tomato and salt, cover, and cook for 4 to 6 minutes, until the tomato has collapsed into a thick mixture. Stir occasionally and, if necessary, lower the heat to prevent the tomato from sticking or scorching.

3 Uncover and add the fish sauce and water. Raise the heat to bring to a boil, and skim off and discard any scum that rises to the surface.

Pour off any water that has drained from the tofu, then add to the soup. Adjust the heat to simmer and cook, uncovered, for about 5 minutes to develop and concentrate the flavors. If you are not serving the soup right away, turn off the heat and cover.

4 Just before serving, bring the soup to a simmer. Taste and add extra salt or fish sauce, if necessary. Turn the heat off. Stir in the dill and transfer to a serving bowl. Garnish with a generous sprinkle of pepper and serve immediately.

Miso Soup MISO SHIRU

SERVES 4 TO 6 WITH 2 OR 3 OTHER DISHES

One of the most popular ways that Japanese cooks use tofu is to include it in miso soup. Whether the tofu is silken or block tofu, it adds visual and textural appeal as well as satisfying protein. You could use julienned fried *abura-age* (see the buying guide, page 11); remember to remove some of its oil by dunking it in boiling water first.

There are innumerable ways to make miso soup and you can use any type of miso, even blending types. I usually have mellow white (*shiro*) and more assertive red (*aka*) on hand.

Instead of the green onion, use 2 to 3 tablespoons of coarsely chopped boldly flavored greens, such as tender leaves of watercress, chrysanthemum, mustard, and celery. If the greens seem at all tough, blanch them before chopping them up and dividing them among the bowls.

6 to 7 ounces silken, medium, or medium-firm tofu
1¹/2 tablespoons dried wakame seaweed or 3 ounces enoki
    mushrooms
1 green onion, white and green parts, cut into thin rings
3¹/2 cups Dashi Stock (page 215)
About 3 tablespoons miso, any type

1 Cut the tofu into large dice. Set aside on a plate.

2 If you are using the seaweed, soak it in cold water for 3 to 5 minutes, until softened. Then drain and set it aside. If you are using the enoki mushrooms, give the cluster a very quick rinse under water, then trim and discard the lower portion of the sandy material that the mushrooms grew in. The cluster should naturally fall apart. Halve them crosswise and put the pieces with the caps into individual soup bowls. Set aside the rest.

Divide the green onion among the soup bowls. Have the bowls near the stove.

3 In a 2-quart saucepan, bring the dashi stock to a boil over high heat. Add the tofu and cook for about 1 minute to warm it up. Lower the heat to medium, then stir in the miso; if your miso is chunky or firm, put it in a bowl and mix in some of the hot stock to break it up before adding back to the pan.

Taste the soup and add extra miso, if needed. Add the seaweed or mushroom and cook for 30 seconds more. Turn off the heat and divide the soup among the bowls. Serve immediately.

Tofu, Seaweed, and Pork Soup GAENG JUED TAO HU SARAI

SERVES 4 TO 6 WITH 2 OR 3 OTHER DISHES

When a Thai meal is full of fiery chile heat, a light clear soup like this one soothes and calms the palate. The term *gaeng jued* often denotes a Chinese-style Thai soup. Here, the silken tofu and soft seaweed provide a velvety backdrop for savory small meatballs of pork, garlic, and cilantro.

Seaweed is commonly prepared with tofu in Chinese and Japanese cooking. Some cooks soak the seaweed before using it, but this Thai approach is to simply drop the dried bits into the broth where it will rehydrate.

When *wakame* seaweed is not available, substitute 2 lightly packed cups of coarsely chopped, mild-flavored leafy greens, such as spinach, chard, or napa cabbage. Minced chicken thigh is an excellent substitute for the pork. You can pair this amicable Thai soup with dishes from other Asian cuisines.

12 ounces silken tofu

4 ounces coarsely ground or hand-chopped pork, fattier kind preferred

1 clove garlic, finely chopped and mashed into a paste

1 tablespoon finely chopped cilantro stems or roots

Sugar

Ground white pepper

3 tablespoons light (regular) soy sauce

5 cups Chicken Stock (page 214), or 3 1/2 cups full-sodium canned chicken broth and 1 1/2 cups water

Salt

3 brimming tablespoons dried wakame seaweed

1 green onion, white and green parts, cut into thin rings

2 tablespoons coarsely chopped cilantro leaves

1 To unmold the tofu, run a knife around the edge of the mold or package and invert onto a plate. Pour off the excess liquid or use paper towels to blot it away. It's okay if the tofu breaks.

2 In a bowl, combine the pork, garlic, cilantro stems, 2 pinches of sugar, 1 pinch of white pepper, and 1 table-spoon of the soy sauce. Vigorously stir with chopsticks or a fork to create a dense mixture. Set aside.

3 Put the chicken stock in a 3-quart saucepan. Add 1 pinch of sugar, 1/4 teaspoon of salt, and the remaining 2 tablespoons of soy sauce. Bring to a boil.

Use 2 teaspoons to scoop up the pork and shape into 1-inch meatballs. Pass the pork back and forth between the spoons to smooth out the surface before casting the meat-ball into the pot. You should have about 16 meatballs.

When the soup returns to a boil, lower the heat to sim-mer for about 4 minutes to cook the pork. Skim and discard any scum that rises to the surface.

4 Meanwhile, cut the tofu into 3/4-inch cubes or break it up into small pieces with your fingers. When the soup has finished simmering, add the tofu. Return the soup to a sim-mer before adding the seaweed. Continue to simmer for 3 to 4 minutes, until the seaweed has expanded and softened.

5 Taste and make any final flavor adjustments with extra salt, sugar, or pepper before ladling into a serving bowl. Garnish with the green onion and cilantro leaves. Serve immediately.

Hot-and-Sour Soup SUAN LA TANG

SERVES 6 GENEROUSLY WITH 2 OR 3 OTHER DISHES

I've been captivated by hot-and-sour soup since I was a teen-ager, preparing it at home for my family and ordering it at Chinese restaurants. It embodies the Asian knack for balanc-ing flavors and textures: bracing white pepper and vinegar are offset by savory pork, shiitake mushrooms, and silky broth. Every spoonful invites another. For a Sichuan meal, pair the soup with *ma po* tofu (page 101) and serve with rice and a simple vegetable, such as steamed squash, to balance the assertive flavors.

There are many ways to prepare this soup and I always include tofu in mine for its color, texture, and protein. Dried lily bulbs, sold at Chinese markets (usually near the dried mush-rooms), impart a mild tang and slight crunch. If they're not available, substitute 1/2 cup of shredded bamboo shoots. For a meatless version, increase the tofu to 12 ounces and use a vegetable stock.

1/4 teaspoon salt, plus more as needed

1 teaspoon plus 1 1/2 tablespoons light (regular) soy sauce

1 teaspoon plus 1 tablespoon Shaoxing rice wine or dry sherry

2 teaspoons plus 1/4 cup cornstarch

1 teaspoon water plus 6 tablespoons

5 to 6 ounces boneless pork shoulder or loin, cut into scant 1/4-inch-thick matchsticks

1 tablespoon canola oil

Chubby 1-inch piece fresh ginger, peeled, halved lengthwise, and bruised

30 dried tiger lily bulbs, reconstituted and trimmed of knobby ends

4 large dried shiitake mushrooms, reconstituted, trimmed, and sliced

6 cups Chicken Stock (page 214), or 4 cups full-sodium canned broth and 2 cups water

About 3/4 teaspoon white pepper

8 ounces medium-firm or firm tofu, cut into 1/4-inch-thick matchsticks

1 large egg beaten with 1 teaspoon sesame oil

About 2 tablespoons Chinkiang vinegar or apple cider vinegar

1 green onion, white and green parts, thinly sliced, for garnish

1 In a bowl, combine the 1/4 teaspoon salt, 1 teaspoon soy sauce, 1 teaspoon rice wine, 2 teaspoons cornstarch, and 1 teaspoon water. Add the pork, stirring to coat well. Set aside.

2 In a 3- or 4-quart pot, heat the oil over high heat. Add the ginger and cook, stirring frequently, for 1 minute, until the ginger is super fragrant. Add the lily bulbs and mushrooms, stir for about 15 seconds until you can smell their perfume, then add the stock.

3 Bring to a boil, lower to a simmer, then add the remaining 1 1/2 tablespoons soy sauce and 1 tablespoon rice wine. Taste and season with salt and white pepper. Aim for a spicy kick and savory depth. If not serving right away, turn off the heat and cover. Before serving, return the soup to a simmer and add the pork and tofu, stirring to separate. Meanwhile, dissolve the remaining 1/4 cup cornstarch in the remaining 6 tablespoons water. Set aside.

4 When the pork has just cooked through and the soup returns to a simmer, give the cornstarch a final stir, then gradually add to the soup. You may not need the entire amount. Aim to create a silky thick soup that's not gloppy. When satisfied, give the egg a final stir, then pour it into the soup pot in a wide circle. Stir gently as the egg solidifies into suspended ribbons. Then add the vinegar, gently stirring. Taste and adjust the flavor with additional salt, white pepper, and/or vinegar. Ladle into a serving bowl or individual soup bowls. Scatter the green onion on top and serve immediately.

Silken Tofu and Edamame Soup EDAMAME NO SURINAGASHI

SERVES 4 TO 6 WITH 2 OR 3 OTHER DISHES

Soybeans are such an integral part of Asian cooking that tofu is often paired with edamame in the same preparation, show-casing the beans' versatility. In this lovely Japanese soup, white silken tofu is surrounded by a green moat of pureed edamame. Traditionally, pods of fresh soybeans would be boiled, shelled, and hand mashed. You can liberate yourself by using frozen edamame and a blender.

This soup comes together in a snap and is elegant enough for company. For extra flair, use homemade Citrus-Scented Silken Tofu (page 29). When making the soup with vegetarian dashi, tester Susan Pi doubled the miso.

1/4 cup packed cooked white rice (short, medium, or long grain)

1/4 teaspoon salt

1 1/2 cups water, filtered or spring preferred

6 ounces (1 rounded cup) frozen edamame, thawed and at room temperature

About 1 1/2 teaspoons white (shiro) miso

About 1 cup Dashi Stock (page 215)

8 ounces silken tofu or Citrus-Scented Silken Tofu (page 29)

Japanese ground chile pepper (ichimi togarashi), fresh citrus zest, or 6 edible flower petals, for garnish

1 In a small saucepan, combine the rice, salt, and water. Bring to a simmer over medium heat. Partially cover, and adjust the heat to allow the mixture to gently bubble for 10 to 12 minutes. The rice will enlarge and release its starch into the water, creating a slightly thick opaque mix-ture similar to a thin gruel. Add the edamame, then turn off the heat. Set aside for 10 minutes.

2 Transfer the rice gruel and edamame to a blender. Add the miso and blend until smooth. Add the dashi stock and continue blending to incorporate the liquid well. Taste and add extra miso or dashi if you want a more savory flavor or thinner soup, respectively. Pour through a mesh strainer positioned over a bowl or saucepan; stir to facilitate strain-ing. Discard the solids. Cover and refrigerate up to a day in advance. You should have about 3 cups.

3 The soup may be served cold, warm, or hot. If you are serving the soup warm or hot, bring the tofu to room temperature or warm it by letting it sit in hot water for about 10 minutes. Regardless, cut the tofu into 4 to 6 blocks (one for each serving); use a crinkle cutter if you want pretty ridged surfaces.

Place each block of tofu in a shallow soup bowl, then ladle the soup around it. Top the tofu with the garnish of your choice and serve.

Tofu Bamboo and Chicken Soup FU ZHU JI TANG

SERVES 4 WITH 2 OR 3 OTHER DISHES

Like the Thai soup on page 81, this homey Chinese soup is meant to be enjoyed during the meal as a complement to other dishes as well as a beverage in lieu of water or tea. Each of the modest ingredients plays an important role. The onion and chicken lay the foundation. The dried tofu sticks, which are literally called tofu bamboo in Chinese, impart an earthy flavor and aroma (see page 211 for information). The Chinese chives give a lively garlicky finish.

1 tablespoon canola oil
1/2 yellow onion, thinly sliced
2 chicken legs (1 pound total)
1 teaspoon salt
5 cups water
1 1/2 ounces dried tofu sticks (2 or 3)
3 Chinese chives, cut into 1-inch pieces, or 2 green onions, white and green parts, thinly sliced on a steep diagonal
Black or white pepper, optional

1 In a 3- or 4-quart pot, heat the oil over medium heat. Add the onion and cook gently, stirring occasionally, for 4 to 5 minutes, until fragrant and soft.

2 Add the chicken, salt, and water. Raise the heat to bring to a boil, skim off and discard any scum, then lower the heat to gently simmer. Cover and cook for 15 to 20 minutes, until you can stick a chopstick into the thickest part of a leg with little resistance. Expect steam to shoot from under the lid.

3 Remove the chicken legs and set them aside until cool enough to handle, 10 to 15 minutes.

Meanwhile, break each dried tofu stick into 2-inch-long sections and drop them into the soup; if you find super-dense-looking pieces, toss them. Gently simmer, uncovered, for 20 to 30 minutes, until the tofu has softened and turned opaque.

When the chicken has cooled enough, remove and discard the skin. Cut or shred the flesh into bite-size pieces. Return the meat (and the bones if you like) to the soup.

4 When the soup finishes simmering, add the chives. Turn off the heat and let the soup sit for about 5 minutes to develop the flavors. Taste and add salt, if necessary. Ladle into a serving bowl, leaving behind any bones. Sprinkle pepper on top and serve.

VARIATION: BURMESE CELLOPHANE NOODLE SOUP

New York–based caterer Irene Khin Wong, a native of Burma, suggests simmering the chicken with 1 1/2 tablespoons fish sauce and 2 large cloves of bruised garlic (omit the salt in step 2). Meanwhile, reconstitute half of one small bundle of cellophane noodles, a dozen dried tiger lily bulbs, and 3 wood ear mushrooms. Cut the noodles into short lengths, trim the lily bulbs of their knobby ends, and slice the mushrooms into thin strips. Add these three ingredients when you return the chicken to the pot. Add salt to taste at the end and garnish with green onion and black pepper.

Warm Simmered Tofu YU DOFU

I did not fully appreciate *yu dofu* until I visited Kyoto and experienced *shojin ryori*, Buddhist vegetarian fare that was introduced to Japan by monks who had studied in China. Buddhist temples abound in Kyoto and its environs. To feed the innumerable religious followers, city dwellers opened up artisanal tofu and *yuba* shops, as well as restaurants specializing in vegetarian cuisine.

One of the dishes created in Kyoto, perhaps at one of its temples, is *yu dofu,* which embodies the purity of flavor that characterizes the cuisine of Japan's ancient capital. Simple to prepare yet brilliant in flavor, it relies on quality ingredients—first and foremost, excellent tofu.

Take the time to make or source good tofu and your efforts will be amply rewarded. The dried kelp boosts the umami in the tofu, which receives a flavor blast from the seasoned soy sauce and garnishes.

There are versions of *yu dofu* that add vegetables and chicken to the hot pot. I prefer to spotlight the tofu. In lieu of the ground chile pepper (*ichimi togarashi*), you can opt for Japanese ground *sansho* or Sichuan peppercorn. Japanese seven-spice pepper blend (*shichimi togarashi*) is good for a mild touch. Tester and stylist Karen Shinto garnished hers with Korean dried chile threads.

1/3 cup thinly sliced green onion, white and green parts

16 square inches dried kelp (kombu)

6 tablespoons Japanese Seasoned Soy Concentrate (page 208)

2 tablespoons Dashi Stock (page 215) or water

1 to 1 1/4 pounds medium or medium-firm tofu, homemade preferred

Japanese ground chile pepper (ichimi togarashi)

1 Put the green onion in a small bowl and add water to cover. Set aside for 10 minutes to soak and reduce its harshness.

2 Meanwhile, set up the hot pot. To simmer and serve the tofu, use a medium (2 1/2- to 3-quart) ceramic Japanese or Korean hot pot, Chinese clay pot, deep casserole dish, or enamel-coated cast-iron pot. Fill halfway with water (filtered or spring preferred). Cut the kelp into 4 pieces and add it to the hot pot. Set aside for 15 to 20 minutes to soak.

3 For a traditional presentation, warm the sauce along with the tofu in the hot pot. Find something to hold the sauce, such as a heatproof glass tumbler, small pitcher, or bowl that is taller than the water line in the hot pot by about 1 inch. Position the sauce container in the center of the hot pot and arrange the kelp pieces around it. Pour the soy concentrate and dashi into the container.

If you like, position and fill the sauce container in the hot pot before adding the kelp to soak. For a modern approach, combine the soy concentrate and dashi in a small bowl and set it at the table.

4 Drain the green onion well, patting it with paper towels to remove excess water. Transfer to a bowl and set at the table.

Cut the tofu into 8 to 12 chunks and arrange in the hot pot. Add extra water to just cover the tofu. It will swell slightly during simmering. Either heat the hot pot at the

CONTINUED

Warm Simmered Tofu

stove and bring it to the table for serving, or use a tabletop portable burner. Regardless, heat over medium heat for about 15 minutes, until the liquid is barely simmering, a sign that the tofu is warmed through. Avoid boiling, as that can cause the tofu to harden.

5 Once the tofu has warmed up, it is ready to serve. If the sauce was warmed in the hot pot, carefully lift it from the water and put it on a plate to catch any drips. Invite guests to use a hot pot strainer or slotted spoon to retrieve a piece of tofu and put it into their rice bowls. Add a drizzle of sauce, shower of green onion, and sprinkling of ground chile pepper. Enjoy with chopsticks and/or spoons. If the sauce is too strong, guests can dilute it with stock from the hot pot.

Silken Tofu and Seasoned Soy Milk Hot Pot TOFU TOUSUI

SERVES 4 WITH 2 OR 3 OTHER DISHES

Elegant yet humble, this specialty of the Tofu-ya Ukai chain of tofu restaurants in Japan blew me away with its clever simplicity. The hot pot of silken tofu surrounded by velvety soy milk came toward the end of a two-hour lunch. I ate nearly all of it. The combination was creamy and rich with an umami undercurrent punctuated by salted kelp (*shio kombu*) added at the table.

That hot pot opened up my palate to the possibilities of tofu—when I returned to the States, *tofu tousui* was the first dish that I recreated in my home kitchen. Instead of the salted kelp, which can be hard to obtain, I used a savory kelp relish and high-quality sea salt. A finely textured salt plays nicely with the tofu and soy milk; a coarser one offers spikes of flavor. Light-colored soy sauce adds depth without darkening the soy milk much. See the ingredients section (page 223) for extra information.

A small quantity of dashi stock is required: try to prepare it with good *kombu* to boost the overall flavor. You can make the soy milk, tofu, stock, and relish days in advance.

3 cups Rich Soy Milk (page 23)

3/4 teaspoon gypsum

1 teaspoon water

1/2 cup Dashi Stock (page 215)

11/2 to 2 teaspoons light-colored soy sauce, such as Japanese usukuchi shoyu or light (regular) Chinese-style soy sauce

4- to 5-inch square kelp (kombu) left over from making Dashi Stock

Sea salt

3 to 4 tablespoons Savory Kelp Relish (page 216), optional

1 Make silken tofu (recipe on page 28) from 11/2 cups of the rich soy milk and the gypsum and water. Choose a mold that will yield a round of tofu about 21/4 inches tall. A small glass bowl or measuring cup works well. Or use a square or rectangular mold. The height is more important: you want the top of the tofu block to peek from the moat of soy milk. Follow the recipe instructions to steam, cool, and chill the tofu. You can make it up to 3 days in advance.

2 Before assembling the hot pot, return the remaining 11/2 cups rich soy milk to room temperature. To easily unmold the silken tofu, let it sit out for about 15 minutes.

3 Meanwhile, select a small (11/2- to 2-quart) ceramic Japanese or Korean hot pot, Chinese clay pot, or deep casserole dish. In a measuring cup combine the 11/2 cups soy milk, dashi stock, and soy sauce. Taste; it should have a light savory quality. You'll be adding hits of salt at the table, so resist extra soy sauce now: the soy milk will darken too much and perhaps separate during heating.

4 Run a knife around the edge of the tofu mold and then unmold it onto the piece of kelp. Center the kelp, with the tofu on top, in the pot. The kelp makes it easier to transfer and place the delicate tofu, and keeps it from sticking to the pot.

CONTINUED

Silken Tofu and Seasoned Soy Milk Hot Pot
CONTINUED

5 Pour the seasoned soy milk around the tofu. Either heat the hot pot at the stove and bring it to the table for serving, or use a tabletop portable burner. Regardless, heat the hot pot over medium-low heat for 15 to 20 minutes, until the liquid is hot but not simmering. Cover the pot if you like, but periodically check its progress. If a film forms on the soy milk, be sure to eat it.

If the soy milk gets overheated, you may see curds form. Avoid this by serving as soon as it has heated through. This is not a dish that waits for you.

6 Serve the hot pot at the table and use a large deep spoon to scoop up some of the tofu into individual rice or soup bowls. Add some soy milk with the same spoon or a ladle. Invite guests to add pinches of salt and the kelp relish.

Soy Milk Lees and Kimchi Hot Pot BIJI CHIGAE

SERVES 4 TO 6 WITH 2 OR 3 OTHER DISHES

I love saying the name of this Korean hot pot—*biji chigae*—as much as I enjoy eating it. *Biji* (like the Bee Gees band but say it faster) is the Korean term for the lees left over from making soy milk and tofu. Just like the Japanese and Chinese, the Koreans put this protein-rich byproduct to great use in satisfying hot pots called *chigae* (chee-GAH), soupy stews packed with contrasting textures and color. For details on the lees, see page 27.

The lees lend body to this dish, which is smoky from the dashi stock and spicy from chile heat. If you are not partial to pork, add manila clams toward the end and let them steam open before serving. When lees are unavailable, substitute 10 ounces of medium, medium-firm, or firm tofu, cut into 3/4-inch cubes. For the Korean radish (called *mu*), head to a Korean market. Daikon is not as sweet, but it is more readily available; or, substitute extra zucchini.

4 ounces (2/3 cup firmly packed) fresh or thawed
    soy milk lees
8 ounces Korean radish or daikon
2 zucchini (8 ounces total)
11/2 teaspoons sesame oil
3 cloves garlic, sliced
1 cup packed napa cabbage kimchi, cut into bite-size pieces
6 ounces boneless pork shoulder, thinly sliced across the
    grain into thin, finger-length strips
3 cups Dashi Stock (page 215)
Salt
2 large green onions, white and green parts, cut on the
    diagonal into 2-inch lengths
1 large moderately hot red chile, such as Fresno, halved
    lengthwise, seeded, and cut on the diagonal into
    1/4-inch pieces

1 Crumble up the lees into a bowl and set aside. Peel the radish and then cut it into rectangular pieces about 1 inch by 11/2 inches by 1/4 inch. Trim the ends off the zucchini and cut them to match the size of the radish pieces. Set the vegetables aside.

2 Choose a medium (21/2- to 3-quart) pot you can take from stovetop to table, such as a ceramic Japanese or Korean hot pot, Chinese clay pot, or enamel-coated cast-iron pot. Heat the sesame oil in the vessel over medium heat, then add the garlic and kimchi.

Cook, stirring, for about 2 minutes, until the vegetables no longer smell raw and harsh. Add the pork and continue cooking for about 2 minutes longer, until just cooked through. Add the radish and zucchini, stir to combine, then pour in the dashi. Bring to a simmer and then cook for about 8 minutes, stirring occasionally, until the pork and vegetables are tender.

3 Add the lees, stirring to combine, and continue simmering for about 2 minutes to allow the flavors to develop. The liquid should have turned creamy and pale orange. Taste and add salt as needed; the amount you need depends on the saltiness of the kimchi. I typically use about 1 teaspoon. When you are satisfied with the flavor, add the green onion and chile, stirring to incorporate and cooking for 1 to 2 minutes, until the green onion has just cooked through but is still bright in color. Turn off the heat and bring the pot to the table, setting it in the center for guests to serve themselves.

Soft Tofu and Seafood Hot Pot SOON DUBU CHIGAE

SERVES 4 TO 6 WITH 2 OR 3 OTHER DISHES, OR 2 OR 3 AS A MAIN COURSE

This preparation of velvety tofu in a bubbly hot pot is perfect on a cold day. Seafood is often featured in this classic Korean hot pot, which can be made with water but I like the depth of dashi stock. *Soon dubu chigae* is typical fare at Korean tofu restaurants and I've enjoyed it at Japanese *izakaya* pubs, too. For a satisfying meal, add some short-grain rice, a pickled vegetable such as kimchi, and cold beer. Korean red pepper powder lends a wonderful earthy bite.

1 tablespoon canola oil

1/2 yellow onion, thinly sliced

1 large clove garlic, minced

3/4 to 11/2 teaspoons Korean red pepper powder (gochu garu)

4 cups Dashi Stock (page 215)

Generous 1/2 teaspoon salt

11/2 tablespoons Korean or Japanese soy sauce

1 pound silken tofu or 2 cups tofu pudding

11/4 pounds shellfish, such as mussels and/or manila clams

6 to 8 medium shrimp, shelled and deveined

1 or 2 large eggs

1 teaspoon sesame oil

1 green onion, white and green parts, cut into rings

1 Choose a medium (21/2- to 3-quart) vessel that you can take from stovetop to table, such as a ceramic Japanese or Korean hot pot, Chinese clay pot, or enamel-coated cast-iron pot. Heat the oil over medium heat and then add the onion. Cook, stirring occasionally, for 3 to 5 minutes, until soft, translucent, and fragrantly sweet. Add the garlic and pepper powder and cook for about 45 seconds, until the mixture has turned pale orange from the pepper.

2 Add the stock, salt, and soy sauce. Increase the heat slightly and bring to a boil. Now use a metal spoon in a horizontal (sideways) motion to scoop up shards of tofu, adding them to the hot pot. Or, coarsely mash the tofu with a fork and add it to the hot pot for a slightly creamier effect. Bring to a simmer, adjust the heat to maintain a soft bubble, then cook for 5 minutes to develop the flavor.

3 Add the shellfish and shrimp and simmer for about 3 minutes, or until the shellfish open up and the shrimp have turned pink or orange, signaling that they are done. Taste for salt.

4 Raise the heat to a vigorous simmer, then turn off the heat. At this point, you can break the eggs into a ladle or small bowl and then slide them into the center of the hot pot. Or, you can bring the bubbling hot pot to the table and let guests crack the eggs right into it. Either way, drizzle on the sesame oil and garnish with a flourish of green onion before presenting to guests. Enjoy immediately with lots of rice. Stir in the eggs as you ladle.

NOTE

If your guests want their eggs to be more cooked, poach the egg in the hot pot. To do that, break the eggs into a ladle or small bowl, and then slide it into the hot pot to gently poach *before* adding the shellfish and shrimp; tuck them around the eggs. When the seafood is cooked, the egg whites should have set but the yolks should remain jiggly.

Stuffed Tofu in Broth NIANG DOU FU

SERVES 4 TO 6 WITH 2 OR 3 OTHER DISHES, OR 2 OR 3 AS A MAIN COURSE

Asian hot pots often include unadulterated tofu, which lends texture, color, and protein. In this Chinese preparation, tofu gets dressed up, cooked twice, and featured in a starring role. Triangles of tofu are stuffed with a shrimp and pork filling and lightly panfried before being simmered in chicken stock along with cellophane noodles and zippy greens. The result is a perfect warming main course. Add a stir-fried vegetable and rice for a satisfying meal.

I've suggested watercress and edible chrysanthemum (*tong ho* in Cantonese) but you could also use mustard greens. Or, go mild with spinach or chard. If you like, simmer the shrimp shells in enough water to cover for about 5 minutes, strain, and add this light stock to the pot. Carving out a pocket in each tofu piece is not as challenging as it sounds. Use the tip of a paring knife and be gentle. Testers Candace and Douglas Grover had good luck with a lobster pick. See the Hakka-Style Stuffed Tofu recipe on page 209 for another variation.

1 pound firm tofu

6 ounces shrimp, shelled and deveined

4 ounces ground pork, fattier kind preferred, roughly chopped to loosen

1 green onion, white and green parts, finely chopped

Salt

White pepper

3/4 teaspoon sugar

31/2 teaspoons light (regular) soy sauce

11/2 teaspoons Shaoxing rice wine or dry sherry

1 teaspoon sesame oil

1/2 teaspoon cornstarch

11/2 teaspoons egg white, optional

Canola oil for panfrying

2 thick slices peeled fresh ginger, bruised with the flat side of a knife

4 cups Chicken Stock (page 214), or 3 cups full-sodium canned broth and 1 cup water

1 small bundle (1.3 ounces) cellophane noodles, soaked in water to soften, drained, and cut into 4- to 5-inch lengths (use scissors)

Leaves and tender stems of 1 bunch watercress or chrysanthemum greens (4 cups lightly packed)

1 Cut the tofu into 16 triangles, each about 3/4 to 1 inch thick. To get that shape and size from a typical squat, squarish block of tofu, first halve it crosswise, then stand each piece on its side and cut lengthwise through the middle. Lay the thick slabs down and halve each crosswise to yield 8 squarish pieces total. Cut each one on the diagonal to create 16 triangles. They do not have to be perfect. (A rectangular bricklike block of tofu will yield 4 larger squarish pieces. Cut each diagonally like an "X" to get the 16 triangles you need.)

2 Put the tofu on a non-terry dishtowel or double layer of paper towels. Set aside to drain for 15 minutes.

3 Meanwhile, make the filling. Rinse and pat the shrimp dry. Coarsely chop the shrimp, then apply a rocking motion to your knife to transform them into a coarse paste. Pause occasionally to use the knife to neaten up and turn the mound of shrimp. Transfer to a bowl.

Add the pork, green onion, heaping 1/4 teaspoon of salt, 1/8 teaspoon of white pepper, 1/4 teaspoon of the sugar,

1½ teaspoons of the soy sauce, rice wine, sesame oil, and cornstarch. Use a fork or chopsticks to briskly stir and combine well. Cover and set aside. The filling may be prepared a day in advance and refrigerated. You should have a scant 1¼ cups.

4 Use the tip of a paring knife to cut and carve out a small pocket on the long side of each piece of tofu. Try to leave a good ¼ inch border all around your pocket. Do your best to avoid piercing through the walls. You'll end up with triangles that look like cinder blocks with gaping mouths. Save the tofu you remove for the next step.

5 Now fill the tofu pieces. Hold each triangle in one hand and use a paring knife in the other to stuff 1 tablespoon of filling into each pocket. (It's akin to spackling a hole in the wall.) Smooth the overflowing mound of filling with your knife blade. Set aside.

Add the tofu bits saved from carving the pockets to the leftover filling. Mash together with a fork, and if you want a silky finish, add the egg white. Cover and set aside if using within the hour, or refrigerate.

6 Pour enough oil into a large nonstick skillet to film the bottom (about 4 tablespoons) and heat over medium heat. Panfry the tofu in 2 batches, filling side down, for about 2 minutes, until browned. Then fry each of the triangular sides for about 2 minutes, until golden, or longer for golden brown. The tofu will not be totally crisp. Aim to firm up the tofu and give it a little color and flavor. Set aside. Add oil, if needed, before frying the second batch. The tofu may be fried up to 2 days in advance. Return to room temperature before finishing the dish.

7 Choose a medium (2½- to 3-quart) pot you can take from stovetop to table, such as a ceramic Japanese or Korean hot pot, Chinese clay pot, or enamel-coated cast-iron pot. Put in the stock, ginger, tofu, ½ teaspoon of salt, ⅛ teaspoon of white pepper, remaining ½ teaspoon sugar, and 2 teaspoons soy sauce. Cover and bring to a simmer over medium heat.

Uncover, and use your hands or 2 teaspoons to form 1-inch meatballs from the reserved filling, adding to the pot as you work. Replace the cover and continue cooking for 5 minutes, adjusting the heat to simmer. Uncover and add the noodles and watercress, stirring gently to distribute. Cover and cook for 5 more minutes, until the noodles are clear and the greens have softened.

8 Taste the broth and add extra salt, if needed. Bring to the table and serve. The tofu is delicate, so use a combination of chopsticks and a ladle to transfer all the goodies and broth to individual bowls.

Main Dishes

"Are you in Chengdu?" the voice said over the phone. Yes, we are here, I responded. "Okay, I will meet you in 45 minutes at the university gate. Bye bye," he replied. That was my first conversation with Xie Qian, a professor of Confucianism and classic Chinese literature at Sichuan University. His English was much better than my rudimentary Mandarin. We had been introduced through a mutual friend, anthropologist Jay Dautcher. The two were graduate school buddies in Beijing decades ago.

On this part of my Asian tofu tour, I was traveling with Beijing food editor Lillian Chou and San Francisco stylist Karen Shinto. Chengdu, the bustling capital city of Sichuan province, is a tofu hot spot—home of piquant savory tofu pudding (page 59) and the ubiquitous *ma po dou fu* (page 101), an out-of-this-world dish of spicy braised tofu and meat. I was on a mission to experience those foods *in situ* and discover others, and my friends were game. Lillian volunteered to translate, too!

Among my goals was to delve into tofu home cooking. I hoped that Jay's *guan xi* (relationship) with Xie Qian would open the door. It's awkward to ask a stranger to cook for you, but over tea we talked about this

book, and Xie Qian tacitly understood my needs and kindly offered to make us lunch. He recruited graduate student Zhong Yi, a woman in her late twenties, to be our guide. "Tell her what you want and she will assist," Xie Qian said. I had a hit list of local specialties and snack shops, and Zhong Yi, an avowed food lover, devised a plan of attack.

The next morning, Karen, Lillian, and I met Xie Qian near his house, located in a new suburb of Chengdu. To get to the morning market, he rode his bike and hired a motorized rickshaw to transport us. Lillian and I squished in and Karen, who is tiny, sat on our laps.

Located among drab new buildings, the market popped with life. There was blaring music and gorgeous vegetables, meats, and snacks from the surrounding area. The farmers had harvested a wealth of late summer produce—various hues of chiles, eggplant, and squash as well as freshly shucked soybeans and corn. The locals were amused at us, three Asian foreigners accompanying Xie Qian and his bike, snapping photos like paparazzi.

Xie Qian inspected several vendors' tofu before he made his selection. The woman simply put the tender white blocks into a small plastic bag. There was no packaging because, as a staple food, tofu is consumed the day it's made. Once home, he set out to make us a sumptuous meal. There was a cold salad of slippery, crunchy wood ear mushroom tossed with garlic and chile, soothing poached cucumber, and sweet boiled winter squash. Dish by dish, he efficiently used his wok to prepare braised eggplant with tomato and stir-fried pork with homemade pickled chiles and ginger. Those dishes, along with a pot of rice, Xie Qian explained, were chosen to offset the heartiness of the main event, bear paw tofu (page 159), a Sichuan panfried tofu seasoned with *dou ban jiang* chile bean sauce. It was wonderfully rich, salty, and spicy.

"Sichuan food is not all about spicy hot. It is about balance," he remarked in a scholarly tone. We opened the meal with toasts of *mou tai*, China's national liquor, and closed with fruit. Reflecting on China's turbulent history, Xie Qian said,

"Twenty years ago, we were not allowed to have foreigners in our homes." I felt extremely fortunate that times had changed.

On our way back to Chengdu, Zhong Yi texted an invitation to her family's Mid-Autumn Festival luncheon. Holy smokes! We hit a double.

When we met Zhong Yi at her aunt's home, there was a party going on. Three generations had gathered, and her aunts and uncle were cooking up a storm in the cramped galley-style kitchen. The prep work spilled out to the dining and living room areas as everyone pitched in. Her parents arrived with *xue dou fu*, a special smoked tofu shaped like a sausage and studded with pork fat. They had brought it from Chongqing, their hometown, for us to sample. It tasted like well-crafted charcuterie.

The family prepared thirteen dishes, including pork-laden ones such as twice-cooked pork belly and red-cooked ribs. To showcase home-style tofu preparations, they made *ma po* tofu, tofu noodles with Sichuan peppercorn, and a terrific smoked tofu stir-fry with pork and red bell pepper

(page 104) that I now make at home. Their menu planning highlighted how meat and tofu can be copacetic in Asian kitchens.

Zhong Yi's grandmother quietly presided over the cooking, verifying the seasonings and nodding in approval. At the table, her mother poured refreshing homemade wine and formally opened the meal with a toast. Everyone then dove into the splendid spread. Zhong Yi's family was delighted by our appetite for their zesty fare. There was so much to try that we forgot to eat any rice. When we said our goodbyes in the mid-afternoon, we were in a reverie, overwhelmed by the conviviality. "Man, Sichuan people really know how to live," Lillian said as we taxied back to our hotel for postprandial naps.

The recipes in this chapter cover a broad range of dishes. Some feature tofu while others use it as a partner with other ingredients or as a seasoning. The varied cooking methods underscore the ways that tofu can be manipulated in wonderful ways.

Stir-Fried Tofu, Shrimp, and Peas XIA REN DOU FU

SERVES 4 WITH 2 OR 3 OTHER DISHES

If you're new to stir-frying tofu, start with this marvelous marriage of land and sea. It is easy and the ingredients are readily available. The results showcase how tofu can absorb the flavors of its companion ingredients while becoming velvety. Include the peas for bright color and a little sweetness. The shrimp shell stock gives the dish a real seafood taste, tester Johanna Nevitt remarked.

14 to 16 ounces medium or medium-firm tofu

About 3 cups very hot or just-boiled water

8 ounces medium shrimp, shelled and deveined, shells reserved

Salt

1 teaspoon minced fresh ginger

1 green onion, white and green parts, finely chopped

1/4 teaspoon sugar

1 tablespoon Shaoxing rice wine or dry sherry

1 tablespoon light (regular) soy sauce

1/2 cup shrimp shell stock (see Note)

1/4 cup frozen peas, thawed, or 3 tablespoons fresh shelled peas, optional

3 tablespoons canola oil

1 tablespoon cornstarch dissolved in 1 tablespoon water and 2 teaspoons sesame oil

White pepper

1 Cut the tofu into 1/2-inch cubes. Put them into a bowl and add the hot water to cover. Set aside.

2 Put the shrimp in a colander. Toss with about 1/2 teaspoon salt, then rinse well. Drain and then blot dry with paper towels. Cut the shrimp crosswise into 1/2-inch nuggets. Set aside near the stove, along with the ginger and green onion.

3 For the sauce, combine 1/2 teaspoon salt and the sugar, rice wine, and soy sauce, stirring to combine. Set aside near the shrimp. Have the peas and stock nearby too, as the first part of this stir-fry comes together quickly. Also, drain the tofu in a strainer or colander and put it near the stove.

4 Heat the oil in a wok or large skillet over high heat. Add the ginger and green onion, stirring a few times to aromatize them. Add the shrimp, stir several times to combine, and then pour in the sauce. When the shrimp starts turning pink, add the stock, and then the tofu and peas. Gently stir to combine the ingredients. When things start bubbling, lower the heat to maintain a vigorous simmer. Cover and cook, adjusting the heat as needed, for 3 minutes. Occasionally uncover and shake the pan a bit to ensure even cooking.

5 Uncover, give the cornstarch mixture one last stir, then pour it in. Gently stir and fold until the sauce has thickened, about 30 seconds. Pour into a shallow serving bowl, sprinkle with some white pepper, and serve hot.

NOTE

For the shrimp shell stock, put the reserved shells in a small saucepan and add 1 cup water. Bring to a boil and cook, uncovered, for 5 minutes. Strain through a cloth or paper towel–lined mesh strainer. Discard the shells. Makes a generous 1/2 cup.

Spicy Tofu with Beef and Sichuan Peppercorn MA PO DOU FU

SERVES 4 WITH 2 OR 3 OTHER DISHES

This is the first tofu dish that I fell in love with. I was a teenager and my dad let me tag along to a Chinese restaurant lunch with him and his friend, Mr. Li. As the adults chatted, I quietly ate up most of this heady Sichuan specialty. The soft tofu and ground meat swimming in a velvety, spicy, unctuous sauce was addictively good. Later, as I was cooking my way through Chinese cookbooks, I realized that the memorable dish was called *ma po dou fu*. It was among the first Chinese recipes I mastered and is one I still regularly make today.

During my visit to Chengdu, I realized how elastic this classic can be. At traditional Sichuan restaurants, it's numbingly hot with a layer of red oil floating on top. Zhong Yi's aunts and uncle favored pork over beef and omitted the chile bean sauce, opting instead for a huge dose of tingly Sichuan peppercorn. When I queried Chef Yu Bo of Yu's Family Kitchen about the key elements of *ma po dou fu*, he responded in his thunderous Sichuan voice, *"Dou fu, niu rou, Pixian dou ban jiang!"* (Tofu, beef, Pixian chile bean sauce!). To make his point, he took my friends and me to visit an artisanal sauce producer in Pixian. Below is my rendition, which provides lots of room for experimentation. Use whichever meat you like, though beef's hearty flavor pairs well with the spicy rich sauce. Add fermented black beans for savory funk and chile flakes for heat.

14 to 16 ounces medium or medium-firm tofu

1 generous teaspoon Sichuan peppercorn

3 tablespoons canola oil

6 ounces ground beef or pork, fattier kind preferred, roughly chopped to loosen

1 teaspoon minced fresh ginger

1/2 teaspoon dried chile flakes, optional

1 tablespoon fermented black beans, optional

2 1/2 to 3 tablespoons chile bean sauce, Pixian kind preferred

1 generous teaspoon sugar

2 teaspoons light (regular) soy sauce

Salt

2 large green onions, white and green parts, cut on the diagonal into pieces about 1 1/2 inches long

1 1/2 tablespoons cornstarch dissolved in 3 tablespoons water

1 Cut the tofu into 1/2-inch cubes and put into a bowl. Bring a kettle of water to a rolling boil. Turn off the heat and when the boiling subsides, pour water over the tofu to cover. Set aside for 15 minutes.

2 Meanwhile, measure out 1 1/3 cups of water (the stuff you just boiled is fine) and set aside near the stove. You'll be using it later for the sauce.

3 In a large wok or skillet, toast the peppercorn over medium heat for 2 to 3 minutes, until richly fragrant and slightly darkened; you may see a wisp of smoke. Let it cool briefly, then pound with a mortar and pestle or grind in a spice grinder. Set aside.

Drain the tofu in a strainer or colander and put it near the stove. As with all stir-fries, assemble your ingredients next to the stove.

4 Heat the oil in the wok or skillet over high heat. Add the beef, stirring and mashing into small pieces until crumbly and cooked through, about 2 minutes. Add the ginger, chile flakes, fermented black beans, and chile sauce. Cook

CONTINUED

Spicy Tofu with Beef and Sichuan Peppercorn
CONTINUED

for about 2 minutes, stirring constantly, until the beef is a rich reddish-brown color and the chile sauce has turned the oil slightly red. Add the sugar and soy sauce, stir to combine, then add the tofu. Gently stir or give the wok a shake to combine without breaking up the tofu much.

5 Pour in the 1¹/₃ cups water you set aside earlier. Bring to a vigorous simmer, and cook for about 3 minutes to allow the tofu to absorb the flavors of the sauce.

6 Taste the sauce and add a pinch of salt or sugar, if needed. Add the green onion and stir to combine. Give the cornstarch one last stir, then pour enough into the wok to thicken the sauce. You may not need to use it all. In Sichuan, the sauce is more soupy than gravylike. Sprinkle in the ground peppercorn, give the mixture one last stir to incorporate, then transfer to a shallow bowl. Serve immediately with lots of hot rice.

Panfried Tofu with Mushroom and Spicy Sesame Sauce
DUBU JEON

Korean and Japanese cooks often top sliced tofu with a sautéed mushroom medley. The main differences are that Koreans panfry the tofu first, and they garnish the dish with *yangnyumjang*, a spicy sesame and soy sauce. The Japanese approach is to warm the tofu and then crown it with the hot mushrooms, which have a delicate coating of savory sauce. Both versions are tasty, but I prefer the textures and punchy flavors of the Korean take.

Many markets nowadays carry a good assortment of fresh Asian mushrooms. The prices at Asian market are often reasonable. I like to use little ones such as flavorful enoki and brown or white *shimeji* (also called beech mushrooms and *pioppini*) so that they retain their distinctive appearances. Small oyster and shiitake would work, too. The size, shape, and color of the mushrooms matter.

1 pound firm or extra-firm tofu

8 ounces assorted fresh mushrooms, such as enoki, shimeji, oyster, and shiitake

2 tablespoons canola oil

2 big pinches salt

2 big pinches black pepper

1/3 cup Korean Seasoned Soy Sauce (page 209)

1 Cut the tofu into chunky matchboxes, each about 1 1/2 inches by 2 inches by 1/2 inch. Line a plate with a non-terry dishtowel or double layer of paper towels. Place the tofu on top to drain for about 15 minutes.

2 Meanwhile, give each type of mushroom a very quick rinse under water to knock off any debris. Hold enoki and *shimeji* by the cluster. If you are using enoki or *shimeji*, trim and discard the sandy material that the mushroom grew in. The cluster should naturally fall apart. Trim oyster mushrooms at the ends and separate into individual ones. Tear large ones lengthwise into bite-size pieces. Trim and discard shiitake stems, then slice the caps a good 1/8 inch thick. Set the mushrooms aside.

3 Heat the oil in a large nonstick skillet over high heat. Blot the tofu pieces before panfrying them until golden, about 3 minutes per side. Transfer to a serving plate and keep warm.

4 Add the mushrooms to the pan and sprinkle in the salt and pepper. Cook, stirring, for about 2 minutes, until the mushroom are soft, fragrant, and about half of their original volume.

5 Arrange the tofu on one large plate or individual plates. Top with the mushrooms and sauce. Serve hot or warm.

Tea-Smoked Tofu with Pepper and Pork

YAN DOU FU GAN ZHAO CAI

SERVES 4 WITH 2 OR 3 OTHER DISHES

At markets in China you'll see many kinds of pressed tofu for sale. In Chengdu, I was delighted to find thin, large squares of smoked pressed tofu. I bought some and ate it in my hotel room. It was lightly smoky, salty, and firm, somewhat like smoked Gouda. It was a terrific snack food, but I wondered how locals cooked with it.

A few days later, I was lucky enough to find out. Zhong Yi, whom I wrote of at the beginning of this chapter, promised to show me some home-style Sichuan dishes, and this one was among them.

It's dead simple and brilliant at the same time. The pork is seasoned with dark soy sauce to pair with the tofu. The bell pepper offers color and flavor. The zingy ground Sichuan peppercorn underscores the smokiness of the tofu. Before I visited Zhong Yi's family, I had already developed a pressed tofu stir-fry recipe for this book. When I tasted theirs, I replaced my previous recipe with it. Recipe tester Georgia Freedman-Wand paired this dish with stir-fried eggplant. It would also be good with the water spinach and fermented tofu preparation on page 147.

10 ounces Tea-Smoked Pressed Tofu or Seasoned Pressed Tofu (pages 40 and 38), or purchased brown (baked) pressed tofu

1 red bell pepper (5 to 6 ounces)

5 ounces boneless pork shoulder

1 1/2 teaspoons dark (black) soy sauce

2 tablespoons canola oil

1/2 teaspoon salt

1/4 teaspoon sugar

1/2 to 3/4 teaspoon Sichuan peppercorn, toasted and ground

1 Cut the tofu into sticks, each about 2 inches long, 1/4 inch wide, and a good 1/8 inch thick. Trim and cut the bell pepper to match the tofu. Set both ingredients aside. Cut the pork about the same length but slightly thicker than the tofu, which swells a bit during cooking. Put the pork in a small bowl and mix it with the dark soy sauce. Set aside.

2 Heat the oil in a wok or large skillet over high heat. Add the pork, spreading it out into one layer. Let it sear for about 30 seconds, undisturbed, then give it a turn or two. Let it sear on the other side for another 15 to 30 seconds, until it no longer looks raw. Add the bell pepper and stir-fry for about 1 1/2 minutes, until the bell pepper has just started to soften. It will release some liquid.

Add the tofu, stir to combine, then sprinkle in the salt and sugar. Stir-fry for about 2 more minutes, until the bell pepper has cooked through and the tofu has softened a bit from absorbing moisture from the other ingredients. If that doesn't happen, splash in 1 tablespoon or so of water.

Sprinkle in the Sichuan peppercorn, stir and/or toss to combine, then transfer the stir-fry to a serving plate. Enjoy hot.

Bitter Melon with Tofu and Pork GOYA CHAMPURU

SERVES 4 WITH 2 OR 3 OTHER DISHES

This classic Japanese preparation hails from Okinawa, a pre-fecture renowned for having a healthy population with a long life expectancy. An easygoing island environment may be the key to Okinawan longevity, but some say that it is the Okinawan diet, which includes a lot of tofu and fresh vegetables, like bitter melon, which is loaded with health benefits.

This everyday Okinawan dish combines bitter melon, tofu, and pork; Spam or bacon may be used, a practice that reflects the Western foodways introduced during the American occu-pation in World War II. I prefer ground pork, whose richness combines well with the scrambled tofu to offset the bitter melon's bite, making the vegetable delectable and accessible. Dashi stock lends tremendous umami depth.

When selecting bitter melon, look for the more mature, pale green or white ones if you want the least bitter specimens. The bumpy variety is less bitter than the spiky-skinned ones.

1 small bitter melon (about 6 ounces)

1/2 teaspoon salt

14 to 16 ounces medium-firm or firm tofu

1 tablespoon sesame oil

3 ounces ground pork, fattier kind preferred, roughly
  chopped to loosen

1 tablespoon sake

1 tablespoon Dashi Stock (page 215)

1 tablespoon Japanese or Korean soy sauce

1 green onion, green and white parts, thinly sliced

Japanese ground red chile (ichimi togarashi), optional

1 Trim the ends and then split each bitter melon lengthwise. Use a spoon to scoop out the seeds and spongy

inside. Discard these. Slice each half on the diagonal into longish thin pieces.

2 Put the bitter melon into a bowl and add water to cover. Gently massage until the water turns opaque; this releases some of the bitterness. Drain and transfer to a bowl. Toss with 1/4 teaspoon of the salt. Set aside for 10 minutes. More bitterness will release in the liquid that will pool in the bowl. Pour off the liquid, rinse, and set aside to drain.

3 Meanwhile, cut the tofu into 2- to 3-inch squares, each about 1 inch thick. Drain the tofu for about 5 minutes atop a non-terry dishtowel or double layer of paper towels set on a plate. Put another towel on top and gently press to expel some moisture. Cut each piece of tofu into 1-inch chunks that will easily mash during cooking.

4 Heat 1 1/2 teaspoons of the sesame oil in a wok or large skillet over high heat. Add the pork, poking and mashing it into small pieces. Sprinkle in the remaining 1/4 teaspoon salt and stir-fry for about 1 minute, until the pork is no longer pink. Add the bitter melon and sake. Continue stir-frying for 1 minute, until the bitter melon has just started to soften.

Add the tofu, gently mashing and stirring to crumble into irregular chunks. Add the remaining 1 1/2 teaspoons sesame oil, then cook for about 2 minutes, stirring, to heat through. Add the dashi stock and soy sauce and cook for 1 minute to allow the tofu to absorb the liquid seasonings and soften. Sprinkle in the green onion, stir to distribute, then transfer to a plate. Offer the ground red chile to guests who want it.

Tofu with Tomato and Green Onion DAU PHU SOT CA CHUA

SERVES 4 WITH 2 OR 3 OTHER DISHES

Tangy-sweet and full of depth, this popular Vietnamese dish borders on addictive, thanks to the umami double whammy of ripe tomato and fish sauce enrobing chewy-rich cubes of fried tofu. Fry the tofu days ahead and assemble everything for an easy meal. When ripe tomatoes are unavailable, use a 14-ounce can of whole peeled tomatoes in juice and include that liquid in your measurement. For heat, add two chopped Thai chiles when cooking the garlic and shallot. Substitute soy sauce for fish sauce if you want a vegetarian version.

14 to 16 ounces firm tofu

About 1 1/2 teaspoons salt

3 cups very hot or just-boiled water

Canola oil for deep-frying and stir-frying

2 large cloves garlic, minced

1 1/2 tablespoons finely chopped shallot

1 1/2 cups chopped, peeled ripe tomato, include the juices

1 tablespoon fish sauce

About 1/2 teaspoon sugar

1/3 cup water

2 slender green onions, white and green parts, cut into 1-inch lengths

1 Cut the tofu into 3/4- to 1-inch cubes. Put them into a bowl. Dissolve the salt in the hot water, then pour over the tofu; it should be just covered. Set aside for 15 minutes.

2 Pour the water from the tofu, then transfer the pieces to a non-terry dishtowel or double layer of paper towels placed atop a plate. Let drain for about 15 minutes.

3 Meanwhile, pour oil to a depth of 1 1/2 inches in a wok, deep skillet, or saucepan. Heat over high heat to between 360° and 370°F. Fry the tofu in batches of 6 to 8 pieces, sliding them into the oil, then gently stirring them with chopsticks or a skimmer to fry evenly and prevent them from sticking. If they stick, let them fry until they are light golden before nudging them apart, or remove them from the oil, separate, and quickly replace in the oil to finish frying. They should be crisp and golden after about 2 minutes. Drain on paper towels. Return the oil to temperature before frying another batch. The tofu can be fried in advance and kept at room temperature for several hours. Or, refrigerate for up to 5 days and return to room temperature before using.

4 Heat 2 tablespoons of oil in a wok or large skillet over medium heat. Add the garlic and shallot and cook, stirring constantly, for about 1 minute, or until fragrant. Add the tomato, fish sauce, and sugar. Increase the heat to medium-high and cook, stirring frequently, for about 5 minutes, until the tomato starts breaking down. Add the water, and when you see bubbling action, add the fried tofu. Cook for 5 minutes, stirring the ingredients frequently, until the sauce has thickened and cooked down to roughly a third of its original volume.

Taste and add extra sugar or salt to balance out the flavors. Toss in the green onion, stir to combine, and cook until they have just wilted. Transfer to a plate or shallow bowl and allow the flavors to settle for a few minutes before serving.

Lemongrass Tofu with Chiles DAU PHU XAO XA OT

SERVES 4 WITH 2 OR 3 OTHER DISHES

I first had this southern Vietnamese dish on Phu Quoc island. Under a spot of shade gazing out at the ocean about thirty feet away, I enjoyed this tofu, a bowl of rice, and a glass of beer on ice. It was one of the best meals I'd ever had, and I was eager to replicate it at home. When the shallot, chile, and lemongrass hit the oil, the fragrant oils release and I anticipate their flavors coating and transforming the triangles of deep-fried tofu into spicy, rich morsels. The touch of coconut milk rounds out the seasonings. Use soy sauce in lieu of fish sauce for a vegetarian approach. Tester Laura McCarthy suggested using snow peas or asparagus instead of the green beans.

14 to 16 ounces firm tofu

1 teaspoon salt, plus more as needed

2 cups very hot or just-boiled water

Canola oil for deep-frying and stir-frying

1 large shallot, finely chopped (about 1/3 cup)

1 or 2 Thai or serrano chiles, finely chopped

1 stalk lemongrass, trimmed and finely chopped
    (about 3 tablespoons)

1/2 red bell pepper, seeded and diagonally cut into
    1/4-inch-wide strips

12 green beans, cut on steep diagonals to match bell
    pepper strips

1/2 teaspoon sugar mixed with 2 teaspoons Madras
    curry powder

1/4 cup coconut milk mixed with 1/4 cup water

1 1/2 teaspoons fish sauce

3 or 4 sprigs cilantro, coarsely chopped

1 Cut the tofu into 2- to 3-inch-square pieces, each 1/2 to 3/4 inch thick. Then cut each square into 2 triangles.

Transfer the tofu to a shallow bowl. Dissolve the 1 teaspoon salt in the hot water, then pour over the tofu. Set aside for 15 minutes to season. Pour off the water, then transfer the tofu to a non-terry dishtowel or double layer of paper towels placed atop a plate. Let drain for about 15 minutes.

2 Heat 1 1/2 inches of oil in a wok, deep skillet, or saucepan over high heat to between 360° and 370°F. Blot excess water from the tofu, then fry the tofu in batches of 5 or 6 pieces, sliding them into the oil, then gently stirring them with chopsticks or a skimmer to fry evenly and prevent them from sticking. If they stick, let them fry until they're light golden before nudging them apart, or remove the pieces from the oil, separate, then quickly replace in the oil to finish frying. They should be crisp and golden after about 2 minutes. Drain on paper towels. Return the oil to temperature before frying another batch. Set aside. Keep the tofu at room temperature, covered, for several hours or refrigerate it for up to 5 days and return it to room temperature before using.

3 Heat 2 tablespoons of oil in a wok or large skillet over high heat. Add the shallot, chile, and lemongrass. Stir-fry for about 1 minute, until fragrant. Add the bell pepper and green beans. Sprinkle on a generous pinch of salt. Stir-fry for about 2 minutes, until the vegetables have slightly softened. Add the tofu, then sprinkle on the mixture of sugar and curry powder. Stir for about 45 seconds to allow the tofu to warm up and absorb the seasonings. Add the coconut milk and fish sauce. Cook for 2 to 3 minutes more, stirring, until there is little liquid visible. Transfer to a serving plate, sprinkle with the cilantro, and enjoy immediately.

Hakka-Style Stuffed Tofu KE JIA NIANG DOU FU

Panfrying stuffed tofu is a simple way to fancy up an everyday ingredient. There are innumerable approaches and cooking methods, but the most popular renditions belong to the Hakka, a nomadic people who long ago migrated from northern China to southern China and many parts of Southeast Asia. Their diaspora—and the fact that stuffed tofu is one of their signature dishes—is why Hakka-style stuffed tofu is what you often encounter at restaurants and food hawker centers. It's commonly referred to as *yong* tofu.

Hakka-style stuffed tofu varies wildly. For example, the Malaysian and Singaporean version features a fish paste that's stuffed into tofu and vegetables, such as okra, bitter melon, and chiles; everything is poached in a fish broth. Other versions use a stuffing of shrimp, pork, or both. Sometimes *yong* tofu is soupy; other times it's saucy.

Hakka food expert and author Linda Anusasananan set me straight on the ubiquitous dish. She explained that although it's hard to pinpoint a quintessential version of *yong* tofu, it typically features a filling of pork and seafood, and the tofu is panfried and then braised with a slightly thickened sauce. "But it really depends on the cook and your tastes," she concluded.

This is my rendition, which combines pork, dried shrimp, and oyster sauce for a delicate yet well-seasoned result. Stuffing triangular pieces of tofu is a classic approach to *yong* tofu. It's not hard to master. See page 94 for a warming hot pot of stuffed tofu.

1 pound firm tofu

1 generous teaspoon dried shrimp

2 whole green onions

1½ teaspoons minced fresh ginger

1/8 teaspoon salt

1/8 teaspoon white pepper, plus extra as needed

1½ teaspoons Shaoxing rice wine or dry sherry

4 to 5 teaspoons oyster sauce

2 teaspoons sesame oil

2 teaspoons cornstarch

6 ounces ground pork, fattier kind preferred, roughly chopped to loosen

Canola oil for panfrying

1 cup Chicken Stock (page 214), or 2/3 cup full-sodium canned broth and 1/3 cup water

1 thick slice peeled fresh ginger, bruised with the flat side of a knife

1½ teaspoons water

1 Cut the tofu into 16 triangles, each about 3/4 to 1 inch thick. To get that shape and size from a typical squat, squarish block of tofu, first halve it crosswise, then stand each piece on its side and cut lengthwise through the middle. Lay the thick slabs down and halve each crosswise to yield 8 squarish pieces total. Cut each one on the diagonal to create 16 triangles. They do not have to be perfect. (A rectangular bricklike block of tofu will yield 4 larger squarish pieces. Cut each diagonally like an "X" to get the 16 triangles you need.) Put the tofu on a lint-free dishtowel or double layer of paper towels. Set aside to drain for 15 minutes.

2 Meanwhile, make the filling. Put the dried shrimp in a small mesh strainer and rinse under hot water for 10 to

CONTINUED

Hakka-Style Stuffed Tofu

15 seconds, until slightly softened. Drain well, then finely chop and transfer to a bowl. Cut one green onion into thick rings and set aside for garnish.

Finely chop the other green onion and then add it to the dried shrimp. Add the minced ginger, salt, white pepper, rice wine, 2 teaspoons of the oyster sauce, 1 teaspoon of the sesame oil, and 1 teaspoon of the cornstarch. Stir with a fork to combine. Add the pork and briskly stir to mix well. Cover and set aside. The filling may be prepared a day in advance and refrigerated. There should be 1 scant cup.

3 Use the tip of a paring knife to cut and carve out a small pocket on the long side of each piece of tofu. Try to leave a good 1/4 inch border all around your pocket. Do your best to avoid piercing through the walls. You'll end up with triangles that look like cinder blocks with gaping mouths. Discard or save the tofu for another use.

4 Now fill the tofu pieces. Hold a triangle in one hand and use a paring knife in the other to stuff 1 tablespoon of filling into each pocket. (It's akin to spackling a hole in the wall.) Smooth the overflowing mound of filling with your knife blade. Set the stuffed tofu pieces aside.

5 Pour enough oil into a large nonstick skillet to film the bottom (about 1/4 cup) and heat over medium heat. Panfry the tofu in 2 batches, filling side down, for about 2 minutes, until browned. Fry each of the triangular sides for about 2 minutes, until golden, or longer for golden brown. Use chopsticks and maybe a spatula, too, to turn

the tofu pieces. The tofu will not be totally crisp; aim to give it a little color and flavor. Set the finished pieces aside. Add oil, if needed, before frying the next batch. The tofu can be fried up to 2 days ahead. Bring to room temperature before proceeding.

6 Pour out all the oil from the skillet; wash it if you like. Put all the fried tofu in the skillet. Stir together the stock and the remaining 2 to 3 teaspoons oyster sauce; taste—you want a light savory-sweet flavor. The liquid will reduce and concentrate, so err on the milder side. When you're satisfied, add to the skillet along with the ginger slice. Cover and bring to a simmer over medium heat. Lower the heat slightly to maintain the simmer.

Cook for 8 minutes, covered; turn the pieces midway. Meanwhile, in a small bowl, dissolve the remaining 1 teaspoon cornstarch with the water and remaining 1 teaspoon sesame oil. Set aside.

7 When the tofu has finished simmering, uncover, lower the heat slightly, then transfer the pieces to a plate or shallow serving bowl. Retrieve the ginger from the skillet and discard. Increase the heat and add the green onion rings to the skillet. When it has just softened, about 15 seconds, give the cornstarch mixture a stir, then add it to the skillet. Cook until thickened, about 30 seconds. Taste the sauce and add a splash of water if it is too salty. If it needs to concentrate in flavor, let it cook down for about 30 seconds. Pour the sauce over the tofu, add a generous sprinkling of white pepper, and serve immediately.

Twice-Cooked Coriander Tofu TAHU GORENG BACEM

MAKES 8 PIECES, ENOUGH FOR 2 AS A MAIN DISH, 4 WITH 2 OR 3 OTHER DISHES

People often describe tofu as bland but I think of it as a blank canvas on which to create delectable masterpieces. This clever Indonesian preparation is one of them; it entails simmering firm tofu in a tangy-sweet-savory-spicy sauce until it reduces to just solids, imbuing the tofu with flavor and color. Then the tofu is deep-fried to a mahogany crisp and the result is a wonderful contrast of flavor and texture between the outer surface of the tofu and its creamy inside.

Galangal is traditionally used for spice heat but I've found that its kin, ginger, works well for a mellower note. How to eat this tofu? I've stolen many chunks straight from the fridge as a snack, but have also eaten it with coconut-scented rice and saucy curries. Tester Alex Ciepley enjoys *tahu goreng bacem* as party fare, cut diagonally, impaled on skewers and served with the relish made from the leftover seasonings (see the Note).

1 pound firm tofu

1/4 teaspoon salt

3 tablespoons packed palm sugar or dark brown sugar

1 1/2 tablespoons ground coriander

2 cloves garlic, coarsely chopped

1 shallot, coarsely chopped (about 1/4 cup)

Chubby 1-inch piece fresh or thawed galangal, or fresh
    ginger, peeled and thinly sliced

1 1/2 tablespoons light (regular) soy sauce

2 tablespoons Tamarind Liquid (page 217)

1 cup water

Canola oil for deep-frying

1 Cut the tofu into 8 rectangular pieces shaped like husky dominoes, each about 1 inch wide, 2 inches long, and 1 inch thick. Let them drain atop a non-terry dishtowel or double thickness of paper towels set on a plate while you prepare the seasoning sauce.

2 Put the salt, sugar, coriander, garlic, shallot, and galangal in a small food processor. Grind to a fine texture, pausing as needed to scrape down the side of the bowl. Add the soy sauce, tamarind liquid, and 1/2 cup of the water. Process to combine well. Pour the sauce into a medium non-stick skillet. Then add the remaining 1/2 cup water, stirring to blend well.

3 Blot the tofu to remove excess moisture, then add it to the skillet. Bring to a simmer over medium heat, then lower the heat to maintain that simmer. Cook for 30 to 40 minutes, carefully turning the tofu pieces every 10 minutes, until the liquid is no longer visible and the sauce has transformed into a wet, soft, dark brown mass. Adjust the heat as needed to keep simmering. Remove the pan from the heat and set aside for about 5 minutes to firm up the tofu.

Transfer the tofu to a plate, leaving behind most of the seasoning mixture and scraping it off the tofu; save the seasoning mixture to make a little relish (see the Note). Do not worry if a bit clings on the tofu. Let the tofu cool completely before deep-frying. You can cover and refrigerate it overnight, returning it to room temperature before continuing.

4 Pour oil to a depth of 1 inch into a medium saucepan, wok, or deep skillet and heat over medium-high heat to between 350° and 360°F. If you don't have a deep-fry thermometer, stick a *dry* bamboo chopstick into the oil; if bubbles rise immediately to the surface and encircle the chopstick, the oil is ready.

Blot away excess moisture from the tofu. When the oil is ready, fry the tofu in batches of 2 or 3 pieces, gently dropping them into the oil. Fry for 3 to 5 minutes, turning frequently with a slotted spoon or skimmer, until crisp and mahogany in color. Drain on paper towels and return the oil to temperature before frying the next batch.

5 Serve warm, at room temperature, or even cold. For a dramatic presentation, cut the tofu on the diagonal to reveal the contrast between the creamy, white inside and nubby, swarthy crust. You can refrigerate this tofu for up to 5 days. It will not be super crisp but will remain well flavored and a treat to eat.

NOTE

Transform the leftover seasoning mixture that remains after simmering the tofu into a sambal-like relish by mixing in squirts of fresh lime juice and 1 or 2 Thai chiles that you have chopped and pounded with a pinch of salt. For a super bright and hot flavor, eat the dip right way. Or, let it sit for about 15 minutes for the flavors to mellow. I like to mix some of this relish into hot rice to eat with or without the *tahu goreng bacem*.

Soy Milk Lees and Vegetable Croquettes UNOHANA KOROKKE

MAKES 8 OR 9 CROQUETTES TO SERVE 4

Japanese cooks refer to the lees left over from soy milk production as *okara*, which literally means honorable shell—the honorific term embodying their respect for soybeans.

Encrusted with panko and deep-fried, these little patties are rich tasting, with the lees absorbing the umami goodness of dashi and soy sauce. They're great with rice, though you can certainly use them as slider burgers, too. For a cocktail party snack, shape 20 small croquettes.

Vegetarians can substitute 1/3 cup chopped rehydrated shiitake mushroom for the ground meat, and reserve 1/2 cup of the mushroom soaking liquid and combine it with 1/2 cup water for a dashi stand-in.

This is one of my favorite uses for the lees leftover from tofu making (see page 27 for details). But you don't have to wait for such an occasion. You can purchase *okara* from Japanese markets or tofu shops.

7 ounces (1 cup firmly packed) thawed or fresh soy milk lees
1 tablespoon sugar
2 tablespoons Japanese or Korean soy sauce
1 tablespoon sake
1 cup Dashi Stock (page 215)
2 tablespoons canola oil, plus more for deep-frying
1 green onion, white and green parts, cut into thin rings
3 ounces fatty ground pork or chicken thigh, roughly
    chopped to loosen
1/2 cup grated carrot (use the largest hole on the grater)
1/4 teaspoon salt
2 large eggs
1/3 cup all-purpose flour

1/2 to 3/4 cup panko or regular breadcrumbs
Lemon wedges, optional
Tonkatsu sauce or Asian chile sauce, such as Sriracha,
    optional

1 If the lees are extremely compact, crumble them up into a bowl and set aside. In another bowl, combine the sugar, soy sauce, sake, and dashi, stirring to dissolve the sugar. Set this seasoned dashi aside.

2 Heat the 2 tablespoons oil in a medium nonstick skillet over medium-high heat. Add the green onion and cook, stirring, for about 15 seconds, until wilted and aromatic. Add the pork, mashing it into small pieces, and cook until it has lost most of its pink color, about 45 seconds. Add the carrot and sprinkle in the salt. Give everything a stir, then add the lees, combining well.

Add the dashi and continue cooking for about 8 minutes, stirring frequently, until the mixture has absorbed all the liquid and resembles mashed potatoes. Remove from the heat and let cool for about 5 minutes, until warm; expect the mixture to dry out and slightly stiffen. Taste and adjust the flavor with sugar and salt, if needed.

3 Beat 1 of the eggs and stir it into the mixture, combining well. Transfer to a bowl and let cool to room temperature before moving on. Once cooled, the croquette mixture can be covered and refrigerated overnight; it can be cold when you form the croquettes.

4 Divide the croquette mixture into 8 portions and form each one into a patty about 2¼ inches wide and a good ½ inch thick. Set aside on a plate as you work. Because the croquettes are very soft, slide them into the freezer for about 10 minutes while you heat up the oil and set up your frying station.

5 Heat 1¼ inches of oil in a saucepan, deep skillet, or wok over medium-high heat to between 350° and 360°F. If you don't have a deep-fry thermometer, stick a *dry* bamboo chopstick into the oil; if bubbles rise immediately to the surface and encircle the chopstick, the oil is ready. Beat the remaining 1 egg in a small bowl and set aside. Have the flour and panko in small bowls nearby, too.

Fry the croquettes in batches of 3 or 4. Lightly coat each one in flour to set the surface, then dip it in egg, and finally encrust it with panko. Pat the croquette at the end to ensure even coverage. Slide it into the oil and fry for 3 to 4 minutes, turning midway, until golden brown. Drain on paper towels. Return the oil to temperature between batches.

Serve warm or at room temperature with lemon wedges and/or one of the sauces, if you like.

NOTE

Refrigerate leftovers and return them to room temperature before reheating in a preheated 350°F toaster oven for 5 to 8 minutes, turning midway, until hot and gently sizzling.

Batter-Fried Tofu with Chile Soy Sauce ZHA DOU FU

SERVES 4 WITH 2 OR 3 OTHER DISHES

Many Asian cooks deep-fry tofu with a coating of cornstarch or flour but the most ethereal approach is a sheath of batter. During the brief time in the hot oil, the batter seals the tofu and allows it to get slightly custardy. Bite into a piece: it lightly shatters before revealing the creamy inside. Wonderful on its own, this batter-fried tofu becomes extra tasty dunked in tangy spicy soy sauce.

Chinese cooks often stuff a bit of minced fish or shrimp into the tofu before frying, but I have never found it to be as spectacular as it sounds. Keep it simple by just highlighting the tofu goodness. Enjoy with rice, a simple stir-fried or boiled green vegetable (dip it in the sauce, too!), and a light soup.

14 to 16 ounces medium or medium-firm tofu

1 tablespoon plus 1 teaspoon cornstarch

2¹/₂ ounces (¹/₂ cup) bleached or unbleached all-purpose flour

¹/₂ teaspoon baking powder

¹/₄ teaspoon salt

1 cup less 1 tablespoon water

1 tablespoon canola oil, plus more for deep-frying

1¹/₂ teaspoons sugar

1¹/₂ teaspoons unseasoned rice vinegar

2 tablespoons regular (light) soy sauce

1 or 2 Thai or serrano chiles, sliced

1 Halve the tofu crosswise, then cut each piece into 4 thick rectangles for a total of 8 pieces. To drain the tofu, place it atop a dishtowel or double thickness of paper towels set on a plate; set aside.

2 For the batter, combine the cornstarch, flour, baking powder, and salt in a bowl. Make a well in the center and gradually whisk in the water until smooth. Whisk in 1 tablespoon of oil to create a silky, slightly thick batter. Set aside.

3 To make the sauce, combine the sugar, rice vinegar, and soy sauce in a small bowl. Stir to dissolve the sugar. Taste and adjust to arrive at a tangy-sweet-salty balance. Add the chiles and set aside.

4 Heat 1¹/₂ inches of oil in a medium saucepan or wok over medium-high heat to between 350° and 360°F. If you don't have a deep-fry thermometer, stick a *dry* bamboo chopstick into the oil; if bubbles rise immediately to the surface and encircle the chopstick, the oil is ready. While the oil heats up, pat the top of the tofu pieces with paper towel to blot off excess moisture. Have the tofu near the stove, along with the batter.

Fry the tofu 2 or 3 pieces at a time to avoid lowering the oil temperature too much. Use one hand to dip and coat each tofu piece in batter, then slide it into the hot oil. Fry for about 3 minutes, turning frequently, until golden brown and crisp. Use a slotted spoon or skimmer to lift the finished tofu from the oil and drain on paper towels. Remove any tendrils of batter in the oil before repeating the frying, and return the oil to temperature between batches. When you're done, if any of the pieces have softened, raise the oil temperature to slightly above 360°F and refry them for about 30 seconds to recrisp.

Serve immediately with the dipping sauce in a communal bowl for guests to help themselves.

Roast Chicken with Red Fermented Tofu GA NUONG CHAO

SERVES 6

Vietnamese cooks love to use fermented tofu to season roasted and grilled meats. The grilled goat skewers (page 63) are a terrific snack; this roast chicken is a more substantial dish. It is easy to throw together and a great introduction to the marvels of red fermented tofu, which gives the flesh a winey, savory depth. Enjoy it as you would any roast chicken. Tester Alec Mitchell said that leftovers were great in sandwiches and on top of dressed salad greens. For the red fermented tofu, see the tofu buying guide on page 13 for selection tips.

3 1/2 pounds chicken legs and/or thighs
1/4 cup mashed red fermented tofu
1 teaspoon Chinese five-spice powder
2 tablespoons honey
2 tablespoons canola oil
Salt as needed

1 Trim the chicken pieces of excess fat or skin. Pat dry and set aside.

2 In a large bowl, combine the fermented tofu, five-spice powder, honey, and oil, mixing well with a fork. The marinade will resemble a thick livery mixture, but taste it. It will be pleasant, I assure you. If needed, add salt by the 1/4 teaspoon to arrive at a deep, savory flavor.

3 Add the chicken pieces and use your fingers to massage the marinade into the flesh, distributing the seasonings as evenly as possible. When possible, peel back the skin to get some marinade between the flesh and skin. Cover and marinate in the refrigerator for at least 2 hours and up to 24 hours for the best flavor.

4 About 30 to 45 minutes before roasting, remove the chicken from the refrigerator. To promote heat circulation and prevent sticking, place a flat roasting or cooling rack on an aluminum foil–lined baking sheet. Put the chicken pieces, skin side down, on the rack. (If you don't have a rack big enough, the chicken can roast on the foil, but it may stick.) Let the chicken sit, uncovered, at room temperature to remove some of the chill.

5 Position a rack in the middle of the oven and preheat to 400°F. Slide the chicken in the oven. Roast for 35 to 40 minutes, flipping the chicken midway, until nicely browned and cooked through; the juices should run clear when a piece is poked in the meatiest part with a toothpick, bamboo skewer, or knife tip.

During the last 10 minutes of roasting, the skin will color quickly to a reddish-brown mahogany. If you want to crisp the skin, switch to broiler heat for the final 3 minutes or so; leave the chicken in the middle of the oven. Monitor the chicken to prevent burning; turn it, as needed. Serve hot, warm, or at room temperature.

Crisp Roasted Pork Belly SHAO ROU

SERVES 4 TO 6 WITH 2 OR 3 OTHER DISHES

Red fermented tofu is often used in Chinese roast pork (*shao rou* in Mandarin, *siu yuk* or *siew yoke* in Cantonese) to impart a lovely mahogany hue and super savory depth. Home cooks can easily apply the technique to pork belly.

One of the measures of good roasted pork belly is in the crispy crackly skin. There are many approaches to producing that finish but I've found that air chilling, cooking smaller pieces, and finishing with a heat blast work well for home kitchens.

You can roast boneless pork belly (aka side pork) but the best cut is pork belly that still has the ribs attached. That cut is thicker, is meaty yet succulent, and won't buckle much during roasting, which unevenly crisps the skin. At a Chinese or Southeast Asian market, bone-in pork belly is sometimes labeled "pork short ribs." Buy it in long pieces that contain two ribs each. If only larger pieces are available, ask the butcher to cut it lengthwise; don't let the butcher cut the meat crosswise into smaller pieces. If you buy boneless belly, cut it yourself.

The quantity required for this recipe is typically two pieces. When selecting the pork, aim for husky cuts with an even distribution of fat and flesh, which will cook up to a wonderful crispness and succulence. Prep the pork a day in advance to ensure the skin dries sufficiently. Crisp roast pork belly is an indulgence. Enjoy it with rice or tucked into a baguette.

2 1/2 to 3 pounds skin-on pork belly, preferably with the ribs attached
Salt
1 1/2 tablespoons mashed red fermented tofu
1 1/2 teaspoons red fermented tofu brine, Shaoxing rice wine, or dry sherry

3/4 teaspoon white pepper
3/4 teaspoon Chinese five-spice powder
About 3/4 teaspoon sugar
Light (regular) soy sauce, optional
2 Thai or serrano chiles, thinly sliced, optional
2 small cucumbers, halved lengthwise, seeded, and thinly sliced, optional

1 Rinse and pat the pork belly dry. With the skin side down, remove the tough white membrane from the underside of each piece. Find a loose edge and slide the tip of a knife underneath the membrane. Use a dishtowel or paper towel to grab the membrane and pull it away from the ribs. Several pulls may be required. Trim any small membrane patches that remain with a knife. (If you are using boneless pork belly, you don't have to remove the membrane.)

Now use a sharp knife to score the skin crosswise at intervals roughly 1/2 to 3/4 inch apart. Aim to cut through the skin and halfway down into the fat. Try not to cut into the flesh. If the score marks are not apparent, run your finger over the skin to reveal them.

2 Rub a generous 1/2 teaspoon of salt into the skin of each piece of pork, doing your best to get some between the score lines. Discard salt that falls off. Set the pork aside.

3 In a small bowl, combine the tofu, brine, white pepper, five-spice powder, and sugar, stirring with a fork to blend well. Taste and add sugar or salt to create a strong savory-sweet flavor.

CONTINUED

Crisp Roasted Pork Belly

CONTINUED

4 Put a rack in a baking pan or on a baking sheet. Holding the pork belly skin side down, smear the fermented tofu seasoning paste on the flesh and fat, coating the bottom and all four sides. Wipe off any paste from the skin.

Place the pork skin side up on the rack. Refrigerate it, uncovered, for about 24 hours, until the skin has dried out, darkened, and shrunk to reveal the fat between the score marks. The skin should feel somewhat leathery. Once the skin is at that stage, it can be refrigerated for a few hours more. Cover it with parchment or wax paper if you are concerned about overdrying.

5 Line a baking sheet with aluminum foil. Remove the pork from the refrigerator and transfer the rack and pork to the baking sheet. Check your score marks to make sure that they have been cut deeply enough into the fat layer. If not, run a knife through them. Later on, the bubbling fat in the score marks helps create blistery skin. If there is excess moisture on the skin, wipe it off with paper towels. Set the pork aside at room temperature for 30 minutes to remove some of the chill. Meanwhile, position a rack in the middle of the oven and preheat to 325°F.

6 Roast the pork for about 1¼ hours, until the flesh is a rich brown. The skin should blister a bit toward the end of the roasting time. Poke a skewer about ½ inch into the fat and you should feel little resistance.

Now, turn on the broiler to blast the skin with super hot heat for about 4 minutes, monitoring it frequently. (I leave the pork to roast in the middle of the oven to avoid burning the skin. If your broiler element is under the oven, drain any fat in the pan before broiling.)

During the broiling, the skin dramatically puffs to form a lovely layer of cracklings. During these final moments, expect rivulets of melting fat, and popping and hissing noises. Tap on the finished skin and it will sound hollow. A little charring is okay. If you accidentally burn the skin, use a knife to gently scrape off the blackened areas.

7 Remove the pork from the oven, and let it rest for 10 minutes. This cut usually has cartilage on one end and bones on the other. Cut the meat off the bone and cartilage areas before cutting it along the skin's score marks into bite-size pieces. Or, you can cut through the cartilage areas and cut the meat off the bone where it is harder to chop. The bones and cartilage are great for guests who enjoy a good gnaw.

Transfer the pork to a platter. Serve immediately with soy sauce and chiles for guests to create a little dip. Offer the cucumber on the side for a refreshing contrast.

NOTES

Reheat uncut pork in a 350°F oven until hot, about 15 minutes. If the skin needs recrisping, assail it with 2 to 3 minutes of heat on broil, as you did during the initial roasting.

Instead of discarding the leftover red fermented tofu brine, turn it into a glaze for barbecued chicken or ribs. For every ¼ cup of brine, stir in about 2 tablespoons of honey and 2 minced cloves of garlic. Season or marinate the meat simply and during cooking, especially during the last 10 to 20 minutes, repeatedly brush on the glaze for a reddish hue and savory-sweet taste.

Simmered Greens with Fried Tofu SAAG SOY PANEER

SERVES 4 WITH 2 OR 3 OTHER DISHES

One of the typical Indian ways to employ tofu is as a substitute for the traditional fresh cheese in *saag paneer*, a classic preparation of spiced leafy greens and fried cheese. "Tofu is perceived as a healthier alternative to paneer and it works for Indian vegans and people with milk allergies," cookbook author Monica Bhide explained, adding that it's often called soya bean curd, bean curd, or soy paneer in India. The term "tofu" has not yet caught on.

When Monica volunteered her family's recipe, she noted, "Saag paneer is a mainstay in the Punjab, where I'm from. Keep it simple because this is not an overly spiced dish." She's right, because when I added tomato or garam masala, those ingredients muffled the vibrant flavors of the greens and caramelized onions. However, for a bit of earthiness, I added cumin. Finishing this dish with butter as Monica's mother loves to do rounds things out beautifully. Enjoy the dish with roti or chapatti flatbread, basmati rice, or even warmed corn or wheat tortillas. Add a dal and sliced cucumbers and onions for an easy vegetarian meal.

Feel free to vary the greens depending on the season. Mustard greens and braising mixes (usually tender leaves of collard greens and various kales) are cool weather crops that lend a slightly bitter bite. You can use all spinach for a milder dish called *palak soy paneer*. The term *saag* refers to a mixture of greens, typically spinach and mustard greens.

12 ounces firm or extra-firm tofu

1½ teaspoons salt

2 cups very hot or just-boiled water, plus more as needed

Chubby 1-inch piece fresh ginger, peeled and coarsely chopped

3 cloves garlic, coarsely chopped

1 yellow onion, coarsely chopped

8 ounces mustard greens, or 6 ounces braising mix

1 pound spinach (2 small or 1 large bunch)

¼ cup canola oil

1 teaspoon cumin seed

2 or 3 green Thai or serrano chiles, finely chopped (seeded for less heat)

¼ teaspoon cayenne

2 tablespoons unsalted butter, optional

1 Cut the tofu into ¾-inch cubes, then put them in a bowl. Dissolve 1 teaspoon of the salt in the 2 cups of hot water. Pour over the tofu; it should be just covered. Set aside for 15 minutes to season. Pour the water off, then transfer the tofu cubes to a non-terry dishtowel or double layer of paper towels placed atop a plate. Set aside to drain.

2 Put the ginger, garlic, and onion in a food processor. Run the machine to yield a finely chopped texture, occasionally pausing to scrape down the sides. Transfer to a bowl and set aside. Reassemble the food processor (you don't have to wash it) for finely chopping the greens later.

3 Rinse the mustard greens well, then coarsely chop, discarding the thick ribs. (If you are using braising mix, rinse, then coarsely chop the entire leaf because the ribs are tender.) Transfer to a 5- or 6-quart pot. Discard any root ends from the spinach, then rinse well. Coarsely chop the leaves and stems, then add to the pot of greens. To facilitate cooking, splash in a little water.

CONTINUED

Simmered Greens with Fried Tofu

Cover and cook over high heat for 5 to 7 minutes, until the greens have wilted and just cooked through. They will turn bright green and collapse to one-fourth to one-third of their original volume. To ensure even cooking, occasionally uncover the pot, stir, then replace the lid. When done, set aside to cool for 5 minutes.

4 Transfer the greens to the food processor, discarding the residual liquid. Process to a rough yet finely chopped texture. Add 1/2 cup water (room temperature is fine) and pulse to blend together. Set aside.

5 Heat the oil in a large nonstick skillet over high heat. Blot the tofu cubes dry, then panfry them in two batches for about 5 minutes, until light golden on 3 or 4 of the sides. Turn the tofu with chopsticks or a spatula during the frying. If the tofu violently sputters and spits, lower the heat slightly. Your aim is to add a bit of character and depth to the tofu, not crisp it all over—it will be soft or crisp in places. Transfer to a plate, leaving the oil behind, and set aside.

6 Adjust the heat to medium-high, then add the mixture of ginger, garlic, and onion. Cook, stirring frequently, for about 8 minutes, until the mixture has browned and begun to caramelize. Add the cumin and chile and continue cooking for 1 to 2 minutes more, until the mixture is highly aromatic and richly browned.

Lower the heat to medium, return the tofu to the skillet, and stir to combine well. Add the greens, stirring to combine. Add the remaining 1/2 teaspoon salt and cayenne. Cook for 2 to 3 minutes, moving the mixture frequently, until heated through. The greens will slightly darken.

Let the mixture sit for a few minutes to meld the flavors. Taste and add salt or cayenne as needed. Stir in the butter, transfer to a communal bowl or individual plates, and serve.

NOTE

The greens and the tofu can be prepared several hours in advance. Let them cool, then cover with plastic wrap and leave at room temperature, if you'll be finishing the dish within 2 hours. Otherwise, refrigerate and return to room temperature before continuing with step 5. Leftovers can be refrigerated for up to 3 days and reheated with a bit of water.

Tofu and Vegetables in Coconut Milk SAYUR LODEH

SERVES 4 AS A MAIN DISH, 6 WITH 2 OR 3 OTHER DISHES

Silky, spicy, and with a touch of good earthy funk, this Malaysian dish is often served for breakfast but it's perfectly at home as lunch or dinner fare. *Sayur lodeh* employs coconut milk, chiles, and other currylike aromatics, but unlike many curries, it is brothy more than saucy, allowing the seasonings to be well absorbed by the tofu.

Some cooks add the tofu to the pot as is, but I like to panfry or deep-fry it to let the tofu pop with texture and color. The recipe below calls for panfrying. Feel free to go the deep-fried route by using the instructions in the lemongrass tofu recipe (page 108); you may need a little less salt because the tofu gets lightly seasoned before deep-frying.

Candlenuts (*kemiri*) and dried shrimp paste (*belacan*) are sold at Chinese and Southeast Asian markets. The nuts slightly thicken the broth and the paste contributes to its briny undercurrent. You can seed all or a portion of the dried chiles, depending on your tolerance for chile heat. Salting the eggplant firms it up, preventing it from turning mushy during cooking.

Sayur lodeh is traditionally enjoyed with *lontong*, slices of compressed cooked rice. Regular boiled long-grain rice works great for soaking up all the delectable flavors. The combination makes for a terrific one-pot meal.

14 to 16 ounces firm tofu

FLAVORING PASTE
1 to 1¹/2 tablespoons dried shrimp paste, or 2 to
   3 teaspoons preroasted dried shrimp paste
1 tablespoon dried shrimp
10 dried red chiles, such as arbol, seeded and coarsely
   chopped

1-inch piece fresh or thawed galangal, or ginger, peeled
   and coarsely chopped, optional
7 candlenuts or unsalted macadamia nuts, coarsely
   chopped
3 large shallots, coarsely chopped (1 cup)
3 cloves garlic, coarsely chopped
2 teaspoons ground turmeric

1/4 cup plus 2 tablespoons canola oil
1 Chinese eggplant (about 6 ounces)
1¹/2 teaspoons salt
2 cups water
1²/3 cups coconut milk (one 13.5-ounce can)
2 carrots, cut into 2-inch sticks, each about 1/3 inch thick
12 to 16 green beans (4 ounces), cut on slight diagonal
   into 2-inch lengths
1/4 small head green cabbage, cored and cut into 1- to
   1¹/2-inch squares
1 to 1¹/2 tablespoons sugar

1 Cut the tofu into 2- to 3-inch squares, each ¹/2 to ³/4 inch thick. Then cut each square into 2 triangles. Put the tofu on a non-terry dishtowel or double layer of paper towels set atop a plate. Set aside to drain while you prepare the flavoring paste.

2 To make the flavoring paste, if you are using unroasted dried shrimp paste, wrap it up in a 3-inch-square piece of aluminum foil like an envelope. Flatten the packet with the heel of your hand. Roast the packet on the stovetop directly over a medium-high flame for 2 to 3 minutes, turning occasionally with tongs, until it is briny smelling; expect steam to shoot from the foil. Remove from the heat and let cool. Blast your exhaust to get rid of the odor. (If you are using preroasted shrimp paste, skip this step.) Transfer to a small food processor. Set aside briefly.

3 Put the dried shrimp in a small mesh strainer and rinse under hot water for 10 to 15 seconds, until slightly softened. Drain well, then coarsely chop and add to the small food processor, along with the dried chiles, galangal, and candlenuts. Process to a coarse texture before adding the shallot, garlic, and turmeric. Run the machine, pausing to push the ingredients down as needed, until the mixture has the texture of oatmeal.

4 Heat the 1/4 cup oil in a 3- or 4-quart pan over medium heat. It is ready when a bit of flavoring paste lightly sizzles upon contact. Add all the paste and gently fry for 5 to 7 minutes, stirring frequently, until fragrant and no longer raw smelling.

5 Meanwhile, halve the eggplant lengthwise and cut crosswise into 1/2- to 3/4-inch-wide half-moons. Put into a bowl and toss with 1/2 teaspoon of the salt. Set aside for 4 to 5 minutes, until the eggplant looks wet from releasing its moisture. Rinse to remove excess salt. Gently squeeze the eggplant by small handfuls to expel liquid; it is fine if some pieces get crushed. Set aside.

6 When the paste has fried sufficiently, add the water. Reserving 1/2 cup of coconut milk for finishing the dish, pour the remainder into the pot. Raise the heat to bring the pot to a simmer, then add the eggplant, carrot, and green beans. Simmer the vegetables for about 10 minutes, until they are just tender but still slightly underdone.

7 While the vegetables cook, panfry the tofu in a large nonstick skillet. Heat the remaining 2 tablespoons oil over high heat. Blot the tofu before panfrying until golden, about 3 minutes per side. Transfer to a plate and set aside.

8 After the initial simmering of the vegetables is done, add the tofu, cabbage, remaining 1 teaspoon salt, and sugar. Simmer for 5 to 8 minutes, until the tofu has puffed up from absorbing the sauce, the cabbage has turned translucent, and the other vegetables are cooked through. Add the reserved 1/2 cup coconut milk and continue cooking for about 2 minutes to heat through.

Remove the pot from the heat and let it sit for about 15 minutes to mellow and develop the flavors. Taste and add salt or sugar as needed. Transfer to a shallow bowl and serve.

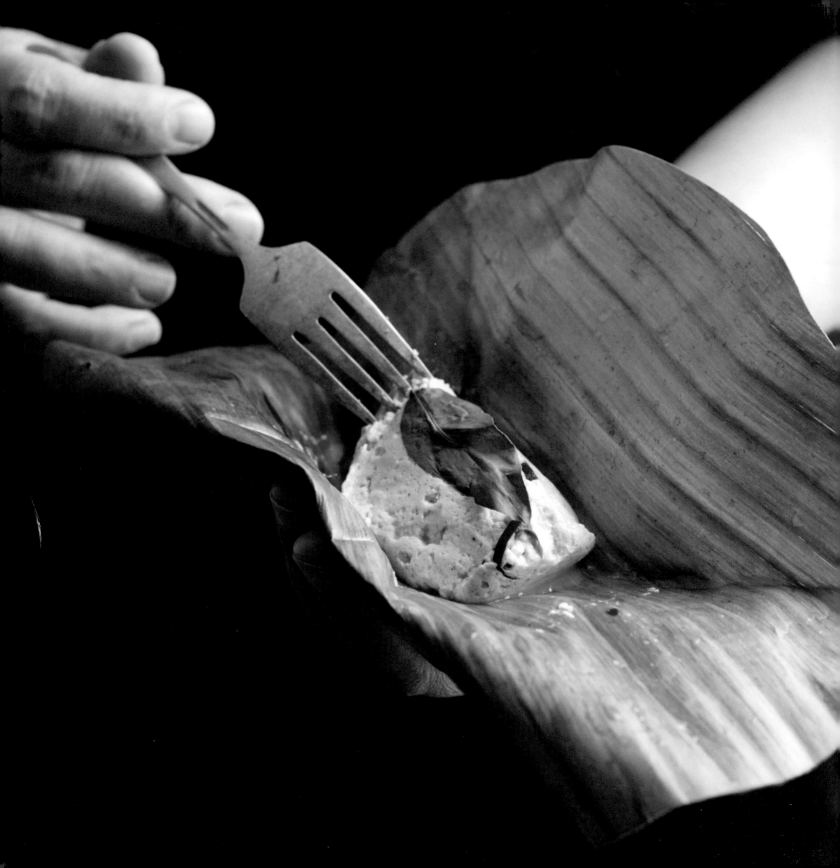

Spiced Tofu and Coconut in Banana Leaf GADON TAHU

MAKES 12 PARCELS, TO SERVE 4

A few years ago, cookbook author Pat Tanumihardja and her mother treated me to a homemade Indonesian feast, which included parcels of steamed tofu in banana leaf. Up until that point, I had never tasted tofu cooked in banana leaf but it suddenly made complete sense. As the mixture of mashed tofu, fragrant aromatics, and rich coconut cream cooked, it picked up some of the tealike fragrance of the leaf. While fresh spices may flavor the tofu, I prefer the earthiness of dried spices. The result is a central Java preparation called *gadon tahu*, according to Indonesian chef and food authority William Wongso.

These parcels are lovely to look at, ridiculously tasty, and easy to prepare. A single *salam* leaf typically adorns the top of each mound of tofu but since it is not available abroad, I instead use a fragrant fresh herb leaf. Some cooks add ground beef or chicken to the mixture to lend texture. If you do that, use 1 pound of tofu and 4 ounces of meat, mixing it in with the chile. You can add 3 minced kaffir lime (*makrut*) leaves to the tofu mixture for extra herbiness. Tester Diane Carlson likes to vary the aromatic garnishes to offer her guests different "flavors."

1¼ pounds firm tofu

1 shallot, chopped (¼ cup)

2 cloves garlic

1 teaspoon salt

½ teaspoon black pepper

1 teaspoon packed dark palm sugar (gula jawa) or dark brown sugar

1 teaspoon ground coriander

¼ teaspoon ground cumin

6 to 7 tablespoons coconut cream (use more for a richer flavor but softer texture)

1 large egg plus 1 large egg white

1 large moderately hot red chile, such as Fresno, halved lengthwise and thinly sliced crosswise

12 (6- by 8-inch) rectangles or (8-inch) circles fresh or thawed frozen banana leaf, trimmed of brown edges, rinsed, and wiped dry

12 fresh herb leaves, such as cilantro, lemon or Thai basil, or Vietnamese coriander

1 To expel water from the tofu and mash it, break it up into 8 to 10 chunks. Working in batches, put the tofu in a lint-free dishtowel or piece of muslin, then gather it up. Standing over a sink, firmly squeeze and massage the tofu. Unwrap and you should have nearly 13 ounces (about 1⅔ cups packed). Transfer the tofu to a bowl.

2 Use a small food processor to grind the shallot, garlic, salt, pepper, palm sugar, coriander, and cumin into a wet paste; pause occasionally to push the ingredients down. Add the coconut cream, whole egg, and egg white, then run the machine or stir to blend well. (This step is also easily done with a mortar and pestle. Just pound the aromatics and then stir in the other ingredients.)

3 Pour these seasonings over the tofu. Add the chile, then use a spatula to combine until there is no visible liquid. You should have about 2⅔ cups.

4 Ready a pot of water and 2 steamer trays for cooking the parcels. While the water comes to a boil, form your parcels. For each one, center a generous 3 tablespoons

CONTINUED

Spiced Tofu and Coconut in Banana Leaf

(3¹/₂ tablespoons, if you want to be exact) on a piece of banana leaf. Neaten up the tofu to form a mound about 2¹/₂ inches long and 2 inches wide. Place a single herb leaf on top.

If you have rectangles, simply fold in the longer sides of the banana leaf, letting them overlap by about ¹/₂ inch. Then fold the ends underneath, letting them overlap. The result looks like a tofu tamale.

If you used circles, imagine the face of a clock. Bring up the edges at 12 and 6 o'clock. Then bring in the edge at 3 o'clock. Two flaps will naturally form. Fold in the back flap away from you. Then fold in the front flap toward you. Now bring in the leaf edge at 9 o'clock and repeat with folding in the flaps. The second set of flaps should overlap the first one a bit. You'll end up with a small pouch. Secure the top closed with a round toothpick. Put the parcels in the steamer trays.

5 Steam the parcels over boiling water for 10 to 12 minutes. The tofu expands slightly during cooking so the parcels will appear enlarged. Turn off the heat and wait for the steam to subside before carefully lifting the lid away from you. Let the parcels cool for a few minutes before serving.

These can be made up to 5 days in advance and refrigerated in an airtight container or zip-top bag. To refresh the parcels, resteam or reheat them in the microwave oven.

BANANA LEAF 101

Foods encased in banana leaves absorb its pale green color and mild tealike flavor and fragrance. Access to fresh leaves is increasing, but frozen ones are much more readily available. Keep a 1-pound package in the freezer, a convenient modern alternative to cutting a leaf from a nearby tree. Look for them in Chinese, Southeast Asian, and Latin markets. Fresh banana leaves are sold at some markets in the US.

When working with frozen banana leaves, partially thaw the package, then gently pry the leaves open. Use scissors to cut off a tear-free section that meets your needs (torn leaves are hard to work with), then refold and refreeze the unused portion. As you trim the section to size, don't let the stiff ribs dictate your cut (or you will get a misshapen piece of leaf) and always remove any dark brown edge. Before using the leaf in cooking, rinse it and then wipe it dry with a paper towel to remove the white residue. If a leaf is particularly stiff, pass it over the flame of a gas stove or a hot electric burner. In general, wrap with the smoother side facing up.

Tofu Chicken Meatballs in Lemongrass Broth

QE NQAIJ QAIB XYAW TAUM PAJ

SERVES 4 WITH 2 OR 3 OTHER DISHES

When I asked Tra Her, a Hmong-American vendor at my local farmers' market, about Hmong tofu dishes, she surprisingly responded, "We like to make meatballs with tofu." The meatballs are a new Hmong-American food that is often prepared for large parties. No one is sure about how these meatballs got their start but they are wonderful—and easy to prepare—and you shouldn't wait for a celebration to make them!

Light in texture, they are packed with flavor, thanks to lots of cilantro and green onion. The tofu functions much like soaked bread does in Italian meatballs: to create a cohesive mixture.

Poaching the meatballs in a fragrant broth is a clever way for the ingredients to exchange flavors yet still remain separate; the poaching liquid is sipped as an accompaniment. Or bake the meatballs: sear them in a skillet, then finish them in a 350°F oven for about 10 minutes. They are good with chile sauce.

4 cups Chicken Stock (page 214), or 2 1/2 cups full-sodium canned chicken broth and 1 1/2 cups water

Chubby 3/4-inch piece thawed or fresh galangal, or ginger

1 hefty stalk lemongrass, loose outer layers removed and cut into 4-inch sections

1 pound medium-firm or firm tofu

1/3 cup finely chopped cilantro leaves and stems

1/3 cup finely chopped green onions, white and green parts

8 ounces ground chicken thigh, roughly chopped to loosen

1 large egg, beaten

1 teaspoon salt

1/2 teaspoon black pepper, plus more as needed

1 tablespoon fish sauce

Sriracha sauce, optional

1 Put the stock into a medium pot. Use the side of a knife to slightly crush the galangal and lemongrass. Add to the stock and bring to a boil over medium-high heat.

2 Meanwhile, break up the tofu into 6 to 8 chunks. Working in batches, put the tofu in a non-terry dishtowel or piece of muslin, then gather it up. Standing over a sink, firmly squeeze and massage the tofu; unwrap and transfer to a bowl. You should have about 11 ounces (1 1/3 cups packed).

3 Add the cilantro, green onion, and chicken to the tofu, then use a fork to mix well. Stir together the egg, salt, pepper, and fish sauce. Pour these seasonings over the tofu and meat mixture. Vigorously stir to create a smooth mixture. There should be about 3 cups.

4 The stock should be boiling now. Raise the heat to high to accommodate cooking the meatballs. Use your hands to form 24 golf ball–size meatballs, dropping each into the stock to poach. (If you prefer, shape a larger number of smaller ones.) The pot will get crowded. After all the meatballs have floated to the top and the broth is simmering, cook for about 10 minutes longer to develop the flavors. The pot should smell of zesty lemongrass and galangal with a delicate cilantro pungency. Taste the broth and add extra salt, if needed.

Present in a large communal bowl, or divide it up among soup bowls. Sip on the broth and dip the meatballs in some Sriracha or black pepper for extra zip.

Salads and Sides

Northern California has long been a weather vane for American food trends. That is particularly applicable to tofu's trajectory. After all, the nation's first tofu manufacturer, Wo Sing & Company, was founded in 1878 in San Francisco. Today, the Bay Area's Quong Hop & Company, established in 1906, is the oldest existing tofu maker in the country.

Modern tofu pioneers William Shurtleff and Akiko Aoyagi, whose *Book of Tofu* (1975) injected tofu into America's modern natural foods movement, still reside locally; Shurtleff maintains the SoyInfo Center, a major virtual information hub. Jeremiah Ridenour and Billy Bramblett's Wildwood Tofu helped set the foundation for manufacturing organic tofu in the United States.

Nowadays, the region's tofu purveyors range from small-batch artisans to state-of-the-art large-scale producers. They are located from Arcata down to Salinas, from Sacramento to San Jose. One of the most interesting newcomers is Hodo Soy Beanery in Oakland, co-founded by Minh Tsai, a Vietnamese-American of Chinese descent. His family immigrated to the United States in 1981 and settled in the Bay Area.

Educated in finance and community development, Tsai was a software design professional who began tinkering with tofu. At first, it was a quest to recreate the excellent food from his youth in Vietnam because he could not readily find it here. "A lot of tofu in America is not very good. People think that it has no taste," he said. "Tofu has taste just like anything else!"

Unlike the Ishijima and Dang families on pages 49 and 194, Tsai did not have a tofu legacy to uphold. He simply wanted to satisfy his palate and let others know about quality tofu. In 2004, he and his cousins prepared weekly batches of tofu to sell at the Palo Alto farmers' market. It was a practical move on Tsai's part because he needed to quickly recoup his expenditures, but it was also a breakout strategy. Tofu makers usually operate small storefronts and distribute to markets and restaurants. This was a way to take their product directly to consumers.

Tsai's farmers' market shoppers were mostly non-Asian and did not quickly warm up to tofu. "Most people did not want to hear the word. Tofu is polarizing," Tsai explained. "So we offered it in ways that people were familiar with, such as smoked tofu, and gave out samples. Customers went for it and we developed a following." With direct customer contact, a friendly staff, and accessible tofu dishes, Tsai's nontraditional approach paid off. In 2005, he left his high-tech career to establish Hodo, which means "good beans" in Cantonese.

Nowadays, Hodo distributes to mainstream retailers and has a kiosk operation at the San Francisco Ferry Building Marketplace. But its farmers' market stands keep busy because people love to taste and purchase various types of prepared tofu dishes, such as the Spicy Yuba Ribbons (page 139), one of my personal favorites. Tsai and his cooks develop the recipes based on Asian flavors and traditions. There are salads and sides of super-firm tofu tossed with heady sauces and braised fried tofu cubes that can be eaten solo or become part of another dish.

The company understands that its customers may not have the time or the know-how to prepare Asian-style tofu dishes. Yet they want healthy, delicious tofu. Hodo's "Grab and Go" line of tofu foods satisfies modern customer demands while at the same time expanding their understanding of tofu's potential. On a monthly basis, curious customers and food industry professionals come to tour the spotless facilities and learn about the tofu making process. Watching the men who cut the tofu or hand pull and fold delicate sheets of tofu skin (yuba) is mesmerizing.

Within the artisanal tofu industry, Hodo is unique in that it is rooted in Asia but not tethered to its traditions. In fact, when Tsai discussed his use of single source organic soybeans, he did not channel the zeal of a man replicating a faraway taste memory, but rather the passion of a Bay Area artisanal food producer. His local models for success include Scharffen Berger Chocolate, Acme Bread, and June Taylor marmalades, conserves, and preserved fruits.

"Good beans make good tofu. It's like Scharffen Berger's focus on excellent beans," Tsai said. "When Robert [Steinberg] and John [Scharffenberger] started out, they just wanted to make good chocolate. Similarly, we produce the best tofu possible." Scharffenberger and Bramblett (formerly of Wildwood Tofu) currently serve as co-CEOs to help Tsai grow the company.

In presenting tofu as an exciting, artisanal product, Hodo elevates tofu's status to a broad audience of hip, food-savvy consumers. Local and national media attention has positioned the company at the forefront of changing American foodways. "If we spawn a generation of tofu makers of higher quality, that is an indicator of our arrival," Tsai said.

Whether or not you are new to tofu, the salads and side dishes in this chapter are sure to please. Enjoy them as a nosh or accompaniment to a bowl of noodles or plate of dumplings. They are also perfectly at home as part of a full meal, where they can add extra protein, texture, and flavor.

Tofu Noodle and Vegetable Salad LIANG BAN QIAN SI

SERVES 4 AS A SIDE DISH

I keep packages of tofu noodles (see page 9) in the fridge to make this quick and easy salad. The flavors are clean, the colors cheery, and the textures varied. Tofu noodles (also called bean curd strips) are cut from very firm sheets of pressed tofu. They have a wonderful springiness and soft chewy quality akin to al dente pasta. This is typically an appetizer or snack kind of salad, but I often serve it along with other dishes, such as dumplings or noodles, as part of a whole meal.

Feel free to vary the vegetables, but keep in mind that they should be colorful and cut to match the thickness of the tofu noodles. Add a teaspoon of chile oil (page 213) for spicy heat.

8 ounces tofu noodles

2 scant teaspoons salt

3/4 teaspoon sugar

1 tablespoon plus 1 teaspoon sesame oil

3-inch section carrot, cut into matchsticks (1/2 cup)

1 large rib celery, cut into matchsticks (1/2 cup)

1/2 small red bell pepper, cut into matchsticks (1/2 cup)

1 Put the tofu noodles in a mesh strainer, fluff them with your fingers, then briefly rinse them under water. Use scissors to cut the noodles into shorter lengths, about 4 inches long. Set aside.

2 Half-fill a 4-quart pot with water and add 1 1/2 teaspoons of the salt. Bring to a boil over high heat. Meanwhile, put the remaining scant 1/2 teaspoon salt, sugar, and sesame oil into a mixing bowl. Stir to combine, then set the dressing aside.

3 When the water is boiling, add the tofu noodles, carrot, celery, and bell pepper. Stir with chopsticks to ensure that they're all swimming freely in the hot water. Cook for 45 to 60 seconds, until the tofu noodles are soft and warm and the vegetables have started to soften. Pick up a piece of one of the vegetables with chopsticks and it should just slightly bend. Immediately drain in the mesh strainer. Rinse under cold water, drain well, then gently press with your hand to expel excess water.

4 Transfer the blanched tofu noodles and vegetables to the bowl of dressing. Use chopsticks or tongs to combine well. Let the salad sit for about 10 minutes to develop the flavors. Taste and adjust the flavors with extra salt or sugar, if needed. Transfer to a dish or shallow bowl and enjoy at room temperature.

White Tofu, Sesame, and Vegetable Salad SHIRA-AE

SERVES 4 TO 6 AS A SIDE DISH

"Food is not just for work. It's a chance to connect with seasonality, loveliness, the body. Enjoy its beauty," Masa Fujiwara explained over a Zen vegetarian lunch in Kyoto. A Japanese cultural liaison, he carefully chose his words and I heeded them. I gazed down at the lacquer bowl containing an artfully placed petite mound of *shira-ae*, a mostly white salad of creamy tofu, nutty sesame, and green beans. With chopsticks, I took a taste. It was sublime, delicate but flavorful.

That day, I gained a greater appreciation for the Japanese approach to savoring small amounts of well-crafted food. I also wanted to make *shira-ae* myself. It is quite easy, and the mashed tofu and sesame dressing can be paired with a wide range of ingredients, though I prefer to focus on a single vegetable.

4 ounces medium-firm or firm tofu

1 tablespoon white sesame seeds

About 1/8 teaspoon salt

1 1/2 teaspoons sugar

About 1 teaspoon light-colored soy sauce, such as Japanese usukuchi shoyu or light (regular) soy sauce

2 tablespoons Dashi Stock (page 215) or water

12 ounces tender green beans

1/4 teaspoon toasted black sesame seeds, optional

1 For the dressing, break up the tofu into large chunks and put them in a non-terry dishtowel or piece of muslin. Gather it up and, standing over a sink, gently squeeze 2 or 3 times. Unwrap, transfer to a small bowl, and set aside.

2 In a small skillet, toast the white sesame seeds, shaking and stirring frequently, for 2 to 3 minutes, until light golden and fragrant. Let cool for 1 minute, then transfer the warm seeds to a small food processor. Add the salt and sugar and grind to a coarse texture. Add the tofu, soy sauce, and dashi. Process to a creamy mixture that is still somewhat coarse. (Or, use a mortar and pestle to pound the sesame seeds with the salt and sugar. Add the tofu and lightly pound and stir to combine. Stir in liquid ingredients.)

Regardless of the method, transfer the tofu to a small bowl and let stand for 5 minutes to develop its flavor. Season with salt or soy sauce, aiming for a pronounced savory and sweet finish. Resist thinning the mixture with dashi because it may dilute the flavors. The dressing may be made 2 days ahead and refrigerated. Return it to room temperature before using; if there is lots of pooled liquid in the container, pour it off. Makes about 1/2 cup.

3 Bring a pot of salted water to a boil. Meanwhile, trim the stem ends from the green beans. Blanch the beans for 1 to 2 minutes, until bright green and still crisp. Drain but do not rinse. Let the beans naturally cool, during which they will finish cooking. Like the dressing, the beans may be prepped up to 2 days ahead. Bring to room temperature before tossing.

4 To serve, you have two options. Short and dainty beans can be presented whole on a serving plate or individual dishes with the dressing spooned across their midline like a big creamy belt; invite guests to mix the ingredients themselves. Or, cut the beans into 2-inch-long pieces and toss in the tofu dressing, coating well; divide among small dishes or offer on a communal plate. Regardless of presentation, garnish with the black sesame seeds.

Greens and Fried Tofu in Mustard Sauce NANOHANA NO KARASHI-AE

SERVES 4 AS A SIDE DISH

When Japanese slices of fried tofu (*abura-age*, page 11) are grilled or toasted, they puff and crisp. The result is akin to an airy crackling that you can cut up into strips to add richness to refreshing sides like this one.

In Japan, cooks employ the tender buds, stems, and leaves of *Brassica napus* (rapeseed) for this springtime favorite. Those mustardy greens are not widely available in the States. My go-to substitute is broccoli rabe (rapini), a close relative. Or you can use a 10-ounce bunch of milder broccolini. Ensure punchy flavor with a hot mustard powder, such as Colman's English mustard powder.

For good character and lovely char, grill the tofu on a Japanese stovetop grill, which looks like an open-wire cooling rack with legs that allow it to sit about 2 inches above the heat source. Sometimes the rack sits in a small pan. Look for the grill at Japanese markets. Otherwise, broil it.

12 ounces broccoli rabe

Salt

1 rectangular fried tofu slice (about 6 by 3 1/2 inches),
     or 2 square fried tofu slices (about 3 inches)

1 1/4 to 1 1/2 teaspoons mustard powder

1 1/2 teaspoons mirin

1 1/2 tablespoons Dashi Stock (page 215) or water

About 2 teaspoons light-colored soy sauce, such as
     Japanese usukuchi shoyu or light (regular) soy sauce

1 Trim the broccoli rabe into 2- to 3-inch lengths. In general, discard stem portions that are more than 1/3 inch thick because they tend to be woody—chew on one to test. Split stems that are 1/3 inch thick so they'll cook evenly.

2 Bring a pot of salted water to a boil. Add the broccoli rabe and blanch for about 1 minute, until bright green and the split stems look translucent on their cut sides. Drain, flush with water, then set aside to drain and cool. By the handful, give the broccoli rabe a couple of gentle squeezes to remove excess water. Transfer to a bowl. Or, store in a lidded container and refrigerate for up to 2 days in advance; return to room temperature before using.

3 Grill or broil the tofu for 1 1/2 to 2 minutes, turning the tofu often, until it is crisp and marked with some charred spots. If you are using a Japanese stovetop grill, use medium-high heat. With a toaster oven, put the tofu directly on the rack and toast with the heat set to broil. In a regular oven, position a rack about 4 inches away from the heat source and broil the tofu on an aluminum foil–lined baking sheet.

Monitor the tofu carefully because it browns quickly. Let it cool to room temperature before cutting it up. It will likely deflate a bit during cooling.

4 Dissolve the mustard powder in the mirin, then stir in the dashi and soy sauce. Set aside for 10 minutes for the flavors to develop.

5 Halve the tofu lengthwise, then cut into strips about 1/3 inch wide. In a bowl, toss the tofu and broccoli rabe with the dressing. I often use my hands to do this. Most of the dressing should be absorbed. Taste and add a few drops of soy sauce, if needed. Transfer to a serving bowl and enjoy.

Spicy Lemongrass Tofu Salad LAAP TAO HOU

Laap is a classic type of salad that is practically the national dish of Laos, a favorite with the Hmong, and synonymous with Issan (northeastern) Thai cooking. It can be prepared many ways and typically features minced meat highly seasoned by chile, lime juice, fish sauce, and tons of freshly chopped herbs. Ground toasted rice imparts a wonderful nuttiness.

It's the seasonings that define *laap*, as the main protein can vary. In this version, I replace the meat with diced homemade pressed tofu, which absorbs the neighboring flavors well. In a pinch, substitute extra-firm tofu that you've squeezed excess water out of and crumbled like you would for Hmong chicken and tofu meatballs (page 129).

Laap is traditionally served with steamed sticky rice and eaten by hand. You can substitute boiled short-grain rice for the sticky rice. Vary the herbs with Vietnamese coriander (*rau ram*) or thorny cilantro (*culantro*). Remember to discard the midrib when prepping the lime leaves.

8 ounces Spicy Lemongrass Pressed Tofu (page 39)

4 dried arbol chiles or other moderately hot dried chile, stemmed, or 1½ teaspoons dried red chile flakes

1½ teaspoons raw long-grain rice

1 shallot or ¼ cup red onion, thinly sliced

1 green onion, white and green parts, thinly sliced

2½ tablespoons fresh lime juice

1½ tablespoons fish sauce

2 kaffir lime leaves, minced, or grated zest of 1 lime

2 tablespoons lightly packed finely chopped mint leaves

1 tablespoon lightly packed finely chopped cilantro

¼ head green cabbage, cut into wedges, or leaves from 1 small head leaf lettuce

6 to 8 cherry tomatoes, halved, optional

6 long beans or 12 regular green beans, cut into 3-inch lengths, optional

1 Cut the tofu into ¼-inch cubes, roughly the size of pencil erasers. Transfer to a bowl.

In a small skillet over medium heat, roast the whole chiles for 5 to 6 minutes, turning them frequently, until aromatic and dark. Transfer to a plate to cool. (Or, roast the chile flakes over medium-low heat for 1 to 2 minutes, stirring constantly.) Add the rice to the skillet and roast for 7 to 8 minutes over medium or medium-low heat, shaking the skillet frequently, until caramel in color. Let cool.

2 Place the chiles in a clean spice grinder (or coffee grinder dedicated to spices) and process to a powder. Transfer to a small bowl. Put the rice in the spice grinder and process to a powder. Transfer to another small bowl. Set both aside, or cover with plastic and keep overnight at room temperature.

3 To assemble the salad, toss the tofu with the shallot, green onion, lime juice, and fish sauce. Set aside for 10 minutes for the flavors to combine. Add the lime leaves, mint, and cilantro, then taste. The salad should be tart, salty, pungent, and herby. Finally, add the ground chile and toasted rice. Toss, taste again, and adjust the seasonings, as needed.

Serve in a shallow bowl or on a plate with the vegetables on the side. Invite guests to wrap the tofu in pieces of cabbage with some tomato and green bean.

Pressed Tofu and Peanuts in Spicy Bean Sauce HUA REN DOU FU GAN

SERVES 4 AS A SIDE DISH

Sichuan preparations such as this one are wickedly addictive, with a range of flavors, from rich to salty to spicy, and a spectrum of textures, from soft to crunchy to chewy. My excuse for finishing every morsel is that even though the refrigerated leftovers are good, the peanuts turn slightly chewy.

Serve this as an appetizer or snack with drinks or alongside dumplings or noodles. Its robust flavors also pep up a simple meal of plain rice and boiled vegetables. Fragrant semirefined peanut oil (see page 213) adds extra nutty flavor.

12 to 14 ounces Seasoned Pressed Tofu or Tea-Smoked Pressed Tofu (pages 38 and 40), or purchased brown (baked) pressed tofu

2/3 cup unsalted roasted peanuts

2 large green onions, white and green parts, cut into 1/4-inch-thick rounds

3 tablespoons fragrant peanut or canola oil

1 teaspoon sesame oil

1 tablespoon fermented black beans, mashed with the broad side of a knife or a mortar and pestle

2 1/2 tablespoons chile bean sauce, Pixian kind preferred

2 teaspoons light (regular) soy sauce

1/2 teaspoon sugar

1 to 2 tablespoons Chile Oil (page 213), with or without chile flakes

1 Cut the tofu into 1/2-inch cubes, roughly the size of a large peanut. Transfer the tofu to a bowl.

2 If you like, refresh the peanuts by toasting them in a dry skillet over medium-high heat for about 3 minutes, until fragrant and slightly darkened. Let the peanuts cool, then add them to the tofu, along with the green onion.

3 In an extra-small saucepan, such as a butter warmer, combine the peanut oil, sesame oil, fermented black beans, and chile bean paste. Heat over medium heat until gently sizzling, about 2 minutes. Continue cooking for 30 to 45 seconds, stirring constantly, until super fragrant. Remove from the heat and stir in the soy sauce and sugar.

Pour the sauce over the tofu, peanuts, and green onion. Add chile oil to taste. Stir with a spatula to distribute the seasonings well. Transfer to a serving plate to enjoy right away or cover with plastic wrap and set aside for up to 2 hours.

Spicy Yuba Ribbons

SERVES 4 WITH 2 OR 3 OTHER DISHES

One of the great benefits of touring commercial food facilities is getting to sample their wares. When I visited Hodo Soy Beanery (see page 131) in Oakland, California, I was instantly captivated by this simple sauté of chewy tofu skin strips. It was a brightly flavored, fresh rendition of a similar preparation I had tasted in China. I could not stop eating it. The tofu skin (*yuba* in Japanese) is initially seared to dry it out a tad, allowing it to absorb the seasonings super well. The subtly rich-tasting result is profoundly satisfying.

It is rare to have artisanal *yuba* like that of Hodo so I buy mine at a Chinese market where there are three tofu skin options to choose from: fresh tofu skin packets (*dou fu bao*), partially-dried rounds of tofu skin (*dou fu pi*), and dried tofu sticks (*fu zhu*); see the buying guide on page 9 for details. In this recipe, the packets yield toothsome ribbons, the rounds of skin yield silky, delicate shreds, and the sticks produce meaty batons. The instructions below are for packets of the fresh tofu skin. See the Note for details on using the rounds and sticks.

8 ounces fresh tofu skin packets

1¹/2 teaspoons sugar

1 tablespoon sake

2 tablespoons light (regular) soy sauce

1 tablespoon unseasoned Japanese rice vinegar

1 teaspoon sesame oil

1 to 1¹/2 tablespoons Chile Oil (page 213), with or without chile flakes

1 tablespoon canola oil

3 tablespoons thinly sliced green onion, green part only

1 Tofu skin packets are typically double folded. To make thin ribbons from them, you have to open each one and cut it into narrow strips. Look on the side of each packet for a seam to pry it open. Lay the opened packet on your work surface and halve it crosswise. Then cut the resulting pieces lengthwise into 1/2-inch-wide strips. Do this with all of the packets.

2 Now you have a bunch of thick, narrow strips. Each strip is made up of many layers of tofu skin. Use your fingers to separate the strips into thin ribbons, gently rubbing and pulling apart. Do your best, but they won't be as thin as a single layer of tofu skin, and they'll be different lengths. As you work, deposit the ribbons, which will resemble wrinkly pasta, into a bowl. When done, set aside.

3 In a medium bowl, combine the sugar, sake, soy sauce, vinegar, sesame oil, and chile oil. Stir to dissolve the sugar. Set these seasonings aside near the stove.

4 Heat 1¹/2 teaspoons of the canola oil in a large non-stick skillet over high heat. Add half of the ribbons and stir and spread the ribbons out on the skillet to sear. Let sit for 10 to 15 seconds, then stir again. Cook the ribbons this way for about 1 minute, until they have softened a bit and stuck together into a loose mass. Transfer to the bowl of seasonings. Add the remaining 1¹/2 teaspoons oil and repeat with the remaining ribbons.

CONTINUED

Spicy Yuba Ribbons

5 Return the skillet to high heat. Give the seared ribbons and seasonings a quick toss, then dump them into the hot skillet. Cook for about 2 minutes, stirring constantly, until most of the liquid has disappeared. Remove from the heat. Taste, and if the ribbons are unpleasantly chewy—they should be toothsome but not rubbery—return the skillet to the burner and splash in water by the tablespoon. Continue cooking over high heat to hydrate and soften the ribbons.

When done, add the green onion, stirring to distribute evenly. Transfer to a plate or shallow bowl. Let cool for about 5 minutes before serving. Refrigerate leftovers and if needed, soften them in a skillet over medium heat with a little water. This dish is great warm, at room temperature, and cold right out of the fridge.

NOTES

To use partially dried tofu skin for this recipe, use three 24-inch rounds. With scissors, quarter the rounds. Trim and discard the hard edges. Then cut the large wedges into 3/4-inch-wide ribbons; you can fold the wedges to make cutting easier. Transfer the ribbons to a large bowl and add enough water to barely cover. Use your hands to massage the ribbons, which will soon rehydrate and soften. When they start turning opaque, drain them and squeeze gently to expel moisture. Then use the noodles like their fresh cousins in the recipe. Cooking time may be a bit shorter than for the fresh tofu packets because these are much thinner. They may stick to the skillet if they've been over-rehydrated but they'll still taste good.

When making this recipe with dried tofu sticks, rehydrate 4 ounces of them in a large pot of just-boiled water, breaking the sticks as needed. Like pasta, the sticks will gradually soften if you poke and push them into the water. Once they are all submerged, weight them down with a lid (use one for a smaller pot) for 30 minutes. They will turn opaque. Drain, then use scissors to cut each stick crosswise into 2-inch pieces; discard any pieces that look dense and potentially difficult to chew. Toss them in the seasonings (step 3), and then cook the sticks in one batch in the skillet. They will take longer than the other kinds of tofu skins because they are thicker and may have residual liquid. Just keep cooking and stirring them until all the seasonings have been absorbed.

Savory Soy Milk Lees with Vegetables UNOHANA

SERVES 4 TO 6 AS A SIDE DISH

If you're unfamiliar with *unohana*, this modest-looking mixture of savory soy milk lees (*okara*, page 27) studded with vegetables may appear mysterious. But nibble on some with beer and sake or enjoy it as a homey side dish, and you'll find this old-fashioned Japanese preparation to be very agreeable.

The cooking process requires an initial dry-roasting to parch the *okara*, which are then cooked with vegetables, dashi stock, and seasonings. The lees absorb the flavors of their companions, and the layering of the stock, sake, mirin, and soy sauce results in a flavorful mixture.

Wash and scrape the root vegetables to retain their earthiness. Feel free to substitute other kinds of fresh mushroom, even non-Asian ones. Chopped green beans or thawed lima beans are worthy stand-ins for the edamame.

4 ounces (2/3 cup packed) thawed or fresh soy milk lees

2 teaspoons sesame oil

2 1/2- to 3-inch section leek, white or pale green part, halved lengthwise and cut crosswise into 1/8- to 1/4-inch-thick half-rounds (1/2 cup)

1/2 cup matchstick-cut or diced root vegetables, such as carrot, parsnip, and/or burdock (gobo)

3 large fresh shiitake mushrooms, stemmed and cut into 1/2- to 3/4-inch dice (brimming 3/4 cup)

2 tablespoons thawed edamame

1 1/3 cups Dashi Stock (page 215)

1 tablespoon sake

About 1 tablespoon plus 1 teaspoon mirin

About 1 tablespoon plus 1 teaspoon light-colored soy sauce, such as Japanese usukuchi shoyu or Chinese regular (light) soy sauce

1 Crumble up the soy milk lees if they are extremely compact. Heat the oil in a large nonstick skillet over high heat, then add the lees. Cook the lees, stirring frequently, for 4 to 5 minutes, until they have gone from being damp clumps to a fluffy fine mixture, like fresh breadcrumbs. Incorporate any crusty bits that form at the bottom and sides of the skillet. Wisps of steam may waft from the skillet.

2 Add the leek, root vegetables, mushrooms, and edamame. Cook for about 1 minute, stirring, until you can smell the vegetables. Pour in the dashi and sake and give the pan a stir to combine. Let things bubble and hiss for about 5 minutes to allow the liquids to cook and season the vegetables and lees. Stir the skillet to ensure even cooking.

The liquid will evaporate and be absorbed during this cooking period. The lees will firm up to resemble a soft mashed mixture. Keep stirring until the root vegetables are tender-crisp and the mushrooms are soft, adding dashi or water by the tablespoon to further cook, if needed.

3 Add the mirin and soy sauce, stirring for about 2 minutes, until the liquid is no longer visible and the vegetables have just cooked through. Aim for a mixture that is moist but not wet.

Remove the skillet from the heat and set aside to cool completely and develop the flavors. After about 10 minutes, give it a taste and add a smidgen of mirin and/or soy sauce, if needed.

Serve as mounded portions in small, individual dishes for each guest. Refrigerate leftovers for up to 3 days and return to room temperature before serving.

Bean Sprouts with Panfried Tofu and Chinese Chives

SERVES 4 AS A SIDE DISH

All over Southeast Asia, from the Philippines to Burma to Indonesia, cooks stir-fry tofu with bean sprouts and Chinese chives. They are inexpensive, everyday ingredients that don't require a huge amount of prep work. Variations of this stir-fry can include shrimp or pork, too. The result is always a lively looking, mild-tasting side dish that pairs well with other dishes.

You can use a wok for this stir-fry but a large skillet is easier for panfrying the tofu and cooking the bean sprouts. To avoid overcooked and weepy bean sprouts, pull the pan from the heat when the sprouts are tender-crisp. Seed the chiles because they can overheat in the presence of the white pepper.

6 ounces firm or extra-firm tofu

Salt

1 cup very hot or just-boiled water

12 ounces bean sprouts

2 large cloves garlic, finely chopped

1 shallot, or 1/4 red onion, thinly sliced

1 large moderately hot chile, such as Fresno or jalapeño, halved lengthwise, seeded, and cut crosswise into half-rings to match the width of a bean sprout

About 1/8 teaspoon white pepper

2 pinches of sugar

2 teaspoons light (regular) soy sauce or fish sauce

6 Chinese chives, cut into 2-inch lengths, or 3 whole slender green onions, cut at a steep diagonal into 2-inch lengths

2 tablespoons fragrant peanut oil or canola oil

1 Cut the tofu into 1/2-inch cubes, then put them in a small bowl. Dissolve 1/4 teaspoon of salt in the hot water. Pour over the tofu to cover. Set aside for 15 minutes.

Pour the water off, then transfer the tofu to a non-terry dishtowel or double layer of paper towels placed atop a plate. Set aside to drain.

2 Pick through the bean sprouts, discarding discolored seed caps and super tired roots. Rinse and let drain well.

Put the garlic, shallot, and chile on a plate. Combine a generous 1/4 teaspoon of salt with the white pepper and sugar. Set these seasonings, along with the soy sauce, plate of aromatics, bean sprouts, and chives, near the stove—this stir-fry comes together quickly.

3 Heat the oil in a large nonstick skillet over high heat. Blot the tofu cubes dry, then panfry them for about 5 minutes, until light golden on 3 or 4 sides. Turn the tofu with a spatula during frying. If it violently sputters and spits, lower the heat and panfry for a little longer. Aim to add a bit of character and depth to the tofu, not fry it to a crisp all over.

4 If needed, adjust the heat to high, then add the garlic, shallot, and chile. Cook, stirring constantly, for 45 to 60 seconds, until fragrant and the shallot has softened. Add the bean sprouts and soy sauce, working the skillet vigorously and constantly to combine the ingredients.

After about 90 seconds, the bean sprouts will have collapsed to roughly two-thirds of their original volume. Add the Chinese chives and sprinkle in the salt, pepper, and sugar.

Keep stirring the skillet for about 30 seconds, until the chives have wilted but remain bright green. Remove the skillet from the heat. Taste and add extra salt or pepper, as needed. Transfer to a shallow bowl and serve immediately.

Tofu with Kimchi and Pork Belly DUBU KIMCHI

"You must have *dubu kimchi* in your book! Tofu and kimchi is a classic pairing. I eat it all the time," my Korean-American friend Linda Lim said to me. And truly this dish of warm tofu and stir-fried kimchi and pork belly is satisfying and addictively good. The tofu acts as a platform to absorb and mellow the tangy, savory, and spicy qualities of the other ingredients. The combination is wonderful with beer. *Dubu kimchi* is a favorite Korean *anju* (drinking snack), though you can enjoy it as a side dish or main course with rice.

To mature kimchi, simply age it for about 4 weeks in the fridge, until it is extra pungent. The kimchi doesn't overwhelm the other ingredients but provides the foundation for the flavors to come together. Some Korean markets label their kimchi according to maturity level for dishes like this one. Fresh pork belly (side pork) is sold at Asian markets. In a pinch, use bacon.

8 to 10 ounces firm tofu

3/4 teaspoon salt, plus more as needed

1 cup very hot or just-boiled water

8 ounces drained mature napa cabbage kimchi (1 cup packed)

About 1/2 teaspoon sugar

1 to 1 1/2 teaspoons Korean red pepper powder (gochu garu)

4 ounces pork belly, with or without skin, cut into 1 1/2-inch-long pieces, each about 1/8 inch thick

1 clove garlic, finely chopped

1 jalapeño chile, cut into 1/8-inch-thick rings, optional

1 to 2 tablespoons kimchi pickling liquid

1 large or extra-large green onion, white and green parts, cut into 1/4-inch-thick rings

1/2 teaspoon sesame oil

1 teaspoon toasted black sesame seeds, for garnish

1 Cut the tofu into super chunky matchbooks, each about 1 1/2 inches by 2 inches by a generous 1/2 inch. Put the pieces in a shallow bowl. Dissolve the 3/4 teaspoon salt in the water, then pour over the tofu; it should be just covered. Set aside to warm and season the tofu while you make the stir-fry.

2 Cut the kimchi into 1- to 1 1/2-inch pieces and transfer to a bowl. Season it with the sugar and red pepper powder to slightly offset the kimchi's tartness and to brighten up its color and heat. I usually add the sugar by the 1/4 teaspoon and the pepper powder by the 1/2 teaspoon. The quantity needed depends on the kimchi's flavor and your preferences. The kimchi should taste pleasantly sour-sweet with a light spicy kick. Set aside.

3 Heat a wok or skillet over high heat. There is no need to add oil because the pork will render its fat. Scatter in the pork, spreading out the pieces to allow them to fry flat. Let them cook for about 1 minute, undisturbed, until the pork has browned a bit. Use a spatula to flip the pork, spreading it out again, and cook undisturbed for another minute. Transition to stir-frying the pork, moving it constantly. If there is more than a tablespoon of fat in the pan, use a spoon to remove it.

4 Add the garlic and chile and give these a few turns. Then add the seasoned kimchi. Cook, stirring frequently, for about 4 minutes to allow the pork to absorb the flavors

CONTINUED

Tofu with Kimchi and Pork Belly

of the kimchi; test by tasting the pork. Splash in the kimchi pickling liquid to inject extra flavor. When you are satisfied, add the green onion. Continue stir-frying for about 30 seconds, until the green onion has softened.

5 Turn off the heat. Taste the kimchi and add sugar and salt, as needed. Add the sesame oil for a fragrant, rich finish. Transfer the kimchi to a plate, mounding it in the center.

6 Pour off the water from the tofu. Arrange the warm tofu pieces around the kimchi. Sprinkle a little black sesame seed atop each piece of tofu before serving.

Invite guests to put a piece of tofu on their plate, then add a copious quantity of the kimchi and pork on top. If the tofu pieces are unwieldy, use chopsticks or a fork to cut them in half before topping with kimchi and pork.

Water Spinach with Fermented Tofu

SERVES 2 OR 3 AS A SIDE DISH

A classic Chinese and Southeast Asian use of white fermented tofu is to employ its savory punchy flavor in a water spinach stir-fry. The tofu lends a creaminess and mellow flavor that is vaguely reminiscent of a light cheese sauce.

When scaling up this recipe for a large group, stir-fry in small batches to avoid overcrowding the wok. If water spinach is unavailable, substitute other kinds of spinach, such as regular or Taiwan spinach. Water spinach is called *kong xin cai* (Mandarin), *ong choy* (Cantonese), *kangkong* (Bahasa, Tagalog), *phak bung* (Thai), and *rau muong* (Vietnamese). Look for it at Chinese and Southeast Asian markets. Examine the cut ends to determine freshness.

12 to 14 ounces water spinach

1½ tablespoons mashed white fermented tofu, with or without chile

1 tablespoon Shaoxing rice wine or dry sherry

½ teaspoon sesame oil

About ⅛ teaspoon salt

Sugar to taste

2 tablespoons canola oil

3 cloves garlic, minced

1 Take each stem of water spinach and snap, twist, or cut off the bottom 4 inches, which tends to be too fibrous to eat. (Chew on some of the hollow stem to see how much you should discard; in general, stems over ¼ inch wide are too tough.) Cut the trimmed water spinach into 3-inch sections and wash well in several changes of water, discarding any unsavory parts. Drain in a colander.

2 In a large pot, bring a generous amount of water (enough to cover the water spinach) to a rolling boil. Add the water spinach, moving it around with chopsticks or a spoon to ensure even cooking. Once it wilts, about 30 seconds, drain it in the colander and flush with cold water.

Gently press to expel excess water, then place near the stove. (You can prep the water spinach a few hours before stir-frying; cool, cover, and keep at room temperature.)

3 In a small dish, combine the tofu, rice wine, sesame oil, and salt. Taste and add pinches of sugar to balance the flavors. Set aside.

4 In a wok or large skillet, heat the oil over medium-high heat until hot but not smoking. Add the garlic and stir-fry for about 15 seconds, or until fragrant. Add the water spinach and stir-fry for 1 minute, until just heated through. Add the mashed tofu, briskly stirring to combine. Cook for about 45 seconds, until the liquid is no longer visible and the water spinach takes on a slightly creamy quality. Turn off the heat, taste, and add extra salt and/or sugar. Transfer to a plate and serve immediately.

Fermented Tofu Simmered in Coconut Milk LON TAO HU YI

SERVES 4 AS A SIDE DISH

Combining pungent fermented tofu and rich coconut milk may seem odd, but the result is this splendid Thai dish. Because *lon tao hu yi* is often served with raw accompaniments, I thought it was a dip. "It could be," said Bangkok-born food writer Pim Techamuanvivit. "But it's really a side dish to be eaten with other foods as part of a meal. You could also mix it into rice noodles."

Indeed, *lon tao hu yi* is a versatile preparation. Treat it like a dressing to accent crisp vegetables and tart fruit, like cucumbers, cabbage, green beans, and Granny Smith apples—spoon it over, or use the veggies to scoop and dunk. It's also a fine relish for grilled foods such as eggplant. Or, use it as a light curry to spark up rice or tender-chewy rice vermicelli.

Don't be deterred by the large amount of white fermented tofu. It provides the savory backbone and its pungency is softened by the coconut milk. The pork and shrimp contribute texture, while the sugar, tamarind, and white pepper help balance the flavors. You have to tweak this dish several times but it's so elastic that you always arrive at a tasty finish. Use a flavorful, rich coconut milk, such as Aroy-D, Chaokoh, or Mae Ploy brands.

2 shallots

Salt

1/3 cup mashed white fermented tofu, with or without chile

12/3 cups coconut milk (one 13.5-ounce can)

2 ounces ground pork, fattier kind preferred

4 large uncooked shrimp, peeled, deveined, and finely chopped

2 to 3 tablespoons packed light palm sugar or light brown sugar

2 to 3 tablespoons Tamarind Liquid (page 217)

About 1/4 teaspoon white pepper

1 or 2 moderately hot chiles, such as Fresno or jalapeño, cut into scant 1/4-inch-thick rounds

2 to 3 tablespoons coarsely chopped cilantro, tender tops only

1 Halve one of the shallots lengthwise, then cut it crosswise into pieces about the width of a bean sprout. Set aside to add toward the end of cooking.

Chop the other shallot, then put into a mortar. Add a pinch of salt, then pound the shallot into a rough texture. Add the tofu and stir to combine. Set aside.

2 Reserve 11/2 tablespoons of the thick coconut cream from the top of the can. Empty the rest of the coconut milk into a small saucepan. Heat over medium-high heat, stirring occasionally, until smooth.

Add the shallot and fermented tofu mixture. Bring to a simmer, then adjust the heat to maintain a steady bubbling. Cook for 5 to 6 minutes, stirring occasionally, until thick. To test, coat the back of a spoon and run your finger through the mixture. The line should hold stiffly.

3 Meanwhile, put the pork and shrimp in a bowl. When the coconut milk mixture has thickened enough, spoon about one-third of it into the pork and shrimp. Use a fork to combine well before adding to the saucepan of coconut milk. This prevents large clumps from forming. Cook for 2 to 3 minutes, stirring occasionally, until the shrimp and pork have changed color and are done. If needed, adjust the heat to barely simmer to make it easier for you to fine-tune flavors in the next step.

4 Season with the palm sugar, tamarind liquid, and pepper to arrive at a sweet-tart-savory finish that has an undercurrent of funky fermented tofu. Start with the smaller quantity and if needed, work up to the maximum. Be generous with the white pepper. The seasonings help further tame the tofu. (When making this dish a day in advance, stop at this point, partially cover, and let cool. Refrigerate and return to room temperature before moving on.)

5 Bring to a simmer, then stir in the sliced shallot and chile. When the mixture returns to a simmer, remove it from the heat. Let it rest for 5 to 10 minutes to concentrate in flavor, thicken further, and lightly cook the shallot and chile. Aim for a thickish, scoopable texture if you intend to enjoy it with raw garnishes. With noodles or rice, it's better to have a thinner consistency; add a splash of water, if needed.

Taste and adjust the flavor as necessary with sugar, tamarind, or white pepper. You can also add a pinch of salt or a teaspoon of the fermented tofu brine. No one flavor dominates in the end, and there's a lovely harmony among the ingredients.

6 Stir half of the cilantro into the sauce, then transfer to a serving bowl. Top with the reserved coconut cream and remaining cilantro. Serve warm.

Mock Meats

You may think of fake meat as veggie patties or soy chorizo, but in many parts of Asia, meat analogues have been elevated to an art form. The Chinese, in particular, excel in manipulating vegetables or vegetable products into realistic and tasty imitations of spareribs, chicken breast, shrimp, and the like. That vast repertoire of meat substitutes supports the vegetarian diets of countless Asian Buddhists all over the world. Buddhism was likely introduced to China during the Han period (206 BCE–220 CE) and its attitudes and beliefs have shaped much of East and Southeast Asian culture and cuisine ever since.

Taiwan, in particular, is a hub for mock meat production, vegetarian restaurants and cafeterias, and vegetarian cooking competitions. To prepare for visiting Taipei, I asked some Taiwanese Facebook acquaintances about their penchant for fake meat. The concept seemed to almost contradict the Buddhist precept of not harming other living beings.

We had a lively conversation during which Christine Tsai, a practicing Buddhist vegetarian, remarked, "In Taiwan, the reason why people try to make vegetarian dishes taste like meat is because they want to draw nonvegetarians' attention to it. They want people to like their food

and see if the food can make them slowly become vegetarian." Buddhism is flexible and some practitioners are full-time vegetarians like her, while others avoid meat only on the first and fifteenth day of the lunar month. She then offered to show me her world of Buddhist cuisine, and became the de facto leader of my Taipei tofu posse, a group of virtual friends who quickly became my tofu buddies after I arrived. With rapid-fire cell phone skills and a sizable address book, Christine helped organize my excursions, including a last-minute visit to the Ming Ji tofu factory. One morning, we rode her scooter to a favorite wholesale food market, where we perused myriad tofu and sampled very persuasive imitation chicken, pork belly, and fish roe.

She also reached out to Lin Mei Hua, the assistant manager of Kuan Shih Yin, a well-regarded Buddhist vegetarian restaurant. Ms. Lin hosted us, along with two of Christine's friends, for a special lunch that turned out to be a tofu banquet.

The restaurant was an upscale, serene establishment with an amicable-yet-formal staff. We were ushered to a private room, and a parade of exquisite food began appearing. Each item was lavishly decorated with carved vegetables that reminded me of elaborate photos I had seen in old Taiwanese cookbooks.

Ms. Lin smiled as she watched us try the appetizer. Everyone's eyes widened as we enjoyed the flavors and textures of the savory-sweet fried morsels. When we correctly guessed that it was mock Japanese-style eel (page 157), she nodded in approval and we all giggled. I asked about how the "eel flesh" tasted so briny, and Ms. Lin matter-of-factly responded, "It's just mashed tofu and seaweed." A braised fish was similarly rendered but garnished with a delicate vegetable stock, colorful mélange of vegetables, goji berries, and Thai basil. Stuffed tofu had been hollowed out like a gift box before being filled. Individual portions of tofu had been steamed in Chinese soupspoons to resemble flower

petals. Ms. Lin also presented homey fare such as egg tofu seasoned with a rich and slightly pungent sauce of ground Chinese toon (*Toona sinensis*). The palate cleanser was a gingery vegan broth that tasted like rich chicken stock.

We ate in amazement, marveling at the range of vegetarian dishes. Evelyn, a nonvegetarian and accomplished home cook, helped me decipher and decode the food. Kara, a slender professional singer, commented on the healthful benefits of being vegetarian. For Christine, the meal illuminated the refinements of Buddhist cuisine. She practically beamed with pride.

I don't know if Christine meant to convert me, but I left Kuan Shih Yin with great esteem for Buddhist vegetarian cooking. The chefs there demonstrated that they follow the same guiding principles as other Chinese chefs, but their vegan fare went beyond being well-crafted food to express Buddhist notions of kindness, harmony, and respect. It was an elegant, delectable, and effective manner of fulfilling their religious requirements. The experience broadened my palate and perspective but didn't ask me to change my lifestyle or belief system.

This chapter's small collection of recipes spotlights interesting Asian approaches to making mock meat. For example, in the photo above the round patties are Japanese mock goose (*ganmodoki*, page 154). Each preparation is delicious in its own right, whether you are familiar with the original or not. I hope that these dishes stoke your further exploration of Asian vegetarian cooking.

Tofu and Vegetable Fritters GANMODOKI

MAKES 12 SMALL FRITTERS, TO SERVE 4 TO 6 AS A SNACK

In Japanese, *ganmodoki* means "mock goose," though it's a stretch of the imagination to say that these chewy-crisp, rich-tasting fritters resemble game. Some say they originated around the 1400s at Buddhist temples and monasteries. During that time, the most prized food for the nobles was wild goose (*gan*). Upon tasting the fried tofu fritters, the monks were so enthralled that they proclaimed the fritters to be surely as good as the best wild goose. Their reaction gave rise to the popular name, *ganmodoki* (also called *ganmo*). In the Kansai region (Osaka and Kyoto), the fritters are called *hiryozu*, meaning "flying dragon heads," because the vegetables sometimes poke out of the tofu after frying.

Ganmodoki are often part of Japanese *oden* hot pots, but when I visited with food authority Elizabeth Andoh in Tokyo, she taught me to savor them simply, dipped in soy sauce with a little grated fresh ginger. I like to dunk them in Sriracha chile sauce, too. Traditionally, the ingredients are bound by grated *yama imo*, a viscous tuber, and fried in low-, then high-temperature oil to force the fritter to puff. Mixing the tofu with egg white and starch and cooking the fritters at a moderately low temperature yields similar results.

Feel free to add a teaspoon of black sesame seeds. To substitute other vegetables, such as cooked *hijiki* seaweed or chopped edamame, use 1/4 to 1/3 cup of such additions to lend umami, texture, and color. Make larger patties than the ones here or try forming different shapes, such as ovals or triangles. Put a surprise in each one, such as roughly chopped fresh *shiso* or a blanched gingko nut. Have fun with this homey, humble treat.

1 pound firm tofu

1/4 teaspoon salt

2 big pinches of sugar

1 tablespoon cornstarch

1 large egg white, beaten

1 tablespoon finely chopped green onion, white and green parts

2 small dried shiitake mushrooms, rehydrated, stemmed, and finely chopped (2 tablespoons)

1 1/2 tablespoons finely grated carrot, parsnip, and/or burdock (gobo); use the smallest hole on a shredder

Canola oil, for deep-frying

1 teaspoon grated fresh ginger

Japanese or Korean soy sauce

1 To quickly expel water from the tofu and begin mashing it, break it up into 6 to 8 chunks. Working in 2 or 3 batches, put the tofu in a non-terry dishtowel or piece of muslin, then gather it up. Standing over a sink, firmly squeeze and massage; you want some moisture left in the tofu but you don't want it wet. Unwrap and you should have about 11 ounces (roughly 1 1/3 cups packed). Transfer to a bowl.

2 Use a potato masher to even out the texture of the tofu. It should only take about 15 seconds. Add the salt, sugar, cornstarch, and 1 1/2 tablespoons of the egg white; discard or save leftover egg white for another use. Mash the mixture again to create a fairly smooth texture that's akin to ricotta cheese. Add the green onion, mushroom, and carrot. Use the potato masher to combine the ingredients. Switch to using one hand to gather, lift, and throw the mixture back into the bowl. Repeat 5 or 6 times to compact.

3 Before forming the fritters, put 1 tablespoon of oil on a small plate and set it aside. Divide the tofu mixture into 12 portions, forming them into rough balls. Throw each back and forth between your hands to compact it. Replace the balls in the bowl. Now lightly press the palms of your hands in the oil to coat them, then roll one of the balls between your hands to smooth its surface and prevent sticking during frying. Gently flatten the ball into a small patty, roughly 1³/₄ inches wide and ³/₄ inch thick. Be mindful of the thickness because it ensures that the fritter sufficiently cooks during frying. Set the formed fritter on your work surface. Repeat with the other balls, reoiling your palms as needed.

4 Heat 2 inches of oil in a wok or medium saucepan over medium-high heat to about 325°F. If you don't have a deep-fry thermometer, stick a *dry* bamboo chopstick into the oil; if bubbles rise to the surface in 1 to 2 seconds, the oil is ready.

Fry the fritters in 2 batches to avoid overcrowding. Slide each fritter into the oil, where it will sit and bubble. After about 1 minute, the entire batch will have risen to the surface. Nudge them a little with a skimmer if they appear to have gathered together.

Fry for another 4 minutes, turning occasionally, until the fritters are golden brown, puffed, and crisp. During the last minute of frying, turn the fritters often to coax them to puff. A ³/₄-inch-thick fritter will puff to about 1¹/₄ inches thick. Drain on a double layer of paper towels, turning them after 30 to 45 seconds to blot oil from the other side. Adjust the oil temperature before frying the second batch. As the fritters cool, they deflate in the center to form their characteristic dimples.

5 Serve hot or warm with grated ginger and soy sauce for dipping. The fritters may be refrigerated for up to 5 days or frozen for a month. Return to room temperature and reheat in a 350°F toaster oven for about 8 minutes, turning them midway, until hot.

Sweet and Savory Tofu Eel UNAGI MODOKI

SERVES 4 WITH 2 OR 3 OTHER DISHES

Asian faux foods can tickle your fancy when they successfully imitate their real counterparts in looks, texture, and flavor. This rendition of Japanese *unagi kabayaki* is a clever copy. My inspiration came from the feast at Kuan Shih Yin vegetarian restaurant in Taipei. (Japan's influence on Taiwanese cuisine is a legacy of its fifty-year colonial history.) To impart a delicate sealike flavor, the chefs mixed dried seaweed into the tofu mixture that formed the eel "flesh." That brininess is reinforced by the strip of nori that serves as the eel "skin." The sweet soy sauce glaze further echoes the real deal.

The plate of mock eel, beautifully arranged on a bed of daikon and garnished with a camellia flower carved from a radish, was the appetizer. Assistant Manager Lin Mei Hua and her staff presented so many dishes that we could not finish all of them. Every morsel of this mock eel, however, was completely eaten up. Serve this as a snack or present it atop a big, deep bowl of hot rice for a vegan *unagi donburi*.

GLAZE

1 tablespoon plus 1 teaspoon sugar
2 1/2 tablespoons mirin
3 tablespoons Japanese or Korean soy sauce

2 full-size sheets toasted nori
1 pound firm tofu
1/8 teaspoon salt
2 big pinches of sugar
1/2 teaspoon Japanese or Korean soy sauce
2 teaspoons plus 1 1/2 tablespoons cornstarch
1 1/2 tablespoons water
Canola oil for shallow-frying

1 For the glaze, combine the sugar, mirin, and soy sauce in a very small pan. Bring to a boil over medium-high heat, stirring to dissolve the sugar. Let boil for about 2 minutes, until tan foam appears on the surface. Lower the heat to vigorously simmer for 1 to 2 minutes, until slightly thickened. Set aside to cool completely. The finished glaze should be syrupy, with a strong salty sweetness. There should be 3 to 4 tablespoons.

2 Use scissors to cut each sheet of nori in half lengthwise. Set aside 1 piece for the moment. Stack the remaining 3 pieces and cut them in half lengthwise to yield 6 strips that are roughly 2 inches wide and 8 inches long. Set them aside in a dry spot.

Tear the reserved piece of nori into 3/4-inch pieces. Put them in a clean, dry spice grinder (or coffee grinder dedicated to spice grinding) and process into small flakes that resemble graphite. Don't worry if they are not a fine size. Transfer to a small bowl and set aside.

3 Break up the tofu into 6 to 8 chunks. Working in 2 or 3 batches, put the tofu in a non-terry dishtowel or piece of muslin, then gather it up. Standing over a sink, firmly squeeze and massage. You want some moisture left in the tofu but you don't want it wet. Unwrap and you should have about 11 ounces (roughly 1 1/3 cups packed). Transfer the tofu to a bowl.

CONTINUED

Sweet and Savory Tofu Eel

4 Use a potato masher to even out the texture of the tofu. Add the salt, sugar, soy sauce, 2 teaspoons of cornstarch, and 1 brimming teaspoon of the seaweed flakes; discard or save leftover flakes for another use. Mash the mixture again to create a fairly smooth mixture. Divide the tofu mixture into 6 even portions.

In a small bowl, dissolve the remaining 1 1/2 tablespoons cornstarch with the water. Set this "glue" and the tofu mixture aside.

5 To assemble the eel, put a nori strip on your work surface, rougher side facing up. Give the cornstarch slurry a stir, then brush it on the seaweed, taking care to cover the edges. Spread a portion of the tofu mixture over the seaweed. Do your best to even out the surface with your fingers, the flat side of the knife blade, or a wooden dowel rolling pin.

Now use the spine of the knife to create a faux eel fillet. Lightly tap out shallow lines across the tofu mixture, working from one end to the other. Then, gently press the knife spine down the middle to evoke the backbone.

Turn your knife over to its normal position, then halve the strip crosswise. Place the 2 strips on a parchment paper–lined baking sheet. Repeat with the remaining seaweed strips and tofu mixture. When done, cover loosely with a dishtowel to prevent drying.

6 Heat 1/3 inch of oil in a medium skillet over medium-high heat to between 350° and 360°F. If you don't have a deep-fry thermometer, gauge the oil temperature by sticking a *dry* bamboo chopstick into the oil; if bubbles rise immediately to the surface, the oil is ready.

Fry the strips 3 at a time, carefully laying each one, tofu side facing down, in the oil. The strip should initially sink, then quickly rise and raucously sizzle. The strip should slightly bend upward, as if it were arching toward you. Oil will naturally pool on the seaweed. Fry for about 2 minutes, until the tofu side is golden, crisp, and puffed up. Use two spatulas to turn the strips over. Fry the nori side for about 45 seconds, until taut and slightly crisp. Drain on paper towel, tofu side up. Return the oil to temperature between batches.

7 The strips are good hot, warm, or at room temperature as long as they are somewhat crisp on the tofu side. To serve, cut each strip crosswise or on a steep diagonal into 3/4- to 1-inch wide pieces. Arrange on a plate (or put atop a bowl of rice) and spoon or drizzle some of the glaze on top. You can also elect to drizzle the glaze on the strips before cutting and plating them.

NOTE

When making the strips in advance, leave them unglazed. Keep them at room temperature for up to 2 hours or refrigerate for up to 2 days. To reheat, put the strips on aluminum foil and broil in a toaster oven for 1 minute per side, until lightly crisp again. Store the glaze at room temperature for up to 2 days.

Bear Paw Tofu XIONG ZHANG DOU FU

SERVES 4 WITH 2 OR 3 OTHER DISHES

Sichuan cooks devised this moderately spicy tofu dish to replicate the essence of bear paw, a delicacy in China that is now banned for conservation reasons. Most of us don't care about eating bear paw, but this favorite can stand on its own.

There are fussed-up restaurant versions that feature a giant slab of tofu sculpted to resemble a full-size paw and mini plastic panda ornaments. I take my cue from home cooks such as Xie Qian (page 97), who simply panfry thick slices of tofu and then infuse them with chile bean sauce, ginger, garlic, and rice wine for savory goodness. A little stock is then added to render the tofu custardy on the inside and create an unctuous, earthy sauce. Some cooks add pork to the dish, but I omit the meat to highlight the tofu's texture and slightly puckered appearance, which the Chinese say is like the real deal. Enjoy this easy dish with rice and a green vegetable.

14 to 16 ounces firm tofu

3 tablespoons canola oil

1 1/2 tablespoons chile bean sauce, Pixian variety preferred

2 teaspoons minced fresh ginger

2 cloves garlic, chopped

About 1/2 teaspoon sugar

2 tablespoons Shaoxing rice wine or dry sherry

1/2 teaspoon cornstarch dissolved in 6 tablespoons lightly
    salted chicken stock, low-sodium canned broth,
    or water

Light (regular) soy sauce, as needed

2 green onions, white and green parts, chopped

1 Cut the tofu into chunky matchboxes, each about 1 1/2 inches by 2 inches by 1/2 inch. Line a plate with a non-terry dish towel or double layer of paper towels, then place the tofu on top to drain for 5 to 10 minutes.

2 Heat the oil in a large nonstick skillet over high heat. Blot the tofu, then panfry until golden and lightly crisp, about 3 minutes per side.

3 Lower the heat slightly, then push the tofu pieces to the edge of the skillet, stacking a few as needed. Add the chile bean sauce, ginger, and garlic to the center opening of the skillet. Sprinkle on the sugar, then cook, stirring constantly, until fragrant, about 1 minute. Flip the tofu a couple of times to coat with the seasonings. Splash in the rice wine to moisten, then cook for about 1 minute, until you no longer smell the alcohol.

Give the cornstarch mixture a stir before adding it to the skillet. Gently combine the ingredients, turning the tofu and shaking the skillet. Cook for 1 to 2 minutes, until the tofu is coated with a lightly thickened sauce.

Taste and if needed, add about 1/2 teaspoon soy sauce for depth. Add extra pinches of sugar to balance the flavors. Aim for a savory-salty-slightly-sweet finish.

Sprinkle in the green onion, gently turning for 10 to 15 seconds, until it has softened. Transfer to a plate and serve. This dish will naturally weep orange-red oil as it sits. Be sure to mix some of that deliciousness into your rice!

Cellophane Noodle and Tofu Rolls BI CUON CHAY

MAKES 12 ROLLS, TO SERVE 4 TO 6 AS A SNACK

These delicate rice paper rolls are wonderful in their own right, but to understand their flavors and textures, a little background is needed. They are a popular vegetarian copycat of the Viet classic, *bi cuon*, which literally means pork skin rolls.

To mimic the chewy shreds of pork skin (*bi*), cooks rehydrate and chop cellophane noodles. Thin strips of fried tofu stand in for the julienned poached pork. Jicama, which turns translucent and becomes rich tasting when sautéed, imitates the slivered pork fat that is integral to the rolls. Mixing the ingredients with nutty roasted rice powder and wrapping everything up in rice paper creates the signature flavor and appearance of all *bi* preparations. When serving strict Buddhists, omit the garlic, because it is among the five pungent spices that are not allowed in their diet.

12 ounces firm or extra-firm tofu

1 small bundle (1.3 ounces) cellophane noodles

Salt

1 tablespoon plus 3/4 teaspoon light (regular) soy sauce

2 tablespoons raw long-grain rice

Canola oil for sautéing and shallow-frying

8 ounces jicama, peeled and cut into matchsticks

2 tablespoons packed light palm sugar or light brown sugar

2 tablespoons fresh lime juice

1 small Thai or serrano chile, thinly sliced

1 small clove garlic, minced, optional

1/2 teaspoon granulated sugar

Generous 1/8 teaspoon white pepper

1 1/2 cups lightly packed thinly sliced iceberg lettuce

2 tablespoons coarsely chopped fresh mint leaves

12 rice paper rounds, about 8 inches in diameter

1 Halve the tofu crosswise, then cut each half crosswise into rectangular slices, each about 1/3 inch thick. Put into a bowl. Put the cellophane noodles in a different bowl.

In a teakettle, bring a generous 4 cups of water to a boil. Turn off the heat and when the boiling has subsided, measure out 2 cups of water. Add 1 teaspoon of salt, stirring to dissolve. Pour the salted water over the tofu. Set aside to soak for 15 minutes.

Return the water to a boil, turn off the heat, then measure out 2 more cups. Add 1/2 teaspoon salt and 1 tablespoon of the soy sauce. Stir to dissolve, then pour over the noodles. Let sit for 6 to 8 minutes, until the noodles are clear, pliable, and al dente. Drain well and set aside.

2 In a small skillet over medium heat, roast the rice for 7 to 8 minutes over medium heat, shaking the skillet frequently, until the grains are caramel in color. Set aside to cool for a few minutes. Working in 2 or 3 batches, transfer to a clean spice grinder (or coffee grinder dedicated to spices) and process to a powder. Transfer to a small bowl and set aside.

3 When the tofu is done soaking, pour off the water. Transfer it to a non-terry dishtowel or double layer of paper towels placed atop a plate. Drain for 10 to 15 minutes.

4 In a large nonstick skillet, heat 2 teaspoons of oil over high heat. Add the jicama, and cook for 10 minutes, stirring occasionally at the beginning and more often toward the end. Spread the jicama out after each stirring to

CONTINUED

Cellophane Noodle and Tofu Rolls

allow it to cook evenly and dry out. When done, the jicama will be soft and translucent, with a little browning. It will be roughly one-third of its original volume. Transfer to a bowl and let cool to room temperature.

5 Lower the heat in the skillet to medium-high and add oil to a depth of $1/4$ inch. Blot the tofu dry one last time. Working in 2 batches, shallow-fry the tofu for about 5 minutes, turning midway, until golden and crisp. Transfer to paper towels to drain and cool.

6 To make the sauce, in a small bowl, stir together a generous $1/4$ teaspoon salt with the palm sugar and lime juice. Use the back of the spoon to mash the ingredients to dissolve the sugar. Add the remaining $3/4$ teaspoon soy sauce and $1/3$ cup water. Taste and adjust the flavors for a tangy-savory finish. Add the chile and garlic, then set aside.

7 Before assembling the rolls, make the "pork" filling. Cut the fried tofu into thin strips, then put in a bowl. Chop the drained noodles into 1- to 2-inch lengths and add to the tofu strips. Add the jicama to the bowl, too. Sprinkle on $1/2$ teaspoon of salt along with the granulated sugar, white pepper, and toasted ground rice. Toss to combine well. Then season with $1\!1/2$ tablespoons of the sauce; try to leave out the chiles or your guests will get a whopping surprise. Combine the lettuce with the mint in bowl. Set near the filling.

8 For each roll, dip a rice paper round in warm water and then place it on your work surface. When the rice paper is pliable and tacky, position about 2 tablespoons of lettuce slightly below the midline of the round, arranging it into a 4-inch-wide rectangular bed. Top with $1/4$ cup of the filling. Spread it out to cover the lettuce and neaten it up, making sure the tofu strips on top lay horizontally for a nicer presentation.

Lift the bottom edge up and over the filling, tucking the edge under it. Give the rice paper a full roll to secure things, then fold in the sides and continue rolling to close. The rice paper is self-sealing. Repeat to make a total of 12 rolls.

9 Serve the rolls whole or halve each one crosswise. Present the rolls with the sauce. Invite guests to drizzle a little sauce into the rolls to prevent the filling from falling out.

NOTE

Lighten your load by preparing the tofu, jicama, and roasted rice powder up to 2 days in advance; refrigerate the tofu and jicama and return them to room temperature before using. The noodles and sauce can be made up to 4 hours before serving. You can assemble the rolls at least 2 hours ahead and cover with plastic wrap; rolls made with rice paper brands such as Three Ladies can sit for as long as 4 hours. Do not refrigerate prepared rolls because they will stiffen and dry out.

Savory Okara Crumbles DOU FU ZHA SONG

One of the popular ways to extend precious protein in Asia is to transform it into salty-sweet, finely textured, preserved bits. That type of food is often referred to as floss or fluff (i.e., pork floss), and is used to season flavor-neutral foods such as rice or creamy rice soup (jook/congee). I grew up with pork, chicken, and fish renditions, but Singaporean food writer Christopher Tan tipped me off to this clever version made from soy milk lees (*okara*, page 27). The result is crumbly like bacon bits. Use a generous amount of the crumbles and some of the cooked green onion to doll up a bowl of plain rice.

5 ounces (3/4 cup packed) fresh or thawed soy milk lees
2 1/4 teaspoons sugar
1/4 teaspoon salt
2 tablespoons canola oil or fragrant peanut oil
2 large green onions, white and green parts, thinly sliced
2 teaspoons light (regular) soy sauce
1 teaspoon dark (black) soy sauce
1 teaspoon sesame oil

1 Put the soy milk lees in a shallow bowl. Mix in the sugar and salt with a fork. Set aside.

2 Heat the oil in a medium nonstick skillet over medium heat until a piece of green onion sizzles upon contact. Add the green onion, then cook for 1 to 2 minutes, stirring frequently, until soft and fragrant. Pour through a mesh strainer positioned over a small bowl, pressing to extract extra oil. Reserve the cooked green onion for later. You'll reuse the skillet, so don't wash it.

3 Add both of the soy sauces and the sesame oil to the green onion oil. Use a spatula to mix these liquid seasonings into the lees, stirring and mashing the ingredients together into a uniformly brown mixture that texturally resembles dry mashed potatoes.

4 Reheat the medium nonstick skillet over medium heat and add the lees, spreading them out flat for maximum heat contact. Cook, stirring occasionally and scraping the bottom as necessary, for 20 to 25 minutes, until the mixture is nearly dry, light, and fluffy. The result will texturally resemble nearly dry instant oatmeal, but will be a rich brown.

Toward the end, press the mixture into a thin pancake that covers the bottom of the skillet and let it get slightly toasty, about 1 minute, before stirring things up. If needed, adjust the heat up or down to coax the lees to dry out into flakes and crumbles.

Transfer the mixture to a large plate or parchment paper–lined baking sheet, spreading it out to cool and finish drying. Store the crumbles and green onion separately in airtight containers. Refrigerate the onion for up to a week. The crumbles keep well at room temperature for just as long, if not longer.

Buns, Dumplings, Crepes, Noodles, and Rice

Many recipes in this book are classics, iconic members of their respective Asian cuisines. But tofu, like any other food, does not stand still. Though it can be frozen, it is not frozen in time.

While working on this book, I met two remarkable Asian-American restaurateurs who are doing new tofu takes on old favorites. They were born on opposite sides of the planet and focus on seemingly opposite types of food, yet their approach is the same.

Eddie Huang, twenty-nine, is the owner and chef of BaoHaus in New York City. His Taiwanese parents immigrated to the US and settled in Florida, where Eddie grew up in the restaurant industry. He was educated to be a lawyer but did not remain on the "model minority" track. In 2009, he decided to open a small hip-hop snack shop dedicated to modern renditions of *gua bao*, a Taiwanese specialty originally comprised of a very large folded steamed bun stuffed with a mess of slow-cooked pork and garnished with pickled mustard greens, ground roasted sweetened peanuts, and cilantro. Given its size and ubiquity, *gua bao* earned the nickname "The Taiwanese Hamburger."

At BaoHaus, Huang presents twists on the classic. "I'm a young guy in downtown New York trying to explore and create modern Chinese-Taiwanese food for me, my family, and friends to eat," he said. "We don't have to eat our parents' food. My goal is to keep the story moving."

Huang's *gua bao* are slider-size, and you can order the fluffy steamed buns (think of it as a roll) filled with pork

belly, hanger steak, free-range chicken, or fried tofu. As much as I love meat, the tofu rendition was the standout, its flavors bright and exciting. With a Chinese bun holding pieces of Japanese-style deep-fried tofu garnished with Taiwanese sweet chile sauce that's akin to the popular Thai condiment, the "Uncle Jesse," as Huang calls his tofu *gua bao*, embodies Taiwanese foodways as a unique crossroads of Chinese, Japanese, and Southeast Asian cultures.

You would expect a tofu version of *gua bao* to entail some kind of mock meat made of tofu, but Huang just fried pieces of tofu and tucked them into the bun.

Meanwhile in Taipei, Wei Shum, thirty-four, had received a lot of attention for his well-crafted hamburgers at California Grill, a stylish hipster burger joint on trendy Yong Kang Street. My Taiwanese friends insisted that I try the tofu burger before I left town. With a modern groovy-retro vibe and dinerlike open kitchen, the small restaurant could have been in Venice Beach, California. There were beef, chicken, and salmon burger options but I was there for the tofu burger, which I ordered without fancy accoutrements.

Expecting a mock meat patty made with soy, I instead received a beautifully grilled slab of marinated tofu on a perfect hamburger bun. I laughed at Shum's brilliance and smiled after my first bite. California Grill's tofu burger was exceptionally good. The tofu wasn't masquerading as meat. It was a fresh-tasting, satisfying sandwich.

"California Grill sells a certain culture. We needed a vegetarian option and I was caught between two worlds. We couldn't do a Tofurky type of meat substitute burger because I believe in honest food, nor could we do a traditional Chinese stir-fry or deep-fried tofu," Shum explained.

Shum was born in Hong Kong and has mostly lived in California, in coastal towns such as Santa Cruz, Santa Monica, and San Clemente. He'd also worked extensively in the food industry and poured that experience, along with his California sensibility, into the restaurant, which he co-owns. The grill's tofu burger is based on one that a Jewish-American vegan friend often made for Shum in California. "It started out as a folksy sandwich, so we kept it that way," he added.

Huang and Shum are part of a generation pioneering new Asian foods, but their tofu philosophy is Asian old school: tofu is not just a meat substitute. It is valuable in its own right. This chapter offers recipes that I hope you'll play with. The dishes are fun and you can serve them as snacks, appetizers, or part of a light meal.

Spicy-Sweet Fried Tofu Buns DOU FU GUA BAO

MAKES 12 BUNS, TO SERVE 4 TO 6 AS A SNACK OR AN APPETIZER

When making Eddie Huang's tofu twist on traditional *gua bao*, I fry up *agedashi dofu* (page 70) and slide the result into Chinese steamed buns. He garnishes with Taiwanese sweet chile sauce, but I prefer to doctor homemade Thai sweet chile sauce with soy sauce. I also offer extra sauce on the side for dipping the buns while eating. The sweet-and-salty ground peanuts add contrasting nutty richness.

For the folded buns, which are like Chinese steamed rolls, buy them at a Chinese market in the refrigerated and frozen sections. Or, follow tester Lea Yancey's lead and make your own; she used the unfilled steamed bun instructions in *Asian Dumplings*. Ideal buns are about 3 inches wide.

14 to 16 ounces firm tofu

Salt

2 cups very hot or just-boiled water

1/2 cup Thai Sweet Chile Sauce (page 210)

1 tablespoon plus 1 teaspoon light (regular) soy sauce

2 tablespoons unsalted roasted peanuts, chopped

1 1/2 teaspoons dark brown sugar

12 Chinese folded buns, fresh or thawed

Canola oil for deep-frying

About 1/3 cup potato starch

1 generous tablespoon chopped cilantro, leafy tops only

1 Cut the tofu crosswise into 2 blocks, then cut each block crosswise into 6 chunky matchbooks, each about 1 1/2 inches by 2 inches by 1/2 inch. Put all 12 pieces of tofu in a bowl. Dissolve 1 1/2 of teaspoons salt in the hot water, then pour over the tofu to cover. Set aside for 15 minutes.

2 Meanwhile, in a small bowl, combine the Thai sweet chile sauce with the soy sauce. Reserve 2 to 3 tablespoons of it in a saucer or small dish that you can later dunk the tofu into. Set aside.

In a small food processor, grind the peanuts, brown sugar, and a pinch of salt to the texture of coarse cornmeal. (Or, use a mortar and pestle.) Transfer to a small bowl and set near the sauce.

3 Before frying the tofu, bring a pot of water to a boil to reheat the buns. Line 2 steamer trays with parchment paper and add the buns. Steam the buns over gently boiling water until soft, fluffy, and hot to the touch, about 5 minutes. Turn off the heat but keep the lid on to ensure that the buns remain soft and warm.

4 Pour off the water from the tofu, then transfer the pieces to a non-terry dishtowel or double layer of paper towels placed atop a plate. Let drain for about 15 minutes.

5 Meanwhile, heat 1 inch of oil in a wok or saucepan over high heat to between 360° and 370°F. As the oil heats up, blot excess moisture from the tofu. Because the starch can turn gummy if it sits too long on the tofu, wait until the oil temperature approaches 340°F before dredging each piece of tofu in the potato starch to coat well. Shake off excess starch, then set aside on a plate near the stove.

When the oil is ready, fry the tofu in 2 or 3 batches, sliding the pieces into the oil, then gently stirring with chopsticks or a skimmer to fry evenly and prevent them

CONTINUED

Spicy-Sweet Fried Tofu Buns

CONTINUED

from sticking. They should be very crisp after 2 to 3 minutes. It's okay if they get just slightly golden. Drain the fried tofu on a paper towel. Return the oil to temperature before frying another batch.

6 For each bun, press one side of a piece of tofu into the saucer of sweet chile sauce, then put the tofu into the bun, sauced side down. Spoon about 1 teaspoon of sauce on top of the tofu, then add a sprinkling of cilantro, then about 3/4 teaspoon of peanuts.

Serve the buns immediately, while the tofu is still warm and chewy-crisp. Let guests add extra sauce to their buns as they wish.

REFRESH NUTS AND SEEDS

To save time, I keep stashes of unsalted, roasted peanuts and toasted sesame seeds in the freezer for preparing Asian food. If their flavor has dulled when I need to use them, I revive them in a dry skillet over medium heat. When they have darkened a bit and are glistening from releasing some of their oils, I pull the skillet off the heat and let the nuts or seeds cool naturally. They're refreshed and ready for action.

Tofu Steak Burgers DOU FU HAN BAO

MAKES 4 BURGERS

The tofu burger at Wei Shum's California Grill in Taipei is not your typical vegetarian fare. There is no mock-meat patty but rather a thick slab of grilled or pan-seared tofu, and you can top it with bacon if you want to. Whether or not there's a porcine element, the tofu is upfront, tasty, and satisfying. Tester Sue Holt converted her husband to tofu with this Asian take on an American classic.

This recipe is built upon what's served at the restaurant. The most important thing is imbuing the tofu with flavor and savory depth. That's achieved through the seasonings and cooking. My preference is to use a cast-iron grill pan, but you can pan-sear the tofu steaks in a skillet for about 2 minutes per side. The glaze from the tofu eel (page 157) adds a terrific savory-sweet note. Feel free to vary the garnishes, toppings, and bread to have it your way.

Instead of discarding the marinade after using it, save it to eat with chilled, unadulterated tofu, or add rice vinegar to dress a sliced cucumber salad. Resist using super-firm tofu because it is too dense to absorb the flavors well.

Two 14- to 16-ounce blocks firm or extra-firm tofu
2 teaspoons sugar
2 pinches of black pepper
2 teaspoons fresh ginger juice (see Note, page 72)
1/4 cup light (regular) soy sauce
1 tablespoon dark (black) soy sauce
3 tablespoons sesame oil
1 tablespoon canola oil, plus extra as needed
4 hamburger buns or Kaiser rolls
Mayonnaise
Iceberg lettuce, for garnish
Sliced tomatoes, for garnish

OPTIONAL TOPPINGS

4 thin slices cheese, such as sharp Cheddar
4 slices cooked bacon, halved crosswise
3 tablespoons Sweet and Savory Tofu Eel Glaze (page 157) (best if no cheese is used)
1 avocado, pitted and sliced

1 Trim each rectangular block of tofu so that it is roughly a 4-inch square. Stand each square on its side and split it down the middle into 2 thick slabs. Each of the resulting 4 pieces of tofu will be a good 3/4 inch thick. There will be a soft cut side and a firmer uncut side. If you trim the tofu to obtain the thickness you want, do it on the cut side. Save the trimmed tofu for another use, or cut it into small squares for tofu mini burgers! Transfer the tofu to a 9-inch-square baking pan.

2 In a small bowl, combine the sugar, pepper, ginger juice, and both kinds of soy sauce, stirring to dissolve. Add the sesame oil and 1 tablespoon canola oil, then pour over the tofu. Turn each piece over to coat well with the marinade. Set aside, uncovered, at room temperature for 1 hour, turning the tofu midway. You can marinate the tofu for up to 2 hours, covered, at room temperature; turn it occasionally to evenly marinate. If the tofu marinates for too long, it may soften too much and become hard to handle during cooking.

3 Before cooking the tofu, toast the buns and have the mayonnaise, lettuce, tomatoes, and any toppings ready to go.

4 Heat a cast-iron grill pan over medium-high heat, brushing on a little oil for good measure. When the pan is hot enough to evaporate a bead of water upon contact, sear the tofu steaks for about 3 minutes per side.

Unless you have a huge pan, you'll be cooking the tofu 2 steaks at a time. There is no need to drain the steaks. Simply pick one up, let excess marinade drip off, then lay it in the pan, uncut side facing down. That side is firmer and will release easily. If you want a pretty side to show off, that uncut side should get cooked first.

To create fancy grill marks, let the tofu sear for about 2 minutes, when it typically releases easily, then use 2 spatulas to lift and rotate each steak by 90 degrees. Cook for 1 more minute before flipping the tofu with the aid of the spatulas. If you don't elect to turn the tofu, let it cook undisturbed for the entire 3 minutes.

During the last minute of cooking the second side, top it with the cheese (if using) to let it melt a bit. You can also reheat the bacon on the grill at this point, too. When done, transfer the tofu to a plate.

5 Spread mayonnaise on each half of the buns (or omit mayonnaise on the top half if avocado will be added). Top each bottom half of a bun with lettuce, tomato, and a tofu steak. Add a drizzle of the glaze, if you like. Then top with the bacon and avocado. Finish with the top half of the bun. Serve immediately.

Vegetarian Wontons in Chile Oil HONG YOU YUN TUN

SERVES 4 AS A SNACK, 6 TO 8 AS A STARTER

The original version of these little poached dumplings included pork, but tofu works as a straight meat substitute here because it's partnered with bold-tasting ingredients. It takes on the earthiness of the greens and the zippiness of the seasonings. Once cooked, the wontons get a luscious coating of soy sauce, garlic, and chile oil. It's a delightful mouthful to snack on or present as an elegant starter.

Whenever you plan to swap tofu for meat in dumpling fillings, be sure to squeeze and season it well. Or, follow the Korean lead in the *mandu* recipe on page 174 and use lots of tofu with a little meat. Feel free to try other kinds of leafy greens; if using frozen ones, you'll need to thaw and squeeze enough for 1/4 firmly packed cup. If you want to cut the richness of the sauce, sprinkle on a little unseasoned rice vinegar.

4 ounces tender leafy greens, such as mustard leaf, baby bok choy, or spinach

3 ounces firm tofu

Generous 1/8 teaspoon salt

1 pinch of white pepper

Scant 1/4 teaspoon sugar

1 1/4 teaspoons plus 1 tablespoon light (regular) soy sauce

1 teaspoon Shaoxing rice wine or dry sherry

1 teaspoon sesame oil, plus extra for garnish

3/4 to 1 teaspoon minced fresh ginger

1 small green onion, finely chopped, white and green parts

24 small (3-inch) square wonton skins

1 to 2 tablespoons Chile Oil (page 213), with chile flakes

2 tablespoons canola or fragrant peanut oil

1 small clove garlic, minced and crushed into a paste

3 or 4 sprigs cilantro, coarsely chopped

1 Fill a saucepan with water and bring to a boil. Add the leafy greens and blanch until tender. Drain immediately, flush with cold water, and drain well. Finely chop, put in a non-terry dishtowel or piece of muslin, and squeeze to remove excess moisture. You should have 1/4 cup firmly packed.

2 To make the filling, break up the tofu into 2 chunks. Put them in the dishtowel or muslin, then gather it up. Standing over a sink, firmly squeeze and massage; leave some moisture in the tofu but it shouldn't be wet. Unwrap and you should have about 2 ounces (roughly 1/4 cup).

Transfer the tofu to a bowl, then sprinkle on the salt, white pepper, sugar, 1 1/4 teaspoons soy sauce, rice wine, and sesame oil. Use a fork to combine. Add the chopped greens, ginger, and green onion, vigorously stirring to create a compact mixture. Cover the filling with plastic wrap and set aside for 30 minutes, or refrigerate overnight, returning it to room temperature before continuing. Makes about 1/2 cup.

3 Fill each wonton skin with about 1 teaspoon of the filling, creating simple triangles. For fancy nurse's caps, form a sealed rectangle, wet one of the folded corners, then bring the two folded corners together, crossing and pinching them together. Remember to moisten the edges with water before folding to seal well. As you work, put the finished wontons on a parchment paper–lined baking sheet that's been lightly dusted with cornstarch. When done, loosely cover with plastic wrap or a dry dishtowel to prevent drying.

4 To cook the wontons, fill a large pot halfway with water and bring to a boil over high heat. Add all the wontons, gently dropping each in. Use a wooden spoon to nudge them to prevent sticking. Return the water to a gentle boil and then lower the heat to medium to maintain it. After the wontons have floated to the top, let them cook for another 3 minutes, until they are translucent.

5 While the wontons cook, combine the remaining 1 tablespoon soy sauce, chile oil, canola oil, and garlic on a serving plate or shallow bowl. Taste and make any flavor adjustments. Add a touch of sesame oil for nutty goodness, if you like. Set near the stove.

6 Use a slotted spoon or skimmer to scoop out the wontons from the pot, pausing above the pot to allow excess water to drip back down. Put the wontons in the dish with the sauce and toss gently to coat. Sprinkle with chopped cilantro and serve immediately.

Tofu, Pork, and Kimchi Dumplings MANDU

MAKES 24 TO 30 DUMPLINGS, TO SERVE 3 OR 4 AS A LIGHT LUNCH, 6 AS AN APPETIZER

Koreans love big flavors but when it comes to dumplings (*mandu*), and they often incorporate mashed tofu to create soft, delicate results. In most cases, the tofu acts as a binder and vehicle for the other seasonings. This dumpling filling, however, is mostly tofu. My inspiration came from Seoul Gom Tang, a hole-in-the-wall Korean restaurant in Oakland, California. After polishing off two orders of *mandu* with a friend, I asked the waitress about the filling. In a sweet, motherly fashion, she responded, "Tofu, pork, and just a *little* kimchi."

The restaurant used purchased wrappers and steamed their dumplings. When making these at home, I found that commercial skins can quickly dry up after steaming so I opted for poaching the dumplings and presenting them in a shallow dish. These dumplings can also be panfried like pot stickers. The dipping sauce is a quickie version of the tangy soy-pickled chiles and garlic that often accompanies *mandu*. Kimchi that's slightly aged (stinky) will impart the best flavor. Tester Georgia Freedman-Wand used young kimchi and suggested adding an extra tablespoon.

DIPPING SAUCE

1/2 teaspoon sugar

1 1/2 tablespoons Korean or Japanese soy sauce

1 1/2 tablespoons unseasoned rice vinegar

1/4 cup water

1/2 clove garlic, thinly sliced

1 jalapeño pepper, cut into thin rounds

8 ounces firm tofu

1/4 teaspoon plus 1/8 teaspoon salt

1/8 teaspoon black pepper

1/4 teaspoon plus 1/8 teaspoon sugar

1 1/2 teaspoons Korean or Japanese soy sauce

1 1/2 teaspoons sesame oil

1/2 teaspoon finely grated fresh ginger

1 clove garlic, minced and crushed into a paste

2 tablespoons lightly packed finely chopped green onion (white and green parts) or Chinese chives

2 tablespoons lightly packed finely chopped napa cabbage kimchi, mature kind preferred

3 ounces ground pork, fattier kind preferred, coarsely chopped to loosen

24 to 30 pot sticker (gyoza) dumpling wrappers

1 For the dipping sauce, in a small bowl, stir together the sugar, soy sauce, vinegar, and water. Add the garlic and jalapeño. Set aside to develop the flavors. The sauce can be made a day in advance, covered, and left at room temperature.

2 For the filling, break up the tofu into 3 or 4 chunks. Put them in a non-terry dishtowel or piece of muslin, then gather it up. Standing over a sink, firmly squeeze and massage; leave some moisture in the tofu, but it shouldn't be wet. Unwrap and there should be about 5 1/2 ounces (2/3 cup packed). Transfer to a bowl.

Sprinkle on the salt, pepper, sugar, soy sauce, and sesame oil. Use a fork to mash and combine. Add the ginger, garlic, green onion, kimchi, and pork, then vigorously stir and mash to create a compact mixture. Cover and set aside for 30 minutes, or refrigerate overnight, returning to room temperature before using. You should have about 1 1/4 cups.

3 Fill each dumpling wrapper with about 2 teaspoons of filling. Depending on the size and elasticity of the skin, you may be able to add a bit more than that. Brush the edge with water and seal to form a half-moon. To form a favorite Korean dumpling shape that's akin to a big hug, hold the dumpling by its two sealed ends. Fold the round sealed edge upward, then wet one of the ends with a dot of water. Bring the ends together as if they're arms and overlap their hands. Press them firmly flat together. (If you plan to panfry the dumplings, make the half-moon, then form 3 or 4 pleats along the rim. See the Note for cooking instructions.)

As you work, put the finished dumplings on a parchment paper–lined baking sheet that's been lightly dusted with flour. When done, loosely cover with plastic wrap or a dry dishtowel to prevent drying.

4 Fill a large pot halfway with water and bring to a boil over high heat. Add half the dumplings, gently dropping each one into the pot and immediately nudging it with a wooden spoon to prevent sticking. Gently cook the dumplings for about 6 minutes, adjusting the heat as needed, until the dumplings have floated to the top, look glossy, and are puffed up and somewhat translucent. Use a slotted spoon or skimmer to scoop the dumplings from the pot, pausing over the pot to let excess water drip back down before putting the dumplings in a shallow bowl or on a plate. Cover with a large inverted bowl to keep warm.

Return the water to a boil and repeat to cook the remaining dumplings. When done, return the first batch to the pot and reheat for a minute or two. There is no need to reboil.

5 Serve the hot dumplings immediately with the dipping sauce in a communal bowl. Invite guests to spoon some of the sauce onto and into the dumpling, or just dunk it and eat. The pickled chiles and garlic are terrific with the dumplings.

NOTE

To panfry the dumplings, use a nonstick skillet. Add enough oil to film the bottom and heat over medium-high heat. Brown the dumplings on two sides, 1 to 2 minutes each. Partially cover with a lid or piece of aluminum foil to minimize cleanup, then add about $1/3$ cup water. Cover with the lid, lower the heat slightly, and let the water bubble away until it is mostly gone, 5 to 6 minutes.

After 4 minutes, move the lid or foil so that it is slightly ajar to allow steam to shoot out from underneath. When you hear sizzling noises (a sign that most of the water is gone), remove the lid. Let the dumplings fry for another minute, until the bottoms are brown and crisp. Turn off the heat, wait for the cooking action to cease, and then use a spatula to transfer the dumplings to a serving plate.

Chinese Chive and Pressed Tofu Turnovers JIU CAI HE ZI

MAKES 8 TURNOVERS, TO SERVE 8 AS A SNACK OR AN APPETIZER

These chewy-crisp pockets of goodness are fun to make and even better to eat. They are a popular Chinese snack filled with the slight garlicky bite of Chinese chives and the savory depth of seasoned pressed tofu. Clear cellophane noodles add body and egg binds the ingredients together. Some cooks add dried shrimp, but I prefer to avoid muddling the flavors.

The turnovers are a great snack or can be served with a bowl of soup, plate of dumplings, and/or a salad. Use regular grocery store flour for the best results. The bit of oil in the dough yields a slightly rich finish.

DOUGH

10 ounces (2 cups) unbleached all-purpose flour, plus
    extra for dusting
1/2 teaspoon salt
Scant 2/3 cup warm water
4 teaspoons canola oil

1 small bundle (1.3 ounces) cellophane noodles, soaked in
    hot water to soften, drained well, and finely chopped
4 to 5 ounces (2 pieces) homemade Seasoned Pressed Tofu
    (page 38) or purchased brown (baked) pressed tofu,
    finely chopped (generous 1 cup)
1 1/2 cups chopped Chinese chives or green onion, green
    and white parts
3/4 teaspoon salt
1/4 to 1/2 teaspoon white pepper
1/2 teaspoon sugar
1 tablespoon cornstarch
1 tablespoon sesame oil
1 large egg
Canola oil for panfrying

1 To prepare the dough in a food processor, put the flour and salt in the processor. Combine the water and oil in a measuring cup. Remove the feed tube and run the machine, adding liquid in a steady stream through the feed tube. Let the machine run for 20 to 30 seconds after a ball of dough forms; don't worry about the straggly bits. Transfer to a work surface.

Or, make the dough by hand. Set a bowl atop a kitchen towel to prevent slippage, then put the flour and salt in the bowl. Make a well in the center. Use a wooden spoon or bamboo rice paddle to stir the flour while adding the water and oil. Add water by the teaspoon if the dough feels dry. Gather the dough and all the bits into a ball.

2 Regardless of method, knead the dough, adding flour as necessary. Work machine-made dough for about 2 minutes and handmade dough for about 8 minutes. The finished dough should feel smooth and be elastic. Place the dough in zip-top plastic bag and seal tightly, expelling excess air. Let rest at room temperature for at least 15 minutes and up to 2 hours. After resting, the dough can be used right away for the turnovers. Or, refrigerate it overnight and return it to room temperature before using.

3 Meanwhile, make the filling. Combine the noodles, tofu, and chives in a bowl. In a smaller bowl, stir together the salt, white pepper, sugar, cornstarch, and sesame oil. Add the egg to the seasonings and mix well, then pour into the bowl with the noodles and tofu and combine well. You should have 2 packed cups. Set aside.

CONTINUED

Chinese Chive and Pressed Tofu Turnovers

4 Make the turnovers in 2 batches. Working with half of the dough, cut it into 4 pieces. Roll each piece into a ball, then smack it down to form a 3-inch-wide disk. Dust both sides with flour.

Use a rolling pin to form a 6½-inch-wide circle, sprinkling on flour as needed. Roll from the center to the edge, giving the dough a quarter turn after each pass. Don't worry if the result is not perfect. Maintaining a "belly" (a thicker area) in the center is not important here.

5 For each turnover, scoop up a packed ¼ cup of the filling and center it on a dough circle. Spread the filling out toward the edge closest to you, leaving a 1-inch border. Bring the upper edge of dough over to meet the lower edge of the dough to form a half-moon. Gently pat the turnover to evenly distribute the filling. Then press the edges closed and use your thumb to seal well. (If the dough does not self-seal, wet the edge with a bit of water.) Check the other side to ensure a good seal. If you want an even, neat edge, invert a bowl over the rim, press, and use a knife to trim off excess dough.

Lightly dust the bottom and put the turnover on a parchment paper–lined baking sheet. Cover with a dishtowel to prevent drying. Repeat to fill and shape the remaining turnovers before working on the other half of the dough. (Once you get the hang of it, panfry the turnovers in pairs as you roll, fill, and seal them.)

6 Pour about ¼ cup of oil into a large nonstick skillet to film the bottom. Heat over medium heat.

Panfry the turnovers in pairs for 3 to 4 minutes per side, flipping them with 2 spatulas when they are crisp and golden brown. They should gently hiss and sizzle while frying; adjust the heat if they don't. Because the turnovers rise up as the second side cooks, that side will not brown all over. Near the end, you can use tongs to hold each turnover upright to cook its spine.

Drain and cool on a rack placed atop a baking sheet. If you want, slide the baking sheet into a warm oven to keep warm as you fry the remaining turnovers. Add more oil as needed and adjust the heat between each batch.

When done frying all of the turnovers, you can make them extra crisp by refrying at high heat for 30 seconds per side. Cut in half or quarters and eat with chopsticks or out of hand.

These turnovers lose some of their charm with refrigeration, so enjoy them the day they are made. You can prepare them several hours in advance, loosely cover them with parchment or plastic wrap, and keep them at room temperature. Reheat them atop the rack in a 350°F oven for 12 to 15 minutes, until hot and crisp. They will turn a lovely golden.

Spiced Chickpea Crepes with Soybean Paneer TOFU CHILLA

MAKES 10 TO 12 CREPES, TO SERVE 4

A chilla is a popular Indian snack that's full of flavor and texture. When the batter is loaded with shredded vegetables, the result is thick and pancakelike. I prefer a thin chilla that's filled like a crepe. Actually, depending on how you fold a chilla (also spelled cheela), you may have something that looks like a taco or an enchilada.

One of the most popular chilla fillings is a mixture of paneer, tomato, and onion. Some modern Indian cooks substitute tofu as a type of "soybean paneer." That approach works really well if you grate super-firm tofu into thick shreds. As the tofu warms up during cooking, it softens to reveal its natural richness, becoming practically indistinguishable from paneer.

Chilla batter is usually made of garbanzo bean flour (besan), available at South Asian, Middle Eastern, and health food markets, or soaked and ground mung beans. I like the ease of using the flour and lighten it with rice flour (Asian and non-Asian brands work), which also helps crisp the crepes. Chillas are terrific as snacks but can be also be part of a breakfast, lunch, or brunch.

6 ounces super-firm tofu

BATTER
6 ounces (1 1/2 cups) garbanzo bean flour
2 1/4 ounces (1/2 cup) rice flour
1 teaspoon cayenne
1 teaspoon ground cumin
Scant 1 teaspoon salt
About 1 1/2 cups water

1/3 cup chopped red onion, rinsed to reduce harshness and drained well
1 Roma tomato, seeded and chopped
2 or 3 green Thai or serrano chiles, chopped
1 1/2 tablespoons chopped cilantro leaves
1/4 to 1/2 teaspoon salt
3 to 4 tablespoons canola oil
2/3 cup Green Chutney (page 218)

1 Despite this being super-firm tofu, let it drain. Put the block on a non-terry dishtowel or double layer of paper towels. Set aside for about 15 minutes.

2 Meanwhile, make the batter. In a bowl, stir together the garbanzo bean flour, rice flour, cayenne, cumin, and salt. Gradually whisk in the water. Pass the batter through a coarse-mesh strainer to smooth it out. You should have about 2 1/4 cups. Set aside.

3 Blot the tofu dry. Use the largest holes on the grater to grate it into thick strands; some crumbles are fine. Transfer to a bowl and add the red onion, tomato, chiles, cilantro, and salt. You should have about 2 cups of filling.

4 Heat 1/2 teaspoon of the oil in a medium nonstick skillet or griddle over medium-high heat. Wipe the oil off with a wadded-up paper towel. The crepe batter will cook better when there's just a bit of oil on the cooking surface. After this initial oiling, you may need just a few drops of oil between crepes.

CONTINUED

Spiced Chickpea Crepes with Soybean Paneer
CONTINUED

For each crepe, stir the batter until there is no more drag, then use a ladle (a wide shallow one works like a charm) to pour a scant 3 tablespoons of batter onto the skillet. Work the bottom of the ladle in a spiral pattern from the center to the edge to spread the batter out to a 5- to 6-inch circle. Drizzle about 1/2 teaspoon of oil around the edge of the crepe.

Then put a good 2 tablespoons of the filling on top. Distribute the filling on one half of the crepe if you want to fold it over like a taco. Or, center the filling if you want to fold the crepe up like an enchilada.

Let the crepe cook for about 2 minutes, until the bottom is crisp and golden or golden brown. Peek underneath with a spatula to check on its progress. These are thin crepes and do not need to cook on the other side. When done, fold the crepe in half or fold in the sides to cover the filling. The crepe may crack a bit at the folds if it has crisped a lot. Transfer to a rack to cool while you make the remaining crepes. Expect the crepes to soften a bit during cooling.

Regulate the heat to prevent the crepes from browning too quickly. If the batter thickens as you work, stir in water by the 1/2 teaspoon. If you have a large griddle, you can make 2 crepes at a time.

5 These crepes are best hot or warm but are fine as a cold snack within a couple hours of being made. Serve with the chutney and eat with a fork or out of hand.

Fried Shrimp Tofu Skin Rolls XIA FU PI JUAN

MAKES 8 ROLLS, TO SERVE 4 TO 6 AS A SNACK

Many of the recipes in this chapter feature tofu as a filling, encased by a dumpling wrapper or tucked into a bun. A Cantonese dim sum favorite and Vietnamese rice plate side dish, this chewy-crisp treat showcases the reverse. Partially-dried rounds of tofu skin (*dou fu pi*, page 11) functions as a pliable wrapper to envelop a fragrant shrimp filling. It's a nifty use of tofu, but better yet, the rolls can be fried in advance and revived in the oven, which makes them perfect for entertaining.

Shell and devein the shrimp for the tastiest results; "E-Z peel" shrimp has a flabby flavor and texture. Worcestershire sauce was introduced to China in the 1800s and a similar kind of black vinegar often accompanies these rolls.

FILLING

8 ounces medium or large shrimp, peeled and deveined
Salt
1/8 teaspoon white pepper
3/4 teaspoon sugar
Scant 1 teaspoon cornstarch
1 teaspoon oyster sauce
1 teaspoon sesame oil
1 teaspoon Shaoxing rice wine or dry sherry
2 tablespoons finely chopped green onion, white and
    green parts
2 tablespoons finely chopped bamboo shoot

1 tofu skin round, 24 inches in diameter
1 tablespoon all-purpose flour mixed with 2 1/4 teaspoons
    water
Canola oil for deep-frying
Chinese black vinegar or Worcestershire sauce

1 To make the filling, refresh the shrimp by putting them in a colander and tossing them with a liberal amount of salt. Rinse immediately under lots of cold water and drain well. Blot dry with paper towels.

2 Coarsely chop the shrimp, then transfer to a bowl. Add a very generous 1/8 teaspoon of salt, then the pepper, sugar, cornstarch, oyster sauce, sesame oil, and rice wine. Put into to a small or regular-size food processor and grind into a stiff and relatively coarse paste; it should not be uniformly smooth because you want a little texture. Transfer to a bowl and stir in the green onion and bamboo shoot. Cover and set aside for 15 to 30 minutes to develop the flavors, or refrigerate overnight, before using. Use at room temperature or cold. You should have about 1 cup.

3 Unfold the tofu skin and use scissors to cut it into 8 pie-shaped wedges. The manufacturer's folds are great guidelines for cutting. Trim and discard the dried wrinkly edges. Don't worry if the wedges are not evenly sized. Slide the cut tofu skin into a large plastic zip-top bag to prevent drying. Have the cut tofu skin, shrimp paste, and flour paste at your work area. Divide up the shrimp paste into 8 portions, each about 2 tablespoons.

4 To make each roll, place a tofu skin wedge on your work surface, curved edge closest to you. Position a portion of the shrimp paste in the center, about 1 1/2 inches from the bottom. Spread the shrimp paste into a rectangular layer, about 4 inches long and 1 1/4 inches wide. Bring up the lower edge to mostly cover the filling. Then gently crease each of the sides before folding them inward. Finally, gently roll up the skin. Stop when there are 2 to 3 inches left. Use your finger to spread the flour paste on that triangular area, then finish rolling up the skin. The paste seals the roll. Set aside, with the pointy tip facing down to maintain the seal, as you repeat this process to make 7 more rolls. Expect the rolls to get wrinkly wherever the flour "glue" was applied.

5 Into a deep skillet or wok, pour enough oil to a depth of 1½ inches and heat over medium-high to about 340°F. If you don't have a deep-fry thermometer, stick a *dry* bamboo chopstick into the oil; if it takes about 1 second for bubbles to rise to the surface and encircle the chopstick, the oil is ready.

Fry the rolls in 1 or 2 batches; in a 14-inch wok, you can fry all the rolls at once. After adding the rolls, lower the heat to medium to prevent the oil temperature from skyrocketing. Fry for 4 to 5 minutes, turning frequently, until crisp, rich golden, and opaque. Though the rolls will turn golden soon after they're in the oil, aim for a longer frying time to help them remain crisp longer. Little bubbles will form on the surface of the tofu skin. Drain briefly on paper towels and then cool on a rack placed atop a baking sheet. Return the oil to temperature if you are frying a second batch.

As the rolls cool, they deflate and turn chewy-crisp. The tofu skin will go from being opaque to translucent.

6 Serve the rolls immediately after frying, while they remain crisp and hot. Or, let them cool, cover them with plastic wrap, and keep at room temperature for up to 3 hours. To revive and reheat, keep the rolls on the rack and bake in a preheated 350°F oven or toaster oven for about 6 minutes, turning midway, until they are crisp and opaque in most places.

To serve, use scissors or a knife to cut each into 3 or 4 pieces. Present with the black vinegar for guests to use as a tangy dipping sauce. They can dunk the rolls into the vinegar or dribble it on. Enjoy with chopsticks or as a finger food.

NOTE

What to do with all those leftover rounds of tofu skin? You can break them up into pieces and deep-fry them into tofu chips or drop them into soup such as the chicken and tofu soup on page 86. They can also be cut up for a batch of Spicy Yuba Ribbons (page 139).

Stir-Fried Thai Noodles PAD THAI

SERVES 2 AS A MAIN DISH, 4 WITH 2 OR 3 OTHER DISHES

The real pad Thai, without the orangey-ness of ketchup, is a splendid stir-fry of chewy noodles seasoned by a nuanced tamarind-based sauce and punctuated by small rods of fried pressed tofu. The tofu functions like croutons and offers a wonderful meatiness to what is traditionally a no-meat affair. In *Thai Street Food*, David Thompson describes pad Thai with fresh shrimp as a gentrified version.

In Thailand, dense cakes of pressed tofu, made yellow by turmeric, are cut up and deep-fried in advance by pad Thai vendors, who then throw a handful into the noodles during cooking. You can do that or shallow-fry them as I've suggested below. The pounded dried shrimp and finely chopped salted radish and peanuts lend savory depth and texture. Head to a Chinese or Southeast Asian market for the dried shrimp, noodles, and preserved salted radish (also called "salted turnip"). You'll find those ingredients in the refrigerator case, dried noodle section, and dried and preserved vegetables aisle, respectively.

Feel free to double or triple the seasoning sauce and fry the tofu in advance. Refrigerate the sauce for up to a month and the tofu for a good week. Use them to quickly satisfy your pad Thai urges.

7 ounces dried medium (1/4-inch-wide) flat rice noodles

3 ounces homemade Spicy Lemongrass Pressed Tofu or Seasoned Pressed Tofu (pages 39 and 38), or purchased brown (baked) pressed tofu

1/2 to 3/4 teaspoon ground, toasted dried red chile flakes or ground cayenne

1/4 cup packed light palm sugar or light brown sugar

2 tablespoons water

1/4 cup Tamarind Liquid (page 217)

1/4 cup fish sauce

2 tablespoons dried shrimp

6 tablespoons canola oil

1 large shallot, chopped (about 1/3 cup)

2 large eggs

2 tablespoons preserved salted radish, rinsed, dried, and chopped

8 Chinese chives, or 12 whole slender green onions, cut into 1-inch lengths

2 cups bean sprouts (about 5 ounces)

3 tablespoons unsalted roasted peanuts, coarsely chopped

1 or 2 limes, quartered

1 Place the noodles in a bowl and cover with hot tap water. Let them soak for 15 to 20 minutes, until they are pliable and opaque. Drain in a colander and set aside.

2 Cut the tofu into 1/4-inch-thick pieces, then crosswise into short rods like the fat end of a chopstick. You should have a good 1/2 cup. Set aside near the stove.

3 In a small saucepan, stir together the chile flakes, palm sugar, water, tamarind liquid, and fish sauce. Taste it and make an initial adjustment for a balance of tart, sweet, briny, and slightly spicy. Bring to a simmer, stir to dissolve the sugar, then remove from the heat. Set aside to cool, then retaste and adjust as needed. You should have about 3/4 cup.

4 Put the dried shrimp in a small mesh strainer and rinse under hot water for 30 to 45 seconds, until pliable. Drain well, then, in batches, pound the shrimp with a mortar and pestle into a fluffy texture. Set aside near the stove.

Ready all the other ingredients near the stove. To avoid overloading the wok, cook the pad Thai in 2 batches. Except for the peanuts, split the other ingredients in half. Divide the peanuts into thirds to save some for garnish.

5 Heat a large wok or skillet over medium-high heat. Add 3 tablespoons of the oil, then half of the tofu. Shallow-fry it for 1 to 2 minutes, until crisped. Use a slotted spoon to transfer to a plate. Add more oil if needed, then repeat to fry the remaining tofu.

6 Lower the heat slightly, then add half of the shallot. Cook, stirring constantly, for 5 to 10 seconds, until aromatic. Then crack an egg into the pan. Stir it gently to form an amorphous omelet. Fry for 30 to 45 seconds, until the egg sets and is no longer runny.

Increase the heat to medium-high, add half of the noodles, and stir to combine, breaking the egg apart. Add half of the sauce and keep stir-frying for about 1 minute, until the noodles have softened. Add a portion of fried tofu, dried shrimp, salted radish, Chinese chives, and bean sprouts. Toss in a third of the peanuts. Stir-fry for another minute, until the bean sprouts have just wilted. If the noodles seem dry, splash in a bit of water.

Transfer to an individual plate or platter, depending on how you'll be serving. Repeat to make the second batch.

7 Garnish with the remaining chopped peanuts. Offer lime wedges on the side for guests to squeeze on. Enjoy with chopsticks or fork and spoon.

Foxy Tofu Noodle Soup KITSUNE UDON

SERVES 3 OR 4

Japanese food is full of symbolism to enhance its enjoyment. For example, the name of this popular preparation reflects the Japanese fondness for foxes (*kitsune*), a common subject of their folklore. Whether the foxes are good or evil, they are portrayed as being fond of fried tofu. In fact, the burnished brown color of the soy-simmered fried tofu that's featured in this dish can be described as *kitsune iro* (fox color). Cooks cut the tofu into triangles to mimic fox ears. Animal imagery aside, this simple noodle soup is a satisfying snack that won't weigh you down.

Udon noodles are sold at specialty grocers, health food stores, and Asian markets. I prefer the fresh or frozen ones over the dried variety. The packs often contain three flats of noodles, enough for this recipe. When making the dashi stock, use 5 cups of water and add extra *kombu* kelp and dried bonito flakes. You'll have enough for the simmered tofu and broth.

4 cups Dashi Stock (page 215)

3/4 to 1 teaspoon salt

2 tablespoons light-colored soy sauce, such as Japanese usukuchi shoyu or light (regular) soy sauce

2 tablespoons mirin

3 large rectangles or 6 large squares Soy-Simmered Fried Tofu (page 46)

3 packages fresh or thawed, frozen udon (about 21 ounces total)

1 green onion, white and green parts, thinly sliced on the diagonal

3/4 to 1 teaspoon peeled grated fresh ginger

Japanese seven-spice pepper blend (shichimi togarashi), optional

1 Bring a pot of water to a boil to cook the noodles. Meanwhile, put the dashi in a saucepan and add the salt, soy sauce, and mirin. Bring to a boil, then lower the heat and cover to keep hot.

2 Cut the tofu into 12 triangles. If you have rectangles, halve each crosswise and then cut each half diagonally. With squares, just cut each piece once on the diagonal. Set aside.

3 Heat the noodles in the boiling water for about 2 minutes, until chewy soft. Drain well and divide among the serving bowls; there's no need to flush the noodles with cold water.

4 Return the broth to a boil. Heat the tofu pieces in the broth for about 20 seconds, then use a slotted spoon or skimmer to transfer them to the bowls, arranging them on top.

Return the broth to a boil, then ladle it into the bowls. Garnish with the green onion and serve immediately. Offer the ginger on the side in a small dish and invite guests to add it and/or a sprinkle of the spice blend.

Sushi Rice in Tofu Pouches INARI-ZUSHI

MAKES 6 LARGE OR 12 SMALL POUCHES, TO SERVE 3 OR 4

When I met up with Elizabeth Andoh in Tokyo, she suggested that we head to a nearby Takashimaya department store's *depachika* (fancy downstairs food hall) for *inari-zushi*. I respectfully agreed, even though my American experiences with the iconic rice-stuffed tofu pouches were of overly sweet tofu pouches filled with so-so sushi rice.

Elizabeth led me to a favorite vendor. The *inari-zushi* were twice the size of the ones back home and shaped as pillows, triangles, and open bags. More importantly, the tofu had great flavor and the rice was seasoned by many things, including vegetables, salmon, herbs, and seaweed. I was converted—and full—after sampling five of them.

I began making them at home, enjoying them for lunch and on road trips. A beginner-level sushi, they are easy to make. Take liberties with seasoning the mildly tart sushi rice, but at minimum, use sesame seeds and chopped pickled ginger.

SUSHI RICE

1 cup short-grain rice

1 cup plus 2 tablespoons water, filtered or spring preferred

1-inch-square dried kelp (kombu), optional

1/2 teaspoon sea salt

1 tablespoon sugar

2 tablespoons unseasoned rice vinegar

SEASONING OPTIONS (CHOOSE AT LEAST TWO)

1 1/2 teaspoons freshly toasted sesame seeds, any kind

1 tablespoon packed finely chopped pickled ginger (blot dry before chopping)

1 1/2 to 2 tablespoons chopped Savory Kelp Relish (page 216)

3 tablespoons Savory Okara Crumbles (page 163), or 1/4 cup seasoned salmon flakes (see Note)

3 or 4 green *shiso* leaves, finely chopped, or generous 1 tablespoon finely chopped fresh herbs, such as dill, red perilla, and Thai lemon basil

6 large squares or 12 medium rectangles or triangles Soy-Simmered Fried Tofu (page 46)

1 For the sushi rice, if you have a preferred method of cooking rice or ratio of rice to water, follow it to prepare the 1 cup of rice with the kelp square. Otherwise, put the rice in a bowl and wash in 3 to 5 changes of water, until the water is mostly clear. Drain in a mesh strainer, shaking it to remove excess water. Transfer the rice to a 1-quart saucepan and add the water and kelp.

Bring to a boil (or near-boil) over medium-high heat. Give a stir with chopsticks to loosen rice grains sticking to the bottom. Lower the heat slightly so the rice simmers vigorously. Cook the rice, stirring 2 or 3 times, for a few minutes, or until most of the water appears to have been absorbed and the surface looks glossy and thick. Small craters may form on the surface.

Decrease the heat to low, cover, and cook for 10 minutes. Then turn off the heat and let the rice sit for 15 to 20 minutes to firm up and finish cooking.

2 Meanwhile, combine the salt, sugar, and vinegar, stirring to dissolve. Set aside. Choose a low, round vessel to efficiently cool and season the rice. Japanese cooks traditionally use a flat-bottomed wooden tub. I've used a 9-inch-wide shallow bowl (ceramic or plastic), glass pie pan, or nonstick cake pan. Find something that will enable you to spread the rice out and quickly introduce air, and set it atop a dishtowel to prevent skidding. Have a rice paddle and handheld fan (or piece of cardboard) nearby.

3 When the rice is done, use chopsticks to fluff and turn it out into the cooling vessel, spreading the rice out; discard the kelp. You'll first partially cool the rice, then work in the vinegar, and finish with a final cooling. This process takes about 10 minutes.

For the initial cool-down, use the paddle to gently and quickly cut and fold the rice. Go up and down and across to

break up clumps of rice and occasionally turn and fold the grains to cool them. Work the paddle with one hand and fan the rice with the other hand. Pausing is okay.

When steam no longer rises from the rice, set the fan aside. Drizzle on half of the vinegar and continue cutting, turning, and folding the rice to season it. After the grains have absorbed the vinegar, they will feel sticky and glisten. At that point, add the remaining vinegar and work it in.

It's hard to fan and stir the ingredients together so I prefer to resume the fanning after all the vinegar has been incorporated. The rice will still feel warm, so keep working the paddle and start fanning again. Taste the rice and when it is at room temperature, you are done! Cover with plastic wrap and leave at room temperature; a little condensation may gather. In moderate (65° to 75°F) conditions, the rice can sit for a good 5 hours. Resist refrigerating it because it will harden.

4 Before stuffing the soy-simmered fried tofu pouches, use paper towels to blot away excess moisture from each one. Set aside near your work area.

Transfer the rice to a large bowl and add your seasonings. Use the rice paddle to gently mix. Divide the rice into 6 large or 12 small portions, depending on the number of your pouches.

Lightly moisten one hand to roughly shape a rice portion into a ball. Put the rice inside one of the tofu pouches, breaking it up to distribute the rice, and then packing it in. You should fill the pouch up to about 1/3 of an inch of the

CONTINUED

Sushi Rice in Tofu Pouches

rim. Swap some rice as you work because the pouches are likely of uneven sizes.

With triangular pouches, close the open ends, one overlapping the other, and place the pouch upright, seam side down. Rectangular and square pouches may be similarly closed or presented unclosed like an open bag (if you like, partially fold back the rim to reveal the inside).

Repeat to fill all the pouches, placing the finished ones on a platter. Serve immediately or cover with plastic and keep at room temperature for up to 4 hours.

NOTE

For the seasoned salmon flakes, use 1 ounce hot smoked salmon. Coarsely chop the fish to break it up, then rub it with your fingers into small pieces to yield about 1/4 cup. Transfer to a small skillet and add 1/8 teaspoon sugar, 1/2 teaspoon sake, and 1/4 teaspoon Japanese or Korean soy sauce. Cook over medium heat for 5 to 8 minutes, stirring and mashing the fish into flakes. When the salmon has darkened and is nearly dry and fluffy, remove from the heat and let cool. It is ready to be used or refrigerated in an airtight container for up to a week.

Fried Rice with Fermented Red Tofu KHAO PHAT TAO HU YI

SERVES 4 WITH 2 OR 3 OTHER DISHES

Tofu can be used as a meat substitute in fried rice but it can also function as a seasoning. In this Thai fried rice, fermented red tofu lays a savory foundation for the remaining flavors to work off of. The remarkable earthy, briny, spicy combination coaxed tester Fanny Pan and a friend into eating the entire batch.

For good fried rice, the grains need to be dryish. Spread freshly made rice on a baking sheet and then refrigerate it overnight, until it barely sticks to your fingers when you pick it up. I occasionally turn the rice during the chilling to evenly dry it. Use your hands to loosen up clumps of rice before measuring it out for this recipe.

Generous 1 tablespoon mashed fermented red tofu

1^{1}/$_{2}$ teaspoons sugar

2 teaspoons fish sauce

1/4 teaspoon white pepper

8 ounces boneless pork shoulder or chicken thigh, cut into peanut-size pieces

4 cups cold cooked rice

2 tablespoons fermented red tofu brine

2 large green onions, green part only, cut into rings to match the meat

1 or 2 green Thai or serrano chiles, chopped

1 large egg

Salt

1 teaspoon plus 3 tablespoons canola oil

2 tablespoons finely chopped garlic

2 tablespoons finely chopped fresh ginger

1 shallot, finely chopped (1/4 cup)

2 tablespoons chopped cilantro, leafy tops only

1 small cucumber, seeded and sliced, optional

1 lime, quartered, optional

1 Mash the fermented tofu with the sugar, fish sauce, and white pepper. Taste and add extra sugar or fish sauce to create an intensely savory-sweet flavor. Add the pork, stir to combine well, and set aside.

2 In a bowl, toss the rice with the brining liquid from the fermented tofu. Add the green onion and chiles to the bowl. Beat the egg with a pinch of salt. Set near the stove.

3 Heat a wok or large nonstick skillet over medium-high heat. Add 1 teaspoon of the oil, then pour in the egg, swirling it to form a pancake. Let it cook for 45 to 60 seconds, until it is no longer runny and is set. Flip it over and cook for another 15 seconds, until done. Transfer to a plate. When cool enough to handle, 3 or 4 minutes later, quarter and cut into pieces a smidgen smaller than the meat. Set aside.

4 Heat a wok or large nonstick skillet over medium-high heat. Add the 3 remaining tablespoons oil, then the garlic, ginger, and shallot. Stir-fry for a good 2 minutes until the aromatics no longer smell raw and are beginning to turn golden. Add the pork, and stir-fry for 2 minutes until just cooked through. Add the rice, and keep stir-frying for 1 to 2 minutes, until it has heated through. The rice will soften and feel weightier in the wok as it revives from its cold, dry state. Add the egg, and continue to work the rice to combine well and heat through, about 30 seconds. Taste and add salt, if needed.

5 Turn off the heat, stir in the cilantro, then transfer to a platter. Garnish with the cucumber slices and lime wedges, or offer them on the side. Enjoy in the Thai tradition with fork and spoon.

AMAZING TRANSFORMATIONS
Sweets and Dessert

Hands down, one of my favorite sweets is a bowl of soft tofu pudding garnished with gingery sugar syrup. The custardy delight from my youth is a reminder of how brilliant simple cooking can be.

I grew up on tofu pudding purchased from Viet markets and tofu shops (*lo dau phu*, literally tofu oven or kiln), which also made loaf-shaped block tofu. Over the years, I developed the Vietnamese-American habit of touching the tofu before buying it. If it felt warm, it was super fresh and I would grab several loaves for dinner and a few tubs of tofu pudding for dessert or an afternoon snack. Just-made tofu is a prized find like any other artisanal product. You eat lots of it as soon as you can.

After I began making tofu at home, a family friend introduced me to former City Councilman Tony Lam, a partner in Dong Phuong Tofu factory, located right off of Bolsa Avenue, the main drag of Little Saigon in Westminster, California. There are several tofu shops in the area and Dong Phuong is among the best. When Lam extended an invitation for a tour, I instantly accepted.

He greeted me at the door with the polish of a politician. In his seventies and smartly dressed, Lam quickly escorted me through the retail

193

storefront and kitchen into the production area. Whereas the shop and kitchen were quiet, the factory was a cacophony of sound—he had to raise his voice to be heard. He led me to a platform surrounding giant vats of soaked soybeans. It was a Willie Wonka-esque scene. The sweet aroma of soy milk filled the air. Machinery and equipment loudly ground beans, spewed out the solids, and cooked up the rich white liquid. Foam quivered atop a humongous percolating kettle of soy milk. Conveyor belts moved along bottles of it. Half a dozen workers diligently and rhythmically tended to the milk, curds, and whey. Light flooded in from a garage door–size opening on a far wall, illuminating the steam emanating from all the activity.

With a grand waving gesture over the factory floor, Lam proclaimed, "We use stainless steel equipment to produce tofu with clean flavors." He then passed me on to plant engineer Simon Wang, who showed me a diagram of the entire operation and guided me through the production space. He explained that owners Tony and Thu Dang aimed to produce traditional Vietnamese tofu but with modern equipment. Tony Dang's family had made tofu in Vietnam for decades and he wanted to continue that trade in America, establishing Dong Phuong over twenty years ago.

Born in Taiwan and trained as an engineer, Wang himself knew little about tofu. However, after spending two months observing Dong Phuong's daily operations, he designed an efficient production line that did not compromise the Dangs' high standards. "This tofu is meant to be eaten fresh. It is best in the first one or two days," he said. Instead of using *nigari* or gypsum, Dong Phuong surprisingly adheres to a long-standing Viet method: employing leftover fermented whey as a coagulant.

"We save some of the whey and let it sour for about three days. It is a good reuse of a resource and gives the tofu a slightly tangy traditional flavor that our customers expect," Wang explained.

Most of the action was around a carousel of six soy milk cauldrons that, at first glance, looked like a mini amusement park ride. Soy milk pumped into the slowly rotating cauldrons. One man agitated the milk and added the whey. On the other side of the carousel, another man scooped up the curds into narrow cloth-lined molds, each about 36 inches long and 4 inches wide. With spellbinding precision and force, he pulled, folded, and pressed on the cloth to shape the curds into a thick white log. After a quick machine pressing, the hot tofu was unmolded at a different station, where two workers cut and encased it in plastic. The finished loaves were placed on baking sheets and slid into speed racks, ready for retail.

Finally, Wang showed me how tofu pudding was made. Coagulant was mixed in a huge stockpot and then placed under a spigot of hot soy milk. The gushing soy milk stirred up the coagulant and then things set. It was simply a large-scale version of what I do at home.

Upon my departure, the woman working the storefront insisted on gifting me tofu pudding, fried tofu, and fresh tofu. Her sincere friendliness reminded me of all the people I'd met while working on this book. Tofu holds special meanings for Asian people. At Dong Phuong, it was about family legacy, evolving traditions, and modern engineering. For other people I'd met, tofu spoke of heritage, religion, ecology, and community.

This chapter of sweets expresses the continuous reinvention of tofu. The recipes begin with an old-fashioned preparation and then segue into modern uses, most of which are tasty Asian interpretations of Western favorites.

Sweet Tofu Pudding with Ginger Syrup DOU HUA

SERVES 6

For many people in Asia, this is the only sweet tofu dish that they know. It is so iconic that it's generically referred to as "dessert tofu." Delicately soft and rich, this Chinese preparation is presented in shallow bowls, oftentimes simply dressed with gingery sugar syrup.

In Asia, sweet tofu pudding is sold in snack shops and by street vendors. Abroad, it's sold at Asian markets catering to Chinese and/or Southeast Asian customers as well as artisanal tofu shops such as Dong Phuong (see page 193). You'll find tofu pudding on dim sum menus, too. But you can easily make it at home to enjoy it whenever you want.

Sweet tofu pudding can be served chilled or with crushed ice, though it's typically presented warm. To ensure that the tofu is well flavored by the syrup, I use a fair amount of ginger and sugar, preferring the flavor of the rock sugar sold at Chinese markets.

Feel free to dilute the syrup or tweak its flavor. For example, add a few pandan leaves or substitute almond extract (about a teaspoon) for the ginger, or use dark palm sugar instead of the light brown sugar. Vary the texture by garnishing each serving with boiled skinned peanuts, adzuki beans, and/or mung beans. Buy the tofu pudding or make it yourself from the recipe on page 30.

6 tablespoons sugar, or 2 1/2 ounces yellow rock sugar, crushed (wrap in a towel and use a hammer or meat tenderizer)
3/4 cup packed light brown sugar
Chubby 2 1/2 inches fresh ginger, peeled, cut into 1/4-inch-thick coins, and smashed with the broad side of a knife
About 3/4 cup water
4 cups tofu pudding

1 To make the syrup, put both types of sugar, ginger, and water in a small saucepan. Cook over medium-high heat, stirring to dissolve the sugar. Bring to a boil, then lower the heat to vigorously simmer for about 5 minutes, until fragrant and slightly thickened. (If you are using rock sugar, it will likely not dissolve until the simmering is over; add water to extend the cooking, if needed.)

Remove from the heat, and set aside, uncovered, to cool completely and concentrate in flavor. If not serving right away, transfer to a jar, straining out the ginger, if you like. Refrigerate and return to room temperature before using. Makes 1 generous cup.

2 If your tofu pudding is cold, reheat it as directed in step 3 of the soft tofu pudding recipe on page 30; or, see page 11 of the buying guide if you purchased the pudding. If lots of sudsy bubbles are at the surface, use a metal spoon to scrape them off. Then scoop up shards of the tofu into individual serving bowls.

Whey will inevitably accumulate in the bowls. Pour it out if you don't want it to dilute the syrup or let its delicate tanginess contribute to the overall flavor. Top with about 3 tablespoons of syrup and enjoy with a spoon.

Tofu Blancmange with Cured Pineapple and Lime

SERVES 4 TO 6

New York–based chef Pichet Ong is a master at presenting hybrid desserts that surprise and titillate. When I told him about this tofu project, he immediately volunteered to contribute this recipe for blancmange, a simple jelled pudding that originated in France.

Ong used tofu and soy milk in lieu of the traditional milk. For the fruit garnish, he slow-roasted pineapple and then added fresh lime zest. The remarkable result is suitable for an afternoon tea or fancy dinner party.

Commercial silken tofu comes in varying textures; use moderately soft silken tofu, such as Nasoya brand, to obtain a tender and delicate texture.

6 ounces silken tofu

1 tablespoon cold water

1 1/4 teaspoons unflavored gelatin

1/2 cup unsweetened soy milk

1/4 teaspoon salt

3/4 to 1 teaspoon vanilla extract

2 to 3 tablespoons plus 1/4 cup sugar

2 large egg whites

12 ounces fresh pineapple chunks

1/3 cup firmly packed light brown sugar

1 tablespoon dark rum or vanilla extract

1 whole lime

1 Cut the tofu into 1-inch chunks and drain on paper towels for 5 minutes; you should net about 5 1/2 ounces (2/3 cup). Meanwhile, put the water in a large bowl, sprinkle on the gelatin, then stir to combine. It will resemble silicone. Set aside.

2 Transfer the tofu to a blender and add the soy milk. Blend for about 1 minute until smooth and silky. Pour the mixture through a mesh strainer into a medium saucepan. Add 1/8 teaspoon of the salt, 3/4 teaspoon vanilla, and 2 tablespoons of the sugar. Taste and adjust the vanilla and sugar, aiming for a mild sweetness. Bring to a boil over medium-high heat, whisking constantly.

3 Remove from the heat, then pour the mixture into the bowl of gelatin, whisking to melt the gelatin. If you're in doubt, whisk a little longer. It won't harm things. Set aside to cool to room temperature, about 45 minutes. Put the egg whites in a bowl and set aside to bring them to room temperature.

4 When the tofu mixture has cooled, use an electric mixer (a hand-held one works great on this small quantity) on low speed to whisk the egg whites until frothy. With the mixer running, slowly add the remaining 1/4 cup sugar; this should take about 1 minute. Continue beating until the egg whites are slightly shiny and stiff peaks form 4 to 5 minutes.

Give the tofu and soy milk mixture a final whisking, then use a spatula to gently fold in the egg whites. Divide among 4 to 6 serving glasses or small dishes.

Refrigerate for at least 4 hours or as long as 2 days. After about 2 hours, the blancmange should be set and you should cover each with plastic wrap.

5 Meanwhile, make the pineapple. Position a rack in the middle of the oven and preheat to 250°F.

Cut the pineapple into 1/2-inch pieces. Aim for perfect dice but expect some pieces to be oddly sized due to the natural shape of pineapple. You should have roughly 2 cups. Transfer to a bowl, along with all the juices. Add the remaining 1/8 teaspoon salt, light brown sugar, and rum. Toss well, then transfer to a 9-inch square or 9 by 13-inch rectangular baking pan.

Bake for about 2 hours, stirring every 30 minutes, until the pineapple pieces look glazed and have shrunk by about a third. After taking the pan out of the oven, stir the pineapple to coat the pieces with any residual syrup in the pan. Set aside to cool completely.

Finely grate the peel of the lime onto the pineapple. Stir to distribute well, then transfer to an airtight container. You should have about 1 cup. Refrigerate for up to 2 weeks.

6 To serve, stir the pineapple, then spoon about 2 tablespoons of the pineapple on top of the blancmange. Serve the remaining pineapple on the side, or save it for another use, such as mixing into the tofu ice cream on page 198.

Essence of Tofu Ice Cream

MAKES ABOUT 3 CUPS

We often think of tofu ice cream in terms of flavors such as vanilla or chocolate but this one is all about tofu. After sampling several in Asia, I wanted to make my own. The ice cream is good alone but amazing when accented by savory garnishes; set out a variety for your guests to explore.

To experiment with the flavor, stir in vanilla extract by the 1/4 teaspoon after blending the mixture in the first step. For a tropical fruit twist, finely chop 1/2 cup of the cured pineapple from the blancmange recipe (page 196) and mix it in after freezing. Serve the ice cream with warm doughnut holes (page 203) for a whole bean experience.

Removing excess water from firm tofu intensifies its flavor, and adding unsweetened soy milk underscores soy's natural richness. I use purchased organic tofu and soy milk for making this ice cream. Select a Grade A dark amber or Grade B (very dark) maple syrup, as they lend deeper savor and contain more invert sugar, which makes the ice cream more scoopable. In a pinch, substitute agave syrup for maple syrup.

1 pound firm tofu

Scant 1/4 teaspoon salt

2 tablespoons sugar

9 tablespoons maple syrup, Grade A dark amber or
    Grade B preferred

1 cup plus 2 tablespoons unsweetened soy milk

TOPPING OPTIONS

1/4 teaspoon mild sea salt, such as Maldon or fleur de sel

1 to 2 teaspoons black sesame seeds, toasted

2 to 3 tablespoons Indonesian sweet soy sauce
    (kecap manis)

1 tablespoon Savory Kelp Relish (page 216)

1 Break the tofu into 6 to 8 chunks. Working in batches, put the tofu in a non-terry dishtowel or piece of muslin, then gather it up. Standing over a sink, firmly squeeze and massage, then unwrap and transfer to a blender. You should have about 11 ounces (1 1/3 cups packed).

2 Add the salt, sugar, maple syrup, and soy milk. Blend until silky. Strain through a fine-mesh strainer, discarding the solids. Cover and chill overnight to develop the flavor and thicken.

3 Freeze the mixture in your ice cream maker. Serve scoops of the ice cream with the toppings for guests to add their own. Advise them to sprinkle on a tiny amount of salt or crush the sesame seeds between their fingers before releasing them onto the ice cream; you can precrush the sesame with a mortar and pestle, too. For sweet-savory notes, they should lightly drizzle on the soy sauce. Extra-adventurous eaters can nibble on the salty kelp relish.

NOTE

For no-machine ice cream, tester Laura McCarthy used a method from davidlebovitz.com.

Tofu Tiramisu

SERVES 6 TO 8

When it comes to Western-style desserts, many Asian cooks do not consider tofu and dairy products to be mutually exclusive. It's acceptable for tofu to be used alongside butter, cream, milk, and cheese. This slightly boozy, flavorful tiramisu is a case in point.

In this recipe, the Japanese technique of combining regular tofu with soy milk and dark brown sugar (*kuro-zato*) creates a deep, round sweetness. Cream cheese and lemon juice mimic Italian mascarpone.

Many cooks in Asia employ slices of spongecake for tiramisu, but purchased Italian savoiardi biscuits (ladyfingers) are what I use. Choose crisp, not spongy, ones. When using tofu-based cream cheese, and add a brimming teaspoon of vanilla.

3/4 cup packed dark brown sugar
1/3 cup unsweetened soy milk
1 pound firm tofu
1/2 cup (4 ounces) cream cheese
2 teaspoons fresh lemon juice
2 tablespoons brandy
1 tablespoon plus 2 1/2 tablespoons dark rum
1 cup cold espresso or strong coffee
6 to 7 ounces (about 20 large) savoiardi biscuits
About 1 1/2 tablespoons unsweetened cocoa powder,
   Dutch-processed (alkalized) preferred

1 Put the sugar and soy milk in a small saucepan. Heat over medium heat, stirring constantly, until the sugar has just dissolved. Set aside to cool.

2 Break the tofu into 6 to 8 chunks. Working in batches, if needed, put the tofu in a non-terry dishtowel or piece of muslin, then gather it up. Standing over a sink, firmly squeeze and massage; unwrap and transfer to a food processor. You should have about 11 ounces (1 1/3 cups packed).

3 Add the sweetened soy milk, cream cheese, lemon juice, brandy, and 1 tablespoon of the rum. Whirl into a very smooth and silky mixture. It will thicken up as it sits.

4 Select an 8-inch square baking pan, casserole, or shallow plastic or glass container to hold the tiramisu. Combine the coffee with the remaining 2 1/2 tablespoons rum. Pour half of it into a shallow bowl.

One at a time, take a biscuit and turn it 2 or 3 times in the coffee to lightly soak. Put it in the pan with the flat (unsugared) side down. Line the bottom of the pan with the biscuits to create a fairly solid layer. As necessary, cut some of the biscuits. When done, sprinkle any leftover coffee over the biscuits.

Spread half of the tofu mixture, about 1 1/4 cups, on top of the biscuits, leveling it as best you can; an offset spatula helps. Sift or strain about 1 1/2 teaspoons of the cocoa over the top.

Repeat to make a second layer of biscuits and tofu mixture, and finish with another coating of cocoa.

5 Refrigerate the tiramisu, uncovered, for about 2 hours, to minimize the condensation that naturally forms; the cocoa layer will darken. Then cover and chill overnight (or even 2 nights) to let flavors bloom.

Before serving, refresh the top of the cold tiramisu with a final layer of cocoa. With a knife, cut the tiramisu into portions. Courageously slide a metal spatula under a portion and lift it out. Use another spatula to push it onto a serving plate.

Cashew and Cardamom Fudge SOY PANEER KAJU BARFI

MAKES 36 SMALL PIECES

Redolent with the richness of cashews and the perfume of cardamom, fudgelike *kaju barfi* is a favorite South Asian sweetmeat. Cooked-down milk, sugar, and ground cashews are combined into a concentrated paste that is seasoned with spices, then pressed into a pan and cooled.

This recipe replaces the milk and sugar with canned sweetened condensed milk and soy paneer (tofu). The modern Indian approach reduces cooking time and adds extra nutrients without compromising flavor and texture. Finely grating the tofu allows it to seamlessly merge with the other ingredients. Edible silver foil typically covers *kaju barfi,* but it remains gorgeous with the simple pistachio garnish.

8 ounces super-firm tofu

3 1/2 ounces unsalted raw cashew pieces or whole nuts

1 (14-ounce) can sweetened condensed milk

3/4 teaspoon ground cardamom

1 1/2 tablespoons chopped raw pistachios

1 Line an 8-inch-square pan with parchment paper to cover the bottom and one side. Set aside.

2 Wipe the tofu dry, then finely shred it using the smallest hole on the grater. Transfer to a bowl and set aside.

Put the cashews in a small or full-size food processor and grind to a texture resembling breadcrumbs or fine cornmeal. Add to the grated tofu and toss to combine.

3 To cook the fudge mixture, use a medium pan, such as 2-quart sauté pan. It's easier to evenly cook the ingredients in that kind of shallow pan. Pour in the sweet-ened condensed milk. Add the tofu and cashew mixture. Over medium heat, stir the ingredients together. Cook the mixture for about 15 minutes, stirring occasionally at the beginning as things heat up, and then frequently, and, eventually, constantly. Prevent scorching by scraping the bottom and sides as you stir. The mixture should not boil, but just thicken at a moderate speed. The mixture will transform into a rough mass resembling very thick, rough oatmeal. When stirring results in the mixture pulling away from the sides or slightly lifting off the bottom of the pan, it's done.

4 Remove from the heat and stir in the cardamom, then transfer the fudge to the lined baking pan. Spread it out evenly, then pat it flat. Sprinkle on the pistachio nuts and gently press into the mixture. Set aside to completely cool. Because this fudge is on the soft side, cover and chill for a few hours or overnight to make it easier to cut; if you're in a hurry, freeze until cold, about 15 minutes. The resting time also develops flavor.

5 Use the parchment paper on the side of the pan to help you remove the fudge. Place it on a cutting board and cut it into 36 small squares for bite-size portions. Or, aim for 16 to 20 large ones. Take liberties with shapes; triangles are easy to achieve, and diamonds are lovely and traditional.

Serve at room temperature or chilled. This fudge keeps well, covered, for up to 5 days in the refrigerator. You can freeze it for up to 1 month but it loses a touch of its oomph. I often eat the fudge as I cut it.

Gingery Chocolate Chip Cookies

MAKES ABOUT 3 DOZEN

These cookies and the tofu doughnuts that follow are prime examples of how Japanese cooks use soy milk lees (*okara*, page 27) for Western-style sweets. In fact, one evening during my visit to Tokyo, food writer Mark Robinson took me to a bakery full of goodies made with tofu, soy milk, and *okara*. The chocolate chip cookies I sampled inspired these, which are a little cakey and chewy, with plenty of chocolate and ginger. Tester Laura McCarthy suggested substituting candied citrus peel, such as *yuzu*, for the ginger.

When I use soy milk lees in baked goods, they partially replace the eggs and flour in the original recipe. Because the lees can weigh things down with moisture, I add extra leavening and tinker with ingredient proportions to avoid compromising flavor and texture. The nutritional advantage of having *okara* in sweets is that you're adding fiber and protein. The ecological payoff is that you're not wasting a valuable food source.

5 ounces (1 cup) bleached or unbleached all-purpose flour
1 teaspoon baking powder
1/4 teaspoon salt
1/2 cup (1 stick) unsalted butter, at room temperature
2 ounces (1/3 cup) packed fresh or thawed soy milk lees,
    at room temperature and fluffed if super compacted
1 cup plus 2 tablespoons packed light brown sugar
1 large egg
1 teaspoon vanilla extract
1 cup bittersweet chocolate chips or mini-chunks, or
    coarsely chopped dark chocolate
2/3 cup chopped crystallized ginger

1 In a bowl, stir or whisk together the flour, baking powder, and salt. Set aside.

2 Using a stand mixer with the paddle attachment, mix the butter, soy milk lees, and sugar until well combined. Low or medium speed works best. Add the egg and vanilla, then beat until they disappear. Add the flour mixture, half at a time, and beat at low speed until just combined. Stir in the chocolate chips and ginger. (Or, make the dough with a hand-held mixer or entirely by hand.) Cover the dough and chill for 2 hours, or even overnight. That firms up the dough, making it easier to shape, and helps develop its flavor. (The dough can also be frozen for up to 3 months. Thaw before using.)

3 Before baking, adjust an oven rack to the middle position. Preheat to 325°F. Line 2 baking sheets with parchment paper.

4 Working with a generous tablespoon of dough at a time, roll the dough into 1¼-inch balls, placing them 2 inches apart on the baking sheet.

5 Bake the cookies, one sheet at a time, for 16 to 18 minutes, until they are light golden brown, have puffed and spread to resemble low domes, and the outer edges start to harden and show some golden brown color. Cool the cookies on the baking sheet. They will deflate a bit.

Once cooled, use a metal spatula to remove them from the parchment paper. Eat right away if you want a chewy, slightly crisp cookie. Or store in an airtight container for several days, during which time the cookies will keep their delightful chewiness. These freeze well, too.

Okara Doughnuts

Japanese cooks do wonders with soy milk lees (*okara*), and these delectable doughnuts are a trendy treat that's often sold at boutique Japanese department store food halls. With the lees added, these seem less sinful than regular doughnuts. They are delicately crisp and pillowy yet toothsome—like a cross between yeast and cake doughnuts. The flavor is not too sweet, reflecting the Asian palate.

Deep-frying is required here, but little oil is absorbed. Use new or very fresh oil for the best clean flavor and texture. These doughnuts are at their peak the day they are fried. They reheat well and are about 85 percent of their prime selves the next day. Remember to bring ingredients to room temperature before using. Regular cow's milk can be used in lieu of the soy milk.

1/4 cup warm (about 110°F) water

1 package instant (fast-acting) dry yeast

1/2 cup lukewarm (about 100°F) unsweetened soy milk

1 large egg

4 ounces (2/3 cup) packed fresh or thawed soy milk lees, at room temperature and fluffed if super compacted

1/2 teaspoon salt

3 tablespoons sugar

131/8 ounces (21/2 cups plus 2 tablespoons) bleached or unbleached all-purpose flour, plus more as needed

6 tablespoons (3/4 stick) unsalted butter, cut into 6 chunks and left at room temperature until very soft but not melting

Canola oil for deep-frying

Sugar or glaze (see Note)

1 To make the dough in a stand mixer, put the warm water into the mixer bowl, then sprinkle the yeast on top. Let it soften for 1 minute. Stir to combine, then add the soy milk, egg, soy milk lees, salt, and sugar.

Put the paddle attachment in place, then beat the ingredients at medium-low speed to combine well, about 15 seconds. Add the flour, a third at a time, to form a soft, sticky dough. Beat in the butter, a chunk at a time; wait for about 10 seconds between additions for the butter to disappear into the dough. Increase the speed to medium and beat for 1 to 2 more minutes to mix the ingredients well and develop a little elasticity. The resulting dough will be sticky and look ragged. Don't expect it to clean the bowl. About a third of the dough will gather up around the paddle. Resist adding more flour at this point.

Scrape the ragged dough onto a well-floured work surface. Knead for about 1 minute to smooth out the surface and work in just a bit more flour. The dough should be slightly sticky.

(Alternatively, make the dough by hand. Use a large bowl and a wooden spoon to stir and then beat the ingredients together; knead the dough for several minutes, until it's smooth and velvety.)

2 Place the soft dough in a clean, lightly oiled bowl. Cover with plastic wrap, and let stand in a warm place until the dough has doubled, about 11/2 hours. (Or let the dough rise in the refrigerator overnight for breakfast doughnuts. Roll and cut the dough cold; the rising time takes about 45 minutes.)

CONTINUED

Okara Doughnuts

3 Turn the dough out onto a lightly floured work surface. Press gently to expel air. Roll it out to a thickness of about 1/2 inch. Use a 2 3/8- or 2 1/2-inch round doughnut cutter to stamp doughnuts and holes, dipping the cutter in flour between stamps. (Or use 2 1/2-inch round and 1-inch round cutters to first cut the large circles, then the smaller holes.) Gather up the remaining dough, knead it a few times, reroll, then cut more; avoid overworking the dough. Repeat once more, using your hands to free-form the last doughnut from the remaining bits.

Place the doughnuts and holes on 2 floured baking sheets, spaced 1 1/2 inches apart. Loosely cover with plastic wrap, and let rise until slightly puffy and nearly double in size, 25 to 30 minutes.

4 Heat 2 inches of oil in a 5- to 6-quart pan over medium-high heat to about 360°F. (Use a deep-fry thermometer, because the oil temperature may vary a lot during frying. If you don't have one, test-fry a doughnut hole; it should be golden brown in about 1 1/2 minutes.) Nearby, have a baking sheet with a rack placed inside.

Fry the doughnuts and holes in batches of 3 or 4, picking up each one with your fingers or a spatula and carefully sliding it into the oil. You may find it easier to fry the doughnuts separately from the holes, which bob around more and require lots of attention.

Fry the doughnuts for about 2 minutes, turning midway, until golden brown. Doughnut holes will take about 30 seconds less; use a slotted spoon to press and rotate the holes in the oil to ensure even frying. When done, use a slotted spoon or chopsticks to transfer to the rack to drain and cool. Return the oil to temperature before repeating.

5 When cool enough to handle, about 10 minutes, roll the doughnuts in sugar or glaze them. These are best within hours of being made. If you want to serve them warm, keep the doughnuts uncoated for up to 5 hours, then reheat them in a 350°F toaster oven for about 5 minutes, flipping them midway, before decorating. Leftovers should be covered and kept overnight at room temperature and reheated. After reheating, let the doughnuts briefly cool before coating them.

NOTE

There are endless ways to enhance and decorate doughnuts. Below are a few suggestions; ready these while the doughnuts rise or cool. Each makes enough to decorate one batch.

Basic sugar: Put about 2/3 cup sugar in a bowl. Shake and roll to coat each doughnut.

Cinnamon sugar: Combine 2/3 cup sugar with 2 teaspoons ground cinnamon in a bowl. Shake and roll to coat each doughnut.

Chocolate glaze: Put 4 ounces dark or bittersweet chocolate chips (or finely chopped dark chocolate) in a bowl. Whisk in 6 tablespoons hot soy milk or whole milk to melt the chocolate. Add 1 1/2 cups sifted confectioner's sugar, a third at a time, and whisk until smooth. To use, dip one side of each doughnut in the glaze, then gently lift and twist to remove the excess. Place the doughnut, glazed side up, on a rack to set; once the chocolate stops dripping, add shredded coconut or chopped unsalted roasted nuts, if you like. If the glaze thickens too much before you use it, whisk in some warm soy milk. Or, set the bowl over a hot water bath and whisk to thin out.

BASICS

Chinese Sweet Fragrant Soy Sauce

MAKES ABOUT 10 TABLESPOONS

Whereas the Japanese seasoned soy sauce on page 208 is full of umami depth, this Chinese one is loaded with aromatic spices. I first tasted *fu zhi jiang you* in Sichuan, where it was the signature sauce for a popular poached dumpling. The alluring sweet-spicy notes added earthiness without over-powering the delicate gingery morsels.

In my home kitchen, I replicated the Sichuanese soy sauce and found it to be a remarkable garnish for chilled and warm tofu. Feel free to vary the spices, but note that they're basically the ones that comprise Chinese five-spice blend. Use a thick-capped mushroom for extra flavor.

1/4 cup dark (black) soy sauce

1 1/2 tablespoons light (regular) soy sauce

2/3 cup water

1 large dried shiitake mushroom, cut into 5 or 6 pieces (use a cleaver)

1/4 cup firmly packed dark brown sugar

1-inch piece cassia bark or cinnamon stick

1 star anise (8 robust points)

1/2 teaspoon fennel seed

1/2 teaspoon Sichuan peppercorn

Chubby 1/2-inch section fresh ginger, unpeeled and crushed with the flat side of a knife

1 In a small saucepan, combine the soy sauces, water, and mushroom. Set aside for at least 1 hour or overnight to rehydrate the mushroom (the longer soak will yield deeper flavor).

2 Add the sugar, cassia, star anise, fennel seed, Sichuan peppercorn, and ginger. Bring to a boil over medium heat, stirring to dissolve the sugar. Lower the heat to gently simmer for 10 to 12 minutes, until the sauce has reduced by about a quarter and is slightly syrupy. Coat the back of a spoon with the sauce and run your finger through it. The line should hold.

3 Set the pan aside to cool. The flavors will concentrate further. Strain through a mesh strainer, then discard the solids. Store the soy sauce in a capped jar and refrigerate for up to 6 months. Return to room temperature before using.

Japanese Seasoned Soy Concentrate

MAKES A GENEROUS 3/4 CUP

Using naturally occurring glutamates to create umami and coax out the maximum flavor from ingredients is basic to Japanese culinary craftsmanship. Called *banno-joyu*, this seasoned soy concentrate—which can be used straight, diluted with water or dashi stock (page 215), or added to marinades—makes for extra tasty tofu dishes. It is phenomenal with freshly made tofu.

For a healthy amount of natural glutamates, soak the larger amount of dried kelp and a big, thick-capped shiitake mushroom.

16 to 20 square inches dried kelp (kombu), cut into 3 or 4 pieces (use scissors)

1 large dried shiitake mushroom, cut into 5 or 6 pieces (use a cleaver)

2/3 cup Japanese or Korean soy sauce

1/3 cup sake

3 tablespoons water

3 tablespoons sugar

2 tablespoons mirin

1/2 cup lightly packed dried bonito flakes (katsuo-bushi)

1 In a saucepan, put the dried kelp, mushroom, soy sauce, sake, and water. Set aside for at least 1 hour, or better yet overnight, to release the deepest flavors from the dried ingredients.

2 Add the sugar and mirin. Bring to a simmer over medium-high heat, then lower the flame to gently simmer for 12 to 15 minutes, until the sauce has reduced by about a quarter and is slightly syrupy. Coat the back of a spoon with the sauce and run your finger through it. The line should just hold.

3 Turn off the heat. Scatter in the dried bonito flakes. Let the sauce sit for 2 or 3 minutes for the fish to release its smoky brininess; resist waiting longer or the sauce will be overly fishy. Some of the flakes will settle to the bottom.

4 Position a muslin- or coffee filter–lined mesh strainer over a jar. Pour the seasoned soy sauce through the strainer. Press on the solids to extract extra liquid, then discard the solids. (The kelp is not reusable here.) Let the soy concentrate sit at room temperature until completely cool. Cap tightly and refrigerate for up to 6 months.

VARIATION: VEGETARIAN SEASONED SOY CONCENTRATE

The concentrate is not as strong, and it lacks the bonito's smokiness, but it still tastes good. Soak 2 thick-capped dried shiitake mushrooms instead of 1, and soak for at least 12 hours to draw out more flavor.

VARIATION: QUICK SEASONED SOY CONCENTRATE

This simplified version will not have as much depth as the ones above but it will do in a pinch. For a generous 1/4 cup, in an extra small saucepan, stir together 4 teaspoons sake, 2 tablespoons sugar, and 3 tablespoons soy sauce. Bring to a boil, remove from the heat, and set aside to cool before using.

Korean Seasoned Soy Sauce

MAKES ABOUT 1/3 CUP

You won't call tofu bland when it's garnished with this robust Korean sauce named *yangnyumjang*. Raw garlic, ground red chile, and green onion contribute a nice bite that's mollified by unctuous sesame oil and crushed sesame seeds. A mainstay in Korean cuisine, this delicious sauce is terrific with chilled or panfried tofu (pages 54 and 103). Its thick consistency means it will not slide off tofu like normal soy sauce would.

2 tablespoons Korean or Japanese soy sauce

1 tablespoon water

1¹/₂ teaspoons sesame oil

1 to 2 teaspoons sugar

1 clove garlic, minced

1 teaspoon Korean red pepper powder (gochu garu)

2 tablespoons lightly packed finely chopped green onion, white and green parts

2 to 3 teaspoons sesame seeds, toasted then crushed with a mortar and pestle

1 In a small bowl, stir together the soy sauce, water, sesame oil, and sugar, until the sugar has dissolved. Add the garlic, red pepper powder, green onion, and sesame seeds. Set aside for about 15 minutes for the flavors to develop. The sauce can be made in advance and refrigerated for up to a week.

2 This sauce can dramatically change its characteristics as it sits. Right before using, taste the sauce again and make any last-minute tweaks. You want a strong savory-spicy-slightly-sweet finish because the tofu that will be served with this is not highly seasoned.

Thai Sweet Chile Sauce

MAKES ABOUT 2 CUPS

Called *nam jim gai wan*, this mildly hot chile sauce is ubiquitous with Thai grilled chicken but is also popular with other foods, such as fried tofu. The ones you'll find in Chinese and Southeast Asian markets can be cloying. If you make it at home you can dial in heat and tang to suit yourself, and build more complex flavors.

Leave about a quarter of the seeds intact for a moderate amount of heat. Tester Lea Yancey makes a salad dressing out of the sweet chile sauce with some lime juice or vinegar and a bit of canola or vegetable oil.

1/3 cup coarsely chopped cilantro stems

2 cups water

3 to 4 tablespoons coarsely chopped garlic

4 ounces medium-hot red chiles, such as Fresno, mostly
    seeded (according to taste) and coarsely chopped

1/8 teaspoon salt

About 13/4 cups distilled white vinegar

11/3 cups sugar

1 Put the cilantro stems and water into a saucepan. Bring to a simmer and cook for 5 minutes. Remove from the heat and cover. Let steep for 20 minutes.

2 Meanwhile, use a small food processor to grind the garlic, chiles, and salt to a coarse texture. Set aside.

3 Strain the cilantro liquid through a mesh strainer. Measure the liquid. You should have about 13/4 cups. Transfer to a saucepan, preferably a shallow, wide one. Pour in the same quantity of vinegar as you have of cilantro liquid. Stir in the sugar and mixture of chile and garlic.

4 Bring to a boil over medium-high heat, then lower the heat and simmer until the volume has reduced by half; the amount of time this takes depends on the size of your saucepan. The resulting sauce should be slightly thick. Coat the back of a spoon and run your finger through it; the line should hold for only a few seconds. The sauce will thicken more and concentrate in flavor during cooling.

Remove from the heat and set aside, uncovered, to cool completely. Use immediately or transfer to a jar and refrigerate. Bring to room temperature before using.

Chile and Sichuan Peppercorn Mix

MAKES 1/3 CUP

I first encountered this fragrant chile mixture—with its crimson color, loamy texture, light toastiness, and mild punches of Sichuan peppercorn and salt—in Chengdu, where it was served to me alongside duck. Once back in the States, I recreated it with Korean *gochu garu* and found it to be fantastic with tofu. You can dip poached chicken or simple boiled vegetables in it, too. It complements all these other foods yet lets them shine.

3 tablespoons Korean red pepper powder (gochu garu)
3/4 to 1 teaspoon Sichuan peppercorn, toasted and ground
3/4 teaspoon white sesame seeds, toasted
1/2 teaspoon sea salt
2 tablespoons canola or fragrant peanut oil
1/2 teaspoon sugar

1 In a small bowl, combine the Korean red pepper powder, Sichuan peppercorn, sesame seeds, and salt. Put the oil in a small saucepan or skillet and heat over medium-high heat until just smoking.

2 Pour half of the oil over the chile powder mixture. Expect some foaming action on the surface. Then give the mixture a quick stir with a spoon. Pour the remaining oil over the mixture and stir again to moisten all the ingredients. Stir in the sugar.

3 Let cool for a few minutes, taste, and adjust the flavor with extra salt or sugar. The slightly loamy mixture is ready to use. Or, transfer to a small container, cap tightly, and store at room temperature for up to 2 days, or refrigerate for up to a week.

Fermented Tofu, Lemongrass, and Chile Sauce

MAKES 6 TABLESPOONS

Fermented tofu's pungent aroma makes it seem like a loner, but it actually plays well with other flavors. In this Vietnamese sauce called *nuoc cham chao*, savory fermented tofu gets blended with tangy lime juice, fresh chile heat, and citrusy lemongrass. The result does not overwhelm, and is perfect with foods such as the goat skewers and green onions on page 63 and with grilled vegetables, such as okra, asparagus, and summer squash. You can also serve it as a dip for tofu, whether unadulterated, grilled, or fried. Tester Diane Carlson used homemade fermented tofu (page 41) with fantastic, nuanced results.

2 tablespoons mashed fermented white tofu, with or
   without chile
2 teaspoons sugar
1¹/₂ teaspoons fresh lime juice
1¹/₂ teaspoons minced fresh lemongrass (use tender white
   and/or pale green parts)
1 Thai or serrano chile, minced
2 to 3 teaspoons water

1 Use a fork to break up the tofu in a small bowl. Add the sugar and lime juice, and blend well. Taste and add extra sugar or lime juice to balance the tangy, savory, and slightly sweet flavors.

2 Add the lemongrass and chile. Then stir in the water to thin out the consistency. Aim for a pourable result, like that of a creamy salad dressing. Set aside for at least 15 minutes to develop the flavors. Transfer to a jar and refrigerate for up to a week. Return to room temperature before using.

Chile Oil

MAKES 1¹/₄ CUPS

Nutty, spicy chile oil turns tofu dishes into wonderful brow-wiping experiences. Used in Chinese, Japanese, and Southeast Asian cooking, homemade chile oil is easy to prepare and better than purchased. Some cooks add aromatics, such as ginger, star anise, and Sichuan peppercorn, to the oil, but I like to keep the chile flavor pure.

Regular supermarket dried chile flakes work great but if you have a favorite variety that's fragrant with some heat, use it! Experiment by blending hot chile flakes with milder Korean red pepper powder for vibrant color. You can use canola, but the result will be spectacular with good peanut oil.

¹/₄ cup dried chile flakes or coarsely ground dried chiles
1 cup fragrant peanut oil

1 Put the chile flakes in a dry, 1¹/₂- or 2-cup glass jar.

2 Attach a deep-fry thermometer to a small saucepan and add the oil. Heat over medium-high heat until smoking hot (the temperature will top 400°F) and remove from the heat. Wait 5 to 7 minutes for the temperature to decrease to 325° to 350°F (drop a chile flake in and it should gently sizzle), and then pour the oil into the jar. The chile flakes will sizzle and swirl and then settle down.

Allow the oil to cool completely before covering and storing. Give it a couple of days to mature before using. Chile oil keeps well for months in the cupboard. Use just the infused oil or include the chile for extra liveliness.

FRAGRANT PEANUT OIL

Whenever you want to add a mild nuttiness to food, use a fragrant peanut oil. The kind sold at Chinese markets is semirefined and filled with the aroma of roasted peanuts. It is texturally light, has a high smoking point, and contributes a wonderful flavor to food. Lion & Globe peanut oil from Hong Kong is terrific, and so is Knife brand. Health food markets sometimes carry unrefined peanut oil; its smoking point is low, so take care. Supermarket refined peanut oil does not have the same taste or fragrance.

Chicken Stock

This is my standard, multipurpose Asian chicken stock. Quality chickens are a premium ingredient, so make the most of your investment. Save and freeze chicken parts as you prepare other dishes. Every once in a while, brew some stock. It freezes beautifully. In a pinch or as a shortcut, use the canned substitute suggested in the recipe.

> 4$^{1/2}$ to 5 pounds chicken parts or bones with some meat on them
> 4 quarts water
> 1 large yellow onion, quartered
> Chubby 3-inch piece fresh ginger, unpeeled and smashed with the flat side of a knife
> 2$^{1/2}$ teaspoons salt

1 Rinse the chicken under cool water to remove any bloody residue. Remove and discard any loose pieces of fat. Wielding a heavy cleaver designed for chopping bones, whack the bones to break them partway or all the way through, making the cuts at 1- to 2-inch intervals, depending on the size of the bone. This exposes the marrow, which enriches the stock.

2 Put the bones in a stockpot, add the water, and place over high heat. Bring almost to a boil, and then lower the heat to a simmer. For the next few minutes, use a ladle or large, shallow spoon to skim off and discard the scum that rises to the top. Add the onion, ginger, and salt and adjust the heat to maintain a simmer. You should have a constant stream of small bubbles breaking lightly on the surface. Let the stock cook, uncovered, for 2$^{1/2}$ hours.

3 Remove the pot from the heat and let stand undisturbed for 30 minutes, to allow the impurities to settle and congeal. Position a fine-mesh strainer (or a coarse-mesh strainer lined with cloth or paper towels) over a large saucepan. Gently ladle the stock through the strainer. Remove and discard the bones as they get in your way. Tilt the stockpot to ladle out as much clear stock as possible, then discard the sediment-laden liquid and any remaining bits at the bottom of the pot.

4 Taste the stock. If it is not as flavorful as you would like, simmer it to reduce the liquid and concentrate the flavors. Once you are satisfied with the flavor, let the stock cool completely, cover, and refrigerate for at least 8 hours, or until the fat solidifies on the surface. Remove and discard the fat. The stock is now ready to use. Or, store in a tightly closed container in the refrigerator for up to 1 week or in the freezer for up to 3 months.

Dashi Stock

MAKES ABOUT 4 CUPS

A little dashi goes a long way toward giving tofu dishes savory depth and a slight smokiness. It is one of the stealth ingredients in Japanese cooking, and it can be made days in advance.

There are only three ingredients involved in dashi. Just like for tofu making, use good water for the best, most delicate results. For information on *kombu* (dried kelp) and *katsuo-bushi* (dried bonito flakes) see the guide to ingredients on page 220. In a pinch, use instant *dashi no moto* powder, preferably one without MSG, and follow the manufacturer's instructions.

15 to 20 square inches dried kelp (kombu)

4 1/2 cups water, filtered or spring water preferred

1/2 cup lightly packed dried bonito flakes (katsuo-bushi)

RECYCLING KOMBU

Don't throw away that kelp when you finish making dashi stock. Follow the lead of frugal Japanese cooks and stockpile the kelp in the refrigerator or freezer, where you can keep it for several days or months, respectively. The kelp may be turned into a savory garnish (page 208) or used to line the hot pot for *tofu tousui* (page 89).

1 If there is a chalky film on the kelp, resist wiping or washing it off because it contains natural glutamates. Put the *kombu* and water in a saucepan and set aside for 15 to 20 minutes to extract flavor from the seaweed. For greater depth, soak for a few hours or cover and refrigerate overnight.

2 Heat over medium heat until small bubbles break at the surface and have formed at the sides of the saucepan; some white foam floating on the surface is okay. Remove the saucepan from the heat and scatter in the *katsuo-bushi*. The flakes will float at the top and then start sinking to the bottom of the saucepan. After waiting 3 to 4 minutes (it is okay if the bonito flakes are still floating on top; don't wait too long or the stock can become overly fishy), remove the kelp and reserve for other purposes. Line a mesh strainer with a coffee filter or muslin, then strain the stock.

The stock is ready to use, or you can refrigerate it in an airtight container for up to 4 days. Sediment gathering at the bottom of the storage container is not a sign of spoilage.

Savory Kelp Relish

This savory-sweet relish employs the kelp left over from making dashi stock (page 215)—a prime example of the thoughtful frugality of the Japanese kitchen. I like to chop the seasoned, preserved kelp (called *tsukuda ni kombu*) and mix it with rice for stuffing into *inari-zushi* (page 188). It's also a terrific, punchy garnish for silky tofu hot pot or even a chaser for ice cream (pages 89 and 198).

Remember to refrigerate or freeze the kelp from making dashi; the quantity here comes from two batches of dashi stock. Or, rehydrate 40 to 50 square inches of dried kelp (cut it into 6 pieces to make it more manageable) in water to cover for 20 minutes before diving into the recipe; you can use the soaking water for step 2.

> 80 to 100 square inches recycled kelp from making
>   Dashi Stock (page 215)
> 1¹/₂ cups water
> 2 tablespoons unseasoned rice vinegar
> 1 generous teaspoon sugar
> 1 teaspoon sake
> 3 tablespoons mirin
> About 3 tablespoons Japanese or Korean soy sauce

1 Use a knife to cut the kelp into thin strips, each about 1¹/₂ inches long and a scant ¹/₈ inch wide. Set aside.

2 In a small saucepan, bring the water to a boil over medium-high heat. Add the vinegar and kelp. Lower the heat and simmer for 6 to 10 minutes, until just tender. You should be able to easily bend a strip with its tips touching without breaking. Drain, rinse under cold water, and drain again.

3 Wipe the saucepan dry and add the sugar, sake, mirin, and soy sauce. Bring to a simmer over medium heat. Add the kelp and adjust the heat to maintain a gentle simmer for 10 to 15 minutes, stirring occasionally, until most of the liquid has evaporated and a light syrup remains. Take care not to burn the mixture. Near the end, taste and add a few pinches of sugar or a splash of soy sauce to adjust the flavors. Continue cooking, stirring to incorporate the extra seasonings.

When done, the kelp strips should be pleasantly tender and well seasoned. They will be dark brown and glazy, like tortoiseshell. Set the pan aside and let it cool to room temperature. The strips will shrink slightly and concentrate in flavor. Use or transfer to a small container and refrigerate for up to 2 months. Return to room temperature before using.

Tamarind Liquid

MAKES ABOUT 3 CUPS

I like to make this Southeast Asian and Indian staple in advance and keep it frozen in cubes, just like how some cooks freeze cubes of stock. Purchase tamarind pulp at Chinese, Indian, and Southeast Asian markets. Each sticky, thick dark brown slab is double-wrapped in plastic.

One 14- or 16-ounce package seedless tamarind pulp, broken up into 6 to 8 chunks
4 cups water

1 In a small saucepan, combine the tamarind pulp and water over medium heat. Bring to a simmer and cook, uncovered, for 10 minutes. Remove from the heat, cover, and set aside to steep and soften for about 30 minutes, or until you can easily press the pulp against the side of the pan with a fork.

2 Roughly break up the pulp to make it easier to strain; if cool enough, massage with your hand. Position a coarse-mesh strainer over a bowl and pour in the tamarind. Using a rubber spatula or metal spoon, vigorously stir and press the solids against the mesh to force as much of the pulp through as possible. Do this in two batches, if it is easier to work the pulp.

Return the pulp to the saucepan. Add some of the already-strained liquid, stir to loosen up more of the pulp, and then work it through the strainer again. Repeat this several times until the pulp is spent. Discard the fibrous leftovers. The resulting liquid will resemble chocolate cake batter.

3 Use the liquid immediately, or pour into ice-cube trays and freeze. Make a note of how much each tamarind cube contains; it is typically about 2 tablespoons. Once the cubes are frozen hard, transfer them to a zip-top plastic bag and store in the freezer for up to 6 months. To make sure you use the correct amount of the liquid, always thaw and measure it again before adding it to any recipe.

Green Chutney

MAKES 2/3 CUP

A simple, everyday relish from India, this condiment adds a wallop of fresh spiciness to foods such as fried tofu *pakora* fritters and chickpea crepes with soybean paneer (pages 71 and 179). Every cook has a different take on green chutney, and many add chopped onion and grated coconut. The straightforward approach here keeps the flavors bright. Green chutney is purposely hot, but you can seed the chiles or use a less alarming chile, such as jalapeño, for mellower results.

1 or 2 hot green chiles, such as Thai or serrano, chopped

1 clove garlic, chopped

1/2 teaspoon salt

1 teaspoon sugar

1 1/2 cups packed coarsely chopped cilantro stems and leaves

1/4 cup packed mint leaves

2 tablespoons fresh lime juice

1 Put the chile, garlic, salt, and sugar in a small food processor. Grind to a finely chopped texture, stopping the machine to scrape down the sides several times. Add the cilantro, mint, and lime juice. Process to a fine, thick texture like that of a thick pesto. The chutney should mound on a spoon. Occasionally stop the machine and scrape down the sides, if necessary.

2 Transfer to a serving bowl and set aside for 5 to 10 minutes to allow the chutney to bloom. Taste and adjust the flavors. Lime and sugar will cut the heat, but you do want a nice salty, sweet, sour, hot, pungent finish. Add water by the teaspoon if the chutney is too thick; however, it should not be liquid.

Set it aside for at least 30 minutes for the flavors to mellow and meld and for the texture to slightly thicken. This chutney is at its zippy best when freshly made, but it can be refrigerated for up to 2 days.

INGREDIENTS

To prepare many of the foods in this book, you just need to venture to a supermarket, health food store, or specialty grocer, where ethnic food aisles are better stocked than ever. But some ingredients will require a trip to an Asian market, where the selection will naturally be broader.

CHILE BEAN SAUCE

This salty, spicy Chinese condiment makes tofu dishes such as *ma po* tofu and pressed tofu and peanuts (pages 101 and 138) sing. Chiles, fava beans, and sometimes soybeans are the main ingredients. Freshly made chile bean sauces are bright red; more mature ones lean toward maroon. Inconsistent labeling can make shopping difficult. At Chinese markets, look in the condiment aisle for jars, bamboo containers, and/or soft plastic packages. It can be called chile bean paste, broad bean chile sauce/paste, *dou ban jiang*, or *toban jhan*. "Pixian" on the label signals a Sichuan version. Taiwanese brands, such as Ming Teh, are reliably good.

CHILES

Tofu is a great vehicle for flavor, including the spicy heat of **fresh and dried chiles**. Fresh chiles are usually used seeds and all, though you may remove the seeds and inner membranes for less heat. For more heat, use fresh Thai chiles or serranos. For moderate heat, look to Fresno (sometimes called red jalapeño), Holland (also called Dutch or finger chiles), or jalapeño.

Dried red chile flakes offer a deep, weighty heat, as does homemade chile oil (page 213). When flakes aren't available, stem whole dried chiles and coarsely grind them.

Ground Japanese *ichimi togarashi* chile, sold in slender small bottles, offers a moderate kick and beautiful red garnish to tofu. The seven-spice pepper blend called *shichimi togarashi* (or *nanami togarashi*) is a milder stand-in.

Korean red pepper powder (*gochu garu*) is used to lend an earthy red color and moderate heat to hot pots, sauces, dumplings, and kimchi. Purchase it in plastic bags at a Korean or well-stocked Chinese market. In a pinch, you can substitute a mild chile powder, crushed Spanish *ñora*, or stemmed, seeded, and ground dried Califonia or New Mexico chiles. If the substitute is finely textured and relatively hot, start with half the quantity called for in the recipe and adjust from there.

CHINESE CHIVES

Resembling dark green, flat blades of grass, Chinese chives are significantly larger than Western chives. They have a delicate garlic, rather than onion, flavor. Many Asian cooks treat the chives like a leafy green vegetable, not a garnish, and judiciously use them in stir-fries and dumpling fillings. With few exceptions, they can be replaced with green onions. They may be known as Chinese garlic chives, *gow choy* and *jiu cai* (China), *kucai* (Indonesia, Malaysia, and Singapore), *nira* (Japan), *buchu* (Korea), *gui chai* (Thailand), and *he* (Vietnam).

COCONUT MILK

The liquid pressed from the grated flesh of mature coconuts enriches many tofu dishes, particularly those from more tropical southern regions. You can render fresh coconut milk but terrific coconut milks include Thai brands Chaokoh and Mae Ploy (in cans, with excellent flavor and creaminess) and Aroy-D (in aseptic boxes and harder to find, but with a bright freshness).

If your recipe calls for coconut cream, don't agitate the container of coconut milk before opening. Spoon the cream from the firm plug at the top. Otherwise, shake or whisk the contents well before measuring the amount needed. Asian recipes employ *unsweetened* coconut milk, not the stuff that goes into a piña colada. Insipid "light" coconut milk is not worth using. Go for the full fat and enjoy.

DRIED BONITO FLAKES

A staple of Japanese kitchens, thin shavings of dried bonito (*katsuo-bushi*) lend a smoky edge to dashi stock (page 215). They are also a go-to garnish for chilled tofu (page 51). While you can spend a fortune for premium *katsuo-bushi*, start out with the flakes available in small plastic envelopes sold four or six to a package. All you need for a batch of dashi is a 5-gram packet (half a lightly packed cup). Look for the flakes at Chinese, Japanese, Korean, and health food markets. Store in the cupboard.

DRIED SEAWEED

Three types of dried seaweed are used in this book and they are among the most common and easy to find. **Dried kelp** (*kombu*) comes in different qualities but unless you are a connoisseur of Japanese ingredients, there is no need to hunt down the high-end stuff. I use *dashi kombu*, a well-priced all-purpose type of dried kelp. It is lower in naturally occurring glutamates than other varieties of *kombu* but it will impart good flavor. Dark toasted sheets of **nori** seaweed are typically employed for sushi making, but in this book, they're as a great fake for eel skin (see page 157).

A full-size sheet is approximately 7½ by 8 inches. While **wakame** seaweed is available fresh and salted, the dried kind will work just fine for adding to soup. Look for bags filled with dark green, nearly black flakes; they are sometimes labeled as a "sea vegetable." Look for *kombu*, nori, and *wakame* at Chinese, Japanese, Korean, and health food markets. After opening the package, store it in a zip-top plastic bag in a dry spot.

DRIED SHRIMP

Tiny and orange in color, dried shrimp are a stealth ingredient in many Asian dishes, contributing an alluring sweet brininess and savory depth. They are usually sold in the cold-food section at Asian markets. Buy whole shrimp (not shrimp powder) that are pinkish-orange; medium or large shrimp have more flavor than small ones. Refrigerate the package to prevent an off-odor from developing.

DRIED SHRIMP PASTE

An essential ingredient for Malayasian, Singaporean, and Indonesian dishes, dried shrimp paste has a challenging (stinky) odor but it lends an umami depth to food. Its pungency dissipates during cooking and it is not consumed alone in huge quanties. It is usually roasted or sautéed before being used; if you don't like its odor, purchase preroasted shrimp paste. Unroasted shrimp paste is soft enough to thinly slice; the hard preroasted version should be pounded or finely chopped before being measured out. Refrigerate shrimp paste in a zip-top plastic bag.

FERMENTED BLACK BEANS

Made from black or yellow soybeans, fermented black beans impart a wonderful pungency and earthiness to foods. They are sold at Chinese markets in plastic or paper containers; transfer the beans to a jar and refrigerate indefinitely. When using the beans in hearty dishes, I do not rinse the salt off.

FISH SAUCE

Used like soy sauce in many Southeast Asian kitchens, fish sauce lends an unmistakable flavor to foods that it touches. If you are unfamiliar with using fish sauce, purchase one that is made in a more delicate, so-called Vietnamese style. Excellent brands are Viet Huong's Three Crabs and Flying Lion.

GINGER

Ginger root is an indispensable ingredient for Asian cooking, so keep plenty on hand. At the store, select heavy, hard rhizomes with taut skin. Wrinkly ones are over the hill. More mature ginger is hotter and more flavorful, but is fibrous (check where the knobs are broken) and may be hard to finely cut. Store ginger in a typical thin produce-section plastic bag in the vegetable crisper, where it will stay fresh for weeks.

MIRIN

A syrupy, low-alcohol Japanese rice wine meant for cooking, not drinking, mirin is available at many health food markets and Asian grocery stores. It is used to add sweetness, curb strong aromas, and glaze foods. Refrigerate mirin to preserve its aroma. Wipe the rim of the bottle after each use or it will get sticky.

MUSHROOMS

The musty fragrance, meaty texture, and deep flavor of mushrooms complement tofu well. Asian cooks use many kinds of fresh and dried mushrooms. Chinese, Korean, and Japanese markets, in particular, have terrific prices and selection. When buying **dried shiitake mushrooms**, select whole, thick-capped ones with deep white fissures on top; the packaged presliced ones are of questionable quality. Store dried shiitake mushrooms, also known as Chinese black mushrooms, in a plastic container at room temperature.

For super deep flavor, reconstitute dried shiitake mushrooms, gills facing down, for 8 hours (or overnight) in water to cover; the temperature of the water doesn't matter. Before using the mushrooms, rinse out any dirt trapped under the gills, give each a gentle squeeze to expel excess water, and slice off the knobby stem. Reconstituted shiitake mushrooms, drained of their soaking water, can be refrigerated for several days.

Black-gray, crunchy, and flavorless, **dried wood ear mushrooms** add terrific texture to foods. Small to midsized ones are most versatile; they keep indefinitely in the cupboard. Reconstitute them in hot water to cover for about 15 minutes, or until they are pliable. If the tough "eye" remains at the center of the mushroom, remove it before cutting up the mushroom for a recipe. If you find **fresh wood ear mushrooms**, store them as you would any fresh mushroom, and trim and cut them up for cooking.

NOODLES

Check your supermarket's Asian food aisle for the noodles needed in these recipes. But go to an Asian market for the best selection and prices. In the dried noodle aisle, you'll find packages of **cellophane noodles** (also called bean thread noodles), **flat rice noodles** (may be labeled *banh pho* or Chantaboon rice sticks), and **rice vermicelli** (also called *bun* and Jiangxi rice vermicelli). Purchase cellophane noodles as a package of eight small bundles. Look for flat, medium-wide rice noodles (think fettucine) for pad Thai (page 184). Small rice vermicelli is great with fermented tofu simmered in coconut milk (page 148). The refrigerated or frozen section is where **udon noodles** will be found; Korean and Japanese brands are excellent.

OYSTER SAUCE

When tofu is seasoned with a little oyster sauce, the resulting flavor is somewhat briny, sweet, and savory. At minimum, buy Lee Kum Kee's basic oyster sauce. Better yet, choose their premium sauce with the woman and boy on the label; it has more oyster extractives and a richer flavor. Once it is opened, oyster sauce will keep indefinitely in the refrigerator. Let it stand at room temperature for several minutes before using so it is easier to pour and measure.

PALM SUGAR

Southeast Asian foods often derive an alluring sweetness from unrefined palm sugar. At Chinese and Southeast Asian markets, you'll find two kinds. **Light palm sugar** ranges from pale yellow to caramel brown in color and from soft and creamy to rock hard in texture; it's sold as disks or mounds or in jars. **Dark palm sugar** (also called *gula jawa*, *gula melaka*, and *gula merah*) is often sold as cylinders. It is reddish-brown, moist, and dark, with the deep flavor of molasses.

To measure palm sugar for cooking, shave off thin pieces, grate or chop small chunks, or scoop up mounds, depending on the sugar's texture. Soften jarred or hardened palm sugar in the microwave oven. Light and dark brown sugar, or coconut sugar crystals, can be substituted for palm sugar, but the flavor will not be as complex.

RICE

The accompaniment for many of the tofu dishes in this book is plain boiled rice. In general, cook **long-grain rice**, such as jasmine, for Chinese and Southeast Asian foods. Japanese and Korean dishes pair better with **short-grain rice**. Lao pressed tofu salad (page 137), however, is splendid with healthy servings of steamed **sticky rice**. As with all Asian ingredients, purchase rice at the upper end of the price range to ensure a high-quality product.

RICE WINE

Aromatic and pleasantly nutty-tasting, **Shaoxing rice wine** is the standard spirit used in many Chinese preparations. It contributes an unmistakable flavor and fragrance to food. I use Pagoda brand, which is actually made in Shaoxing, in Zhejiang Province. The tall 750-milliliter bottles are sold at Chinese markets. Pay a little more for the aged version, which tastes like a good dry sherry. Avoid Shaoxing "cooking wine" and "cooking sherry," which are salted. For Japanese dishes, use dry **sake** for its clean flavor and nuanced sweetness. Keep a large mid-priced bottle for cooking.

SESAME OIL

This rich, nutty, amber-colored oil made from toasted sesame seeds is often used to enrich and perfume East and Southeast Asian dishes. Japanese sesame oils are excellent, particularly Kadoya brand. Asian markets have the best prices. Store in a dark, cool spot for up to six months or refrigerate for longer. Only the dark, toasted sesame oil is employed in this book. Toasted black sesame oil can be used, though it has a slight bitter edge.

SESAME SEEDS

Sesame seeds, commonly associated with Asian food, are thought to be native to Africa, Iran, or India. They were probably introduced to China by Persian traders about two thousand years ago. **White sesame seeds** are mostly used in this book, but on occasion, **black sesame seeds** spark up a tofu preparation.

To toast white sesame seeds, put them in a skillet over medium heat, stirring frequently, until they are lightly golden (about 8 minutes for 1 cup toasted in a 12-inch skillet); let the seeds cool before using. Black sesame seeds take about as long but it is hard to tell when they're done; I monitor them extra carefully and pull them off the heat when I detect a bit of vapor rising from the skillet. To save time, keep a small stash of toasted sesame seeds in the freezer. Keep raw seeds frozen, too.

SICHUAN PEPPERCORNS

Sichuan peppercorns, enjoyed in many parts of Asia, have an appealing, distinctive pungency that is spicy and tingly on the tongue; they're a must-have for an authentic version of *ma po tofu* (page 101). These dried dark-red berries are typically toasted in a dry pan and then ground before they're used in cooking. Use medium heat and stir or shake the skillet frequently for about 3 minutes, until the peppercorns are very fragrant and slightly darkened; a little smoking is okay but avoid burning them. Then grind them fine in a spice grinder or pound with a mortar and pestle. Look for them in plastic bags at Chinese markets and specialty grocers. Whole pods and berries, also called Chinese prickly-ash, have a strong flavor that is preferred for Chinese dishes. For a milder bite, use Japanese ground *sansho*, which is just the berries.

SOY SAUCE

There are many types of soy sauces, and they all taste different. Chinese soy sauces are used in most of the recipes here. **Light (regular) soy sauce**, sometimes called thin soy sauce, is light in color, not low in sodium. **Dark (black) soy sauce** is slightly sweet, and deeper in flavor and color. It is great for robust dishes and produces a lovely mahogany color.

Pearl River Bridge (found at Chinese and Southeast Asian markets) makes excellent soy sauces: the superior is good, but golden label superior is more complex and costs pennies more. In your supermarket, choose Kikkoman. Everyday **Japanese** and **Korean soy sauces** (called *shoyu* and *ganjang,* respectively) are similar to Chinese light soy sauce but darker, a touch sweeter, and less salty; in a pinch substitute light soy sauce. Japanese *usukuchi shoyu* is a light soy sauce used when cooks do not want to darken foods too much. Japanese and Korean markets have the best selection of soy sauces for those cuisines. Thick and delicious **Indonesian sweet soy sauce** (*kecap manis*) lends a distinctive molasses-like flavor to certain Southeast Asian dishes.

Pay attention to the sodium content when buying soy sauces. The brands I mostly use have around 900 milligrams per tablespoon, so if you use saltier soy sauces, use a little less or lower the amount of salt, if it is part of the seasonings.

STARCH

Asian cooks use a variety of starches but for the recipes in this book, all you need is cornstarch and potato starch. **Cornstarch** is a great multipurpose thickener that you likely have on hand; some people prefer to thicken sauces with **tapioca starch,** so feel free to follow suit. **Potato starch,** available at health food markets and Asian grocery stores, is useful to finely coat tofu right before deep-frying, creating a delicate, chewy-crisp shell for classics such as Japanese *agedashi dofu* (page 70).

TOFU

See the Tofu Buying Guide on page 7.

VINEGAR

Many Asian dishes depend on the delicate tartness of **unseasoned rice vinegar** to create a balance of flavors. Keep a big bottle on hand. Japanese brands, such as Marukan, are excellent.

On the opposite end of the spectrum is inky **Chinkiang vinegar**, named after an area in China renowned for vinegar production. It is wonderful for hot-and-sour soup (page 82) and other piquant Chinese tofu dishes. Italian balsamic vinegar is an okay substitute, though it is a tad sweeter; unseasoned rice vinegar can also stand in. Chinkiang vinegar is sold at Chinese markets. Gold Plum brand is excellent.

SELECTED BIBLIOGRAPHY

Personal interviews as well as printed resources helped me explore Asian food culture, research ingredients, and crystallize my own tofu making techniques. Here are a number of the works that were especially illuminating.

Andoh, Elizabeth. *Kansha: Celebrating Japan's Vegan and Vegetarian Traditions*. Berkeley: Ten Speed Press, 2010.

———. *Washoku: Recipes from the Japanese Home Kitchen*. Berkeley: Ten Speed Press, 2005.

Boga, Yasa. *The Best of Indonesian Cooking*. Singapore: Marshall Cavendish, 2007.

Chun, Injoo, Jaewoon Lee, and Youngran Baek. *Authentic Recipes from Korea*. Singapore: Periplus, 2004.

Du Bois, Christine M., Chee-Beng Tan, and Sidney Mintz, eds. *The World of Soy*. Urbana: University of Illinois Press, 2008.

Dunlop, Fucshia. *Land of Plenty: A Treasury of Authentic Sichuan Cooking*. New York: W.W. Norton & Company, 2003.

Han, Bei-Zhong. "Characterization and Product Innovation of Sufu: A Chinese Fermented Soybean Food." Ph.D diss., Wageningen University, 2003.

Huang, Hsing-Tsung. *Science & Civilisation in China: Volume 6, Biology and Biological Technology, Part V, Fermentation and Food Science*. Cambridge: Cambridge University Press, 2000.

Kongpan, Sisamon. *The Best of Thai Cuisine*. Bangkok: Sangdad Publishing, 2004.

Lager, Mildred. *The Useful Soybean: A Plus Factor in Modern Nutrition*. New York: McGraw-Hill, 1945.

Lee, Mu-Tsun. *Tofu! Tofu! Tofu!* Taipei: Wei-Chuan Publishing, 1994.

Lin, Florence. *Florence Lin's Chinese Vegetarian Cookbook*. New York: Hawthorn Books, Inc., 1976.

Oseland, James. *Cradle of Flavor: Home Cooking from the Spice Islands of Indonesia, Malaysia, and Singapore*. New York: W.W. Norton & Company, 2006.

Piper, Charles V., and William Morse. *The Soybean*. New York: McGraw-Hill, 1923.

Reddy, Kavitha. *The Indian Soy Cookbook*. New Delhi: Rupa & Co., 2002.

Sahni, Julie. *Classic Indian Vegetarian and Grain Cooking*. New York: William A. Morrow, 1985.

Saito, Tausuo, and Raul Simoes. *Traditional Japanese Recipe Book with English Translation*. Japan: Seibido Shuppan, 2008.

Shurtleff, William, and Akiko Aoyagi. *The Book of Tofu*. Berkeley: Ten Speed Press, 1998.

Takagi, Junko. *The Best of Tofu*. Tokyo: Japan Publishing Company, 2004.

Thompson, David. *Thai Street Food: Authentic Recipes, Vibrant Traditions*. Berkeley: Ten Speed Press, 2009.

Tsuji, Shizuo. *Japanese Cooking: A Simple Art*. Tokyo: Kodansha International, 2006.

ACKNOWLEDGMENTS

Researching and writing this book has been a most excellent tofu adventure. I've had the pleasure to meet with and learn from lots of generous individuals. Many thanks to Aaron Wehner and Melissa Moore at Ten Speed Press for championing and shepherding this project from inception to birth.

Publishing is a team effort and this work greatly benefited from the expertise of creative director Nancy Austin, art director Betsy Stromberg, copy editor Clancy Drake, proofreader Karen Levy, indexer Ken Della Penta, and publicist Kristin Casemore. Many others at Ten Speed Press contributed their time and energy, and I very much appreciate their support.

The artful and informative photos represent the hard work of an extraordinary group of professionals: photographer Maren Caruso and assistants Harrison Budd and Austin Goldin, food stylist Karen Shinto and assistant Fanny Pan, and prop stylist Dani Fisher. Thanks, Karen, for going the extra mile.

These dedicated volunteer testers kept me on my toes: Diane Carlson, Alex Ciepley, Georgia Freedman-Wand, Candace and Douglas Grover, Sue Holt, Laura McCarthy, Alec Mitchell, Johanna Nevitt, Fanny Pan, Susan Pi, Karen Shinto, Ju Sohn, Makiko Tsuzuki, Dave Weinstein, and Lea Yancey. They helped me fine-tune instructions and flavors.

Others shared their knowledge and contacts, took me on tofu tours, and served as translators. Jonathan Chambers, Jeremiah Ridenour, William Shurtleff, Minh Tsai, and Simon Wang contributed their Stateside tofu making and soybean farming expertise. In Taipei, Huang Xiao Chen and Xu Xin Nian graciously opened Ming Ji Tofu factory for an impromptu visit. In Tokyo, Katsuji and Masako Ishijima conducted a tofu making lesson and Toshio and Kyoko Kanemoto generously discussed their techniques.

What began as a Facebook conversation with Katy Biggs developed into a Taipei tofu posse comprised of Anita Chang, Holly Harrington, Sara Lin, Christine Tsai, and Curis Wang. Thank you for the introduction to Lin Mei Hua and Wei Shum. Eddie Huang rounded things out with his Taiwanese-American perspective.

Lillian Chou watched out for me in Beijing and Chengdu. Yu Bo, Carl Chu, Jay Dautcher, Fuchsia Dunlop, Linda Lau Anusasananan, Max Levy, Dai Xuang, and Grace Young greatly enhanced my understanding of Chinese tofu and ingredients. Thank you to Xie Qian and Zhong Yi for inviting me into your homes.

Elizabeth Andoh enthusiastically lent a hand from the beginning. Michael Baxter, Masa Fujiwara, Eric Gower, Junko Nakahama, Mark Robinson, Yukari Sakamoto, Harumi Shimizu, and Mayu Yoshikawa enriched my Japan experience with their cultural and culinary insights. Linda Lim offered her personal story on Korean-American foodways. Meanwhile, Yun Ho Rhee responded to my endless questions from his home in Seoul.

Christopher Tan emailed recipes and snail mailed books from Singapore. Amy Besa, Robyn Eckhardt, Irene Khin Wong, Tony Lam, Loan Luong, Nancie McDermott, Pichet Ong, James Oseland, Tracey Paska, Daniel Sudar, Pim Techamuanvivit, David Thompson, and William Wongso helped me tackle tofu in Southeast Asia. Monica Bhide, Niloufer King, and Julie Sahni lent their thoughtful knowledge on evolving foodways in India. In Australia, Luke Nguyen toured me through his Little Saigon and Tim White guided me toward rare tofu publications. David Lebovitz and Harold McGee answered my technical queries.

Several years ago, my mother, Tuyet Thi Nguyen, planted the seed for this project by asking me about how to make tofu at home. *Cam on Me Gia.*

Finally, I am most grateful to Rory O'Brien for indulging my craft and sharing my appetite for tofu.

INDEX

A

Abura-age, 11, 46
Agedashi dofu, 70
Andoh, Elizabeth, 29, 154, 188
Anusasananan, Linda, 109
Aoyagi, Akiko, 4, 131

B

Banana leaves
    frozen, 128
    Spiced Tofu and Coconut in Banana Leaf,
      127–28
Banno-joyu, 208
BaoHaus, 165–66
Bean flower, 37
Beans
    fermented black, 220
    Lemongrass Tofu with Chiles, 108
    Spicy Lemongrass Tofu Salad, 137
    Tofu and Vegetables in Coconut Milk, 124–25
    White Tofu, Sesame, and Vegetable
      Salad, 135
    See also Soybeans
Bean sprouts
    Bean Sprouts with Panfried Tofu and
      Chinese Chives, 143
    Grilled Crisp Tofu Pockets, 67–68
    Stir-Fried Thai Noodles, 184–85
Bear Paw Tofu, 159
Beef, Spicy Tofu with Sichuan Peppercorn and,
    101–2
Bell peppers
    Lemongrass Tofu with Chiles, 108
    Tea-Smoked Tofu with Pepper and Pork, 104
    Tofu Noodle and Vegetable Salad, 133
Bhide, Monica, 121
Bi cuon chay, 161–62
Biji chigae, 91

Bitter Melon with Tofu and Pork, 106
Block tofu
    alternatives to, 37
    Bitter Melon with Tofu and Pork, 106
    buying, 7–8
    Cashew and Cardamom Fudge, 201
    Cellophane Noodle and Tofu Rolls, 161–62
    Confetti Tofu, 36
    Essence of Tofu Ice Cream, 198
    Fresh Tofu with Sauces and Toppings, 75
    Grilled Crisp Tofu Pockets, 67–68
    Hot-and-Sour Soup, 82–83
    Lemongrass Tofu with Chiles, 108
    making, 32–37
    Miso-Glazed Broiled Tofu, 61–62
    Miso Soup, 80
    protein in, 7
    shaping, 22
    Silken Tofu, 28–29
    Spiced Chickpea Crepes with Soybean
      Paneer, 179–80
    Spiced Tofu and Coconut in Banana Leaf,
      127–28
    Spiced Tofu and Vegetable Fritters, 71–72
    Spicy Tofu with Beef and Sichuan
      Peppercorn, 101–2
    Stir-Fried Tofu, Shrimp, and Peas, 100
    Stuffed Tofu in Broth, 94–95
    Sweet and Savory Tofu Eel, 157–58
    textures of, 7, 8
    Tofu and Vegetable Fritters, 154–55
    Tofu and Vegetables in Coconut Milk, 124–25
    Tofu Chicken Meatballs in Lemongrass
      Broth, 129
    Tofu, Pork, and Kimchi Dumplings, 174–75
    Tofu Steak Burgers, 170–71
    Tofu Tiramisu, 199
    Tofu, Tomato, and Dill Soup, 79

Tofu with Century Eggs, 56–57
Tofu with Kimchi and Pork Belly, 145–46
Tofu with Tomato and Green Onion, 107
Twice-Cooked Coriander Tofu, 112–13
Vegetarian Wontons in Chile Oil, 172–73
Warm Simmered Tofu, 87–88
White Tofu, Sesame, and Vegetable
    Salad, 135
See also Chilled tofu; Fermented tofu;
    Fried tofu; Silken tofu
Bonito flakes, dried, 220
    Dashi Stock, 215
Bowen, Samuel, 3
Bramblett, Billy, 131, 132
Broccoli rabe
    Greens and Fried Tofu in Mustard Sauce, 136
Buns, Spicy-Sweet Fried Tofu, 167–68
Burgers, Tofu Steak, 170–71

C

Cabbage
    Spicy Lemongrass Tofu Salad, 137
    Tofu and Vegetables in Coconut Milk, 124–25
    See also Kimchi
California Grill, 166, 170
Candlenuts
    Tofu and Vegetables in Coconut Milk, 124–25
Canh dau phu, 79
Carlson, Diane, 41, 127, 212
Carrots
    Soy Milk Lees and Vegetable Croquettes,
      114–15
    Tofu and Vegetables in Coconut Milk, 124–25
    Tofu Noodle and Vegetable Salad, 133
Carver, George Washington, 4
Cashew and Cardamom Fudge, 201
Cellophane noodles, 221
    Burmese Cellophane Noodle Soup, 86

Cellophane Noodle and Tofu Rolls, 161–62
Chinese Chive and Pressed Tofu Turnovers, 177–78
Stuffed Tofu in Broth, 94–95
Chicken
    Burmese Cellophane Noodle Soup, 86
    Chicken Stock, 214
    Fried Rice with Fermented Red Tofu, 191
    Roast Chicken with Red Fermented Tofu, 117
    Savory Tofu Pudding with Spicy Meat Topping, 59–60
    Soy Milk Lees and Vegetable Croquettes, 114–15
    Tofu Bamboo and Chicken Soup, 86
    Tofu Chicken Meatballs in Lemongrass Broth, 129
Chickpea Crepes, Spiced, with Soybean Paneer, 179–80
Chile bean sauce, 219
Chiles, 219
    Chile and Sichuan Peppercorn Mix, 211
    Chile Oil, 213
    Chile Peanut Sauce, 69
    Fermented Tofu, Lemongrass, and Chile Sauce, 212
    Thai Sweet Chile Sauce, 210
Chilla, 179–80
Chilled tofu
    Chilled Tofu with Crunchy Baby Sardines, 53
    Chilled Tofu with Spicy Sauce, 54
    Japanese Chilled Tofu, 51
Chinese chives, 219
    Bean Sprouts with Panfried Tofu and Chinese Chives, 143
    Chinese Chive and Pressed Tofu Turnovers, 177–78
    Stir-Fried Thai Noodles, 184–85
Chocolate
    Chocolate Glaze, 204
    Gingery Chocolate Chip Cookies, 202
Chou, Lillian, 97–99
Chutney, Green, 218
Ciepley, Alex, 112
Clams
    Soft Tofu and Seafood Hot Pot, 93
Coagulants, 18–19
Coconut milk or cream, 220
    Fermented Tofu Simmered in Coconut Milk, 148–49
    Lemongrass Tofu with Chiles, 108
    Spiced Tofu and Coconut in Banana Leaf, 127–28
    Tofu and Vegetables in Coconut Milk, 124–25

Coffee
    Tofu Tiramisu, 199
Confetti Tofu, 36
Cookies, Gingery Chocolate Chip, 202
Cornstarch, 223
Crepes, Spiced Chickpea, with Soybean Paneer, 179–80
Croquettes, Soy Milk Lees and Vegetable, 114–15

D

Dang, Tony and Thu, 194
Dashi Stock, 215
Dau phu sot ca chua, 107
Dau phu xao xa ot, 108
Dautcher, Jay, 97
De nuong chao, 63–64
Desserts
    Cashew and Cardamom Fudge, 201
    Essence of Tofu Ice Cream, 198
    Gingery Chocolate Chip Cookies, 202
    Okara Doughnuts, 203–4
    Sweet Tofu Pudding with Ginger Syrup, 195
    Tofu Blancmange with Cured Pineapple and Lime, 196–97
    Tofu Tiramisu, 199
Dong Phuong Tofu, 193–94
Dou fu gua bao, 167–68
Dou fu han bao, 170–71
Dou fu zha song, 163
Doughnuts, Okara, 203–4
Dou hua, 59–60, 195
Dubu jeon, 103
Dubu kimchi, 145–46
Dumplings, Tofu, Pork, and Kimchi, 174–75

E

Eckhardt, Robyn, 67
Edamame no surinagashi, 84
Eggplant
    Tofu and Vegetables in Coconut Milk, 124–25
Eggs
    Soft Tofu and Seafood Hot Pot, 93
    Tofu with Century Eggs, 56–57
Epsom salts, 18–19
Equipment, 20–22
Essence of Tofu Ice Cream, 198

F

Fermented tofu
    buying, 12, 13
    Crisp Roasted Pork Belly, 119–20

Fermented Tofu, Lemongrass, and Chile Sauce, 212
Fermented Tofu, Lemongrass, and Goat Skewers, 63–64
Fermented Tofu Simmered in Coconut Milk, 148–49
Fried Rice with Fermented Red Tofu, 191
Roast Chicken with Red Fermented Tofu, 117
Water Spinach with Fermented Tofu, 147
White Fermented Tofu, 41–42
Fish
    Chilled Tofu with Crunchy Baby Sardines, 53
    salmon flakes, seasoned, 190
Fish sauce, 221
Ford, Henry, 4
Foxy Tofu Noodle Soup, 187
Franklin, Benjamin, 3
Freedman-Wand, Georgia, 104, 174
French Fries, Tofu, 74
Fried tofu
    Batter-Fried Tofu with Chile Soy Sauce, 116
    Bean Sprouts with Panfried Tofu and Chinese Chives, 143
    Bear Paw Tofu, 159
    buying, 10, 11
    Deep-Fried Tofu, 70
    Foxy Tofu Noodle Soup, 187
    Fried Tofu with Chile Peanut Sauce, 69
    Greens and Fried Tofu in Mustard Sauce, 136
    Hakka-Style Stuffed Tofu, 109–10
    making, 15
    Panfried Tofu with Mushroom and Spicy Sesame Sauce, 103
    Simmered Greens with Fried Tofu, 121–22
    Soy-Simmered Fried Tofu, 46–47
    Spicy-Sweet Fried Tofu Buns, 167–68
    Sushi Rice in Tofu Pouches, 188–90
    Tofu French Fries, 74
Fritters
    Spiced Tofu and Vegetable Fritters, 71–72
    Tofu and Vegetable Fritters, 154–55
Fudge, Cashew and Cardamom, 201
Fujiwara, Masa, 135
Fu zhi jiang you, 207
Fu zhu ji tang, 86

G

Gadon tahu, 127–28
Gaeng jued tao hu sarai, 81
Ganmodoki, 154–55
Ga nuong chao, 117

Ginger, 221
    Gingery Chocolate Chip Cookies, 202
    Gingery Miso Sauce, 62
    juice, extracting, 72
    Sweet Tofu Pudding with Ginger Syrup, 195
Goat, Fermented Tofu, and Lemongrass
    Skewers, 63–64
Goya champuru, 106
Greens
    Greens and Fried Tofu in Mustard
        Sauce, 136
    Simmered Greens with Fried Tofu, 121–22
    Stuffed Tofu in Broth, 94–95
    Vegetarian Wontons in Chile Oil, 172–73
    See also individual greens
Grover, Candace and Douglas, 94
Gypsum, 18–19

H

Her, Tra, 129
Hiya yakko, 51
Hodo Soy Beanery, 55, 131–32, 139
Holt, Sue, 170
Hong you yun tun, 172–73
Hot-and-Sour Soup, 82–83
Hot pots
    Silken Tofu and Seasoned Soy Milk Hot Pot,
        89–90
    Soft Tofu and Seafood Hot Pot, 93
    Soy Milk Lees and Kimchi Hot Pot, 91
    Stuffed Tofu in Broth, 94–95
    Warm Simmered Tofu, 87–88
Huang, Eddie, 165–66, 167
Hua ren dou fu gan, 138

I

Ice Cream, Essence of Tofu, 198
Inari-zushi, 188–90
Ishijima, Katsuji and Masako, 49–50

J

Jako hiya yakko, 53
Jiu cai he zi, 177–78

K

Ka Hitsujun, 1
Kaju barfi, 201
Kanemoto, Toshio and Kyoko, 29
Ke jia niang dou fu, 109–10
Kelp (kombu), 220
    Dashi Stock, 215
    recycling, 215
    Savory Kelp Relish, 216

Silken Tofu and Seasoned Soy Milk Hot Pot,
    89–90
Khao phat tao hu yi, 191
Kimchi
    Soy Milk Lees and Kimchi Hot Pot, 91
    Tofu, Pork, and Kimchi Dumplings, 174–75
    Tofu with Kimchi and Pork Belly, 145–46
Kitsune udon, 187
Ku, Dean, 55
Kuan Shih Yin, 152–53, 157

L

Laap tao hou, 137
Lager, Mildred, 4
Lam, Tony, 193–94
Lappe, Frances Moore, 4
Lemongrass
    Fermented Tofu, Lemongrass, and Chile
        Sauce, 212
    Fermented Tofu, Lemongrass, and Goat
        Skewers, 63–64
    Lemongrass Tofu with Chiles, 108
    Spicy Lemongrass Pressed Tofu, 39
    Spicy Lemongrass Tofu Salad, 137
    Tofu Chicken Meatballs in Lemongrass
        Broth, 129
Le Thi Phuong, 56
Levy, Max, 75
Liang ban qian si, 133
Lime, Tofu Blancmange with Cured Pineapple
    and, 196–97
Lim family, 77–78, 145
Lin, Florence, 41
Lin Mei Hua, 152–53, 157
Liu An, 1
Lon tao hu yi, 148–49

M

Mandu, 174–75
Ma po dou fu, 101–2
McCarthy, Laura, 108, 198, 202
Meatballs, Tofu Chicken, in Lemongrass
    Broth, 129
Messinger, Lisa, 5
Mirin, 221
Miso
    Citrusy Miso Sauce, 62
    Gingery Miso Sauce, 62
    Miso-Glazed Broiled Tofu, 61–62
    Miso Soup, 80
Miso shiru, 80
Mitchell, Alec, 117

Mock meats
    in Asia, 151–53
    Bear Paw Tofu, 159
    Cellophane Noodle and Tofu Rolls, 161–62
    Savory Okara Crumbles, 163
    Sweet and Savory Tofu Eel, 157–58
    Tofu and Vegetable Fritters, 154–55
Molds, 21, 22
Morse, William, 4
Musha, 74
Mushrooms, 221
    Burmese Cellophane Noodle Soup, 86
    Hot-and-Sour Soup, 82–83
    Miso Soup, 80
    Panfried Tofu with Mushroom and Spicy
        Sesame Sauce, 103
    Savory Soy Milk Lees with Vegetables, 142
Mussels
    Soft Tofu and Seafood Hot Pot, 93

N

Nakahama, Junko, 49
Nama yuba, 55
Nam jim gai wan, 210
Nanohana no karashi-ae, 136
Navarette, Domingo, 3
Nevitt, Johanna, 100
Nguyen, Luke, 63
Niang dou fu, 94–95
Nigari, 18–19
Noodles. *See* Cellophane noodles; Rice noodles;
    Tofu noodles; Udon noodles
Nori, 220
    Sweet and Savory Tofu Eel, 157–58
Nuoc cham chao, 212
Nuts, refreshing frozen, 168

O

Oboro tofu, 37
Oils
    Chile Oil, 213
    peanut, 213
    sesame, 222
Okara. See Soy milk lees
Ong, Pichet, 196
Oyster sauce, 221

P

Pad Thai, 184–85
Paino, John, 5
Pakoras, Soy Paneer, 71–72
Pan, Fanny, 191
Paska, Tracey, 3

Peanut oil, 213
Peanuts
    Chile Peanut Sauce, 69
    Pressed Tofu and Peanuts in Spicy Bean
        Sauce, 138
    Stir-Fried Thai Noodles, 184–85
Peas, Stir-Fried Tofu, Shrimp, and, 100
Perry, Matthew, 3
Pi, Susan, 84
Pi dan dou fu, 56
Pineapple, Cured, Tofu Blancmange with Lime
    and, 196–97
Piper, Charles, 4
Po, Yu, 101
Pork
    Bitter Melon with Tofu and Pork, 106
    Crisp Roasted Pork Belly, 119–20
    Fermented Tofu Simmered in Coconut Milk,
        148–49
    Fried Rice with Fermented Red Tofu, 191
    Hakka-Style Stuffed Tofu, 109–10
    Hot-and-Sour Soup, 82–83
    Savory Tofu Pudding with Spicy Meat
        Topping, 60
    Soy Milk Lees and Kimchi Hot Pot, 91
    Soy Milk Lees and Vegetable Croquettes,
        114–15
    Spicy Tofu with Beef and Sichuan
        Peppercorn, 101–2
    Stuffed Tofu in Broth, 94–95
    Tea-Smoked Tofu with Pepper and Pork, 104
    Tofu, Pork, and Kimchi Dumplings, 174–75
    Tofu, Seaweed, and Pork Soup, 81
    Tofu, Tomato, and Dill Soup, 79
    Tofu with Kimchi and Pork Belly, 145–46
Potato starch, 223
Pressed tofu
    buying, 8–9
    Chinese Chive and Pressed Tofu Turnovers,
        177–78
    Pressed Tofu and Peanuts in Spicy Bean
        Sauce, 138
    Seasoned Pressed Tofu, 38–39
    Spicy Lemongrass Pressed Tofu, 39
    Spicy Lemongrass Tofu Salad, 137
    Stir-Fried Thai Noodles, 184–85
    Tea-Smoked Pressed Tofu, 40
    Tea-Smoked Tofu with Pepper and Pork, 104

Q

Qe nqaij qaib xyaw taum paj, 129
Qian, Xie, 97–99
Quong Hop & Company, 131

R

Relishes
    Green Chutney, 218
    Savory Kelp Relish, 216
Rice, 222
    Fried Rice with Fermented Red Tofu, 191
    Silken Tofu and Edamame Soup, 84
    Sushi Rice in Tofu Pouches, 188–90
Rice noodles, 221
    Stir-Fried Thai Noodles, 184–85
Rice wine, 222
Ridenour, Jeremiah, 4–5, 131
Robinson, Mark, 202
Rojak Sauce, 67
Rolls
    Cellophane Noodle and Tofu Rolls, 161–62
    Fried Shrimp Tofu Skin Rolls, 182–83

S

Saag soy paneer, 121–22
Sahni, Julie, 3
Salads
    Spicy Lemongrass Tofu Salad, 137
    Tofu Noodle and Vegetable Salad, 133
    White Tofu, Sesame, and Vegetable Salad, 135
Salmon flakes, seasoned, 190
Sardines, Crunchy Baby, Chilled Tofu with, 53
Sauces
    Chile Peanut Sauce, 69
    Citrusy Miso Sauce, 62
    Fermented Tofu, Lemongrass, and Chile
        Sauce, 212
    fish, 221
    Gingery Miso Sauce, 62
    oyster, 221
    Rojak Sauce, 67
    Thai Sweet Chile Sauce, 210
    See also Soy sauce
Sayur lodeh, 124–25
Scharffenberger, John, 132
Seeds, refreshing frozen, 168
Seoul Gom Tang, 174
Sesame oil, 222
Sesame seeds, 222
Shao rou, 119–20
Shinto, Karen, 87, 97–99
Shira-ae, 135
Shrimp
    dried, 220
    Fermented Tofu Simmered in Coconut Milk,
        148–49
    Fried Shrimp Tofu Skin Rolls, 182–83

paste, dried, 220
    shell stock, 100
    Soft Tofu and Seafood Hot Pot, 93
    Stir-Fried Tofu, Shrimp, and Peas, 100
    Stuffed Tofu in Broth, 94–95
Shum, Wei, 166, 170
Shurtleff, William, 4–5, 131
Sichuan peppercorns, 222–23
Silken tofu
    buying, 8
    Citrus-Scented Silken Tofu, 29
    freezing, 42
    Fresh Tofu with Sauces and Toppings, 75
    making, 28–29
    Miso Soup, 80
    protein in, 7
    Silken Tofu and Edamame Soup, 84
    Silken Tofu and Seasoned Soy Milk Hot Pot,
        89–90
    Soft Tofu and Seafood Hot Pot, 93
    Tofu Blancmange with Cured Pineapple and
        Lime, 196–97
    Tofu, Seaweed, and Pork Soup, 81
    See also Chilled tofu
Soon dubu chigae, 93
Soups
    Burmese Cellophane Noodle Soup, 86
    Foxy Tofu Noodle Soup, 187
    Hot-and-Sour Soup, 82–83
    Silken Tofu and Edamame Soup, 84
    Tofu Bamboo and Chicken Soup, 86
    Tofu, Seaweed, and Pork Soup, 81
    Tofu, Tomato, and Dill Soup, 79
Soybeans
    buying dried, 17–18
    canned, 22
    grinding, 20
    Silken Tofu and Edamame Soup, 84
    soaking, 24–25
Soy flour, 22
SoyInfo Center, 131
Soy milk
    buying, 13, 22
    cooking, 20
    draining, 20
    machines, 20
    Master Soy Milk Recipe, 23–27
    Silken Tofu and Seasoned Soy Milk Hot Pot,
        89–90
Soy milk lees
    Gingery Chocolate Chip Cookies, 202
    Okara Doughnuts, 203–4
    Savory Okara Crumbles, 163

Soy milk lees, *continued*
    Savory Soy Milk Lees with Vegetables, 142
    Soy Milk Lees and Kimchi Hot Pot, 91
    Soy Milk Lees and Vegetable Croquettes, 114–15
    storing, 27
    uses for, 27
Soy paneer kaju barfi, 201
Soy Paneer Pakoras, 71–72
Soy sauce, 223
    Chinese Sweet Fragrant Soy Sauce, 207
    Japanese Seasoned Soy Concentrate, 208
    Korean Seasoned Soy Sauce, 209
    Quick Seasoned Soy Concentrate, 208
    Vegetarian Seasoned Soy Concentrate, 208
Spinach
    Simmered Greens with Fried Tofu, 121–22
Stocks
    Chicken Stock, 214
    Dashi Stock, 215
    shrimp shell, 100
Suan la tang, 82–83
Sugar, palm, 222
Sushi-age, 11, 46
Sushi Rice in Tofu Pouches, 188–90

T

Tahu bakar, 67–68
Tahu goreng bacem, 112–13
Takeya Tofu, 49–50
Tamarind Liquid, 217
Tan, Christopher, 163
Tanumihardja, Pat, 127
Tao hu thot, 69
Tapioca starch, 223
Tea
    Tea-Smoked Pressed Tofu, 40
    Tea-Smoked Tofu with Pepper and Pork, 104
Techamuanvivit, Pim, 148
Thompson, David, 2, 184
Tiramisu, Tofu, 199
Tofu
    buying, 7–13
    cooking tips for, 14–15
    cutting, 14
    draining, 14–15

    equipment for making, 20–22
    freezing, 42
    history of, 1–5
    ingredients for, 17–19
    popularity of, 1
    today, 5
    See also Block tofu; Chilled tofu; Fermented tofu; Fried tofu; Pressed tofu; Silken tofu; Tofu noodles; Tofu pudding; Tofu skin
Tofu brains, 37
Tofu chilla, 179–80
Tofu dengaku, 61–62
Tofu noodles
    buying, 9, 10
    Tofu Noodle and Vegetable Salad, 133
Tofu pudding
    buying, 11, 12, 13
    making, 30–31
    Savory Tofu Pudding, 59–60
    Soft Tofu and Seafood Hot Pot, 93
    Sour Tofu Pudding, 60
    Spicy Tofu Pudding, 60
    Sweet Tofu Pudding, 60
    Sweet Tofu Pudding with Ginger Syrup, 195
    See also Chilled tofu
Tofu skin
    buying, 9, 10, 11
    Fresh Tofu Skin, 44–45
    Fried Shrimp Tofu Skin Rolls, 182–83
    Spicy Yuba Ribbons, 139–40
    Tofu Skin Sashimi, 55
Tofu sticks, dried
    buying, 10, 11
    Tofu Bamboo and Chicken Soup, 86
Tofu toushi, 89–90
Tofu-ya-Ukai, 89
Tomatoes
    Spiced Chickpea Crepes with Soybean Paneer, 179–80
    Spicy Lemongrass Tofu Salad, 137
    Tofu, Tomato, and Dill Soup, 79
    Tofu with Tomato and Green Onion, 107
Tsai, Christine, 151–53
Tsai, Minh, 131
Tsuzuki, Makiko, 29
Turnovers, Chinese Chive and Pressed Tofu, 177–78

U

Udon noodles, 221
    Foxy Tofu Noodle Soup, 187
Unagi modoki, 157–58
Unohana, 142
Unohana korokke, 114–15

V

Vinegar, 223

W

Wakame seaweed, 220
    Tofu, Seaweed, and Pork Soup, 81
Wang, Simon, 194
Wang Fen Ji, 56
Wasabi mayonnaise, 74
Water, 18
Water Spinach with Fermented Tofu, 147
Whey, 36
Wildwood Tofu, 131
Wong, Irene Khin, 3, 86
Wongso, William, 127
Wontons, Vegetarian, in Chile Oil, 172–73
Wo Sing & Company, 131

X

Xia fu pi juan, 182–83
Xiao Tan Dou Hua (Mr. Tan's Bean Flower), 59
Xia ren dou fu, 100
Xiong zhang dou fu, 159

Y

Yancey, Lea, 167
Yan dou fu gan zhao cai, 104
Yangnyum dubu, 54
Yangnyumjang, 209
Yi, Zhong, 98–99, 101–2, 104
Yong tofu, 109
Yu dofu, 87–88

Z

Zaru tofu, 37
Zha dou fu, 116
Zucchini
    Soy Milk Lees and Kimchi Hot Pot, 91

MEASUREMENT CONVERSION CHARTS

Volume

U.S.	Imperial	Metric
1 tablespoon	1/2 fl oz	15 ml
2 tablespoons	1 fl oz	30 ml
1/4 cup	2 fl oz	60 ml
1/3 cup	3 fl oz	90 ml
1/2 cup	4 fl oz	120 ml
2/3 cup	5 fl oz (1/4 pint)	150 ml
3/4 cup	6 fl oz	180 ml
1 cup	8 fl oz (1/3 pint)	240 ml
1 1/4 cups	10 fl oz (1/2 pint)	300 ml
2 cups (1 pint)	16 fl oz (2/3 pint)	480 ml
2 1/2 cups	20 fl oz (1 pint)	600 ml
1 quart	32 fl oz (1 2/3 pint)	1 L

Temperature

Fahrenheit	Celsius/Gas Mark
250°F	120°C/gas mark 1/2
275°F	135°C/gas mark 1
300°F	150°C/gas mark 2
325°F	160°C/gas mark 3
350°F	180 or 175°C/gas mark 4
375°F	190°C/gas mark 5
400°F	200°C/gas mark 6
425°F	220°C/gas mark 7
450°F	230°C/gas mark 8
475°F	245°C/gas mark 9
500°F	260°C

Length

Inch	Metric
1/4 inch	6 mm
1/2 inch	1.25 cm
3/4 inch	2 cm
1 inch	2.5 cm
6 inches (1/2 foot)	15 cm
12 inches (1 foot)	30 cm

Weight

U.S./Imperial	Metric
1/2 oz	15 g
1 oz	30 g
2 oz	60 g
1/4 lb	115 g
1/3 lb	150 g
1/2 lb	225 g
3/4 lb	350 g
1 lb	450 g

Published in the United States by Ten Speed Press, an imprint of the Crown Publishing Group, a division of Random House, Inc., New York.
www.crownpublishing.com
www.tenspeed.com

Ten Speed Press and the Ten Speed Press colophon are registered trademarks of Random House, Inc.

With the exception of the photographs listed below, all others are studio photographs by Maren Caruso or location photographs by Andrea Nguyen.

Photographs pages ii, iv (top center, top right, bottom left), 96 (top left, bottom left, top right, bottom right), 99, 102, 150 (middle right), and 206 (top left) courtesy Karen Shinto

Photographs pages 14, 60, 96 (middle right), and 98 courtesy Lillian Chou

Photographs pages 76 and 78 courtesy Linda Lim

2005 LA Tofu Festival poster, page 4, courtesy Rodney Hom and Robby Djendrono

2006 LA Tofu Festival poster, page 4, courtesy Little Tokyo Service Center

Library of Congress Cataloging-in-Publication Data

Nguyen, Andrea Quynhgiao.
  Asian tofu / Andrea Nguyen ; photography by Maren Caruso. — 1st ed.
     p. cm.
  Includes bibliographical references and index.
  Summary: "A guide to making and cooking tofu, with nearly 100 horizon-expanding recipes from one of the country's leading voices on Asian cuisine"—Provided by publisher.
  1. Cooking (Tofu) 2. Tofu. 3. Cookbooks. I. Title.
  TX814.5.T63N48 2012
  641.6'5655—dc23

                          2011041480

ISBN 978-1-60774-025-4
eISBN 978-1-60774-203-6

Printed in China

Design by Betsy Stromberg
Food styling by Karen Shinto
Prop styling by Dani Fisher

10 9 8 7 6 5 4 3 2 1

First Edition